Holding Sacred Ground

Holding Sacred Ground

Essays on Leadership, Courage, and Endurance in Our Schools

Carl D. Glickman

JOSSEY-BASS
A Wiley Imprint
www.josseybass.com

Published by Jossey-Bass
A Wiley Imprint
989 Market Street, San Francisco, CA 94103-1741   www.josseybass.com

Jossey-Bass books and products are available through most bookstores. To contact Jossey-Bass directly call our Customer Care Department within the U.S. at 800-956-7739, outside the U.S. at 317-572-3986 or fax 317-572-4002.

Jossey-Bass also publishes its books in a variety of electronic formats. Some content that appears in print may not be available in electronic books.

Library of Congress Cataloging-in-Publication Data

Glickman, Carl D.
     Holding sacred ground: essays on leadership, courage, and endurance in our schools/ Carl D. Glickman.
       p. cm.—(The Jossey-Bass education series)
     Includes bibliographical references and index.
     ISBN 0-7879-5671-6 (alk. paper)
     1. Educational leadership—United States. 2. School improvement programs—United States. 3. Education—Aims and objectives—United States. 4. Democracy—Study and teaching—United States. I. Title. II. Series.
LB2805 .G537 2003
371.2'00973—dc21
                                              2002153514

Printed in the United States of America
FIRST EDITION
HB Printing   10 9 8 7 6 5 4 3 2 1

The Jossey-Bass Education Series

Contents

List of Tables, Figures, and Exhibits

Tables

Figures

Exhibits

Acknowledgments

Thanks to all the parents, students, citizens, educators, policymakers, and friends who have made a direct contribution to my thinking about education, schools, and democracy. Special mention to Lew Allen, Derrick Aldridge, Jackie Ancess, Ron Butchart, Emily Calhoun, Warren Chapman, David Chojnacki, Cheryl Craig, Linda Darling-Hammond, Lisa Delpit, Paula Evans, John Glenn, and all the other members and staff of the National Commission on Service Learning, John Goodlad, Steven Gross, Steve Gordon, Leslie Hergert, Larraine Hong, Jackie Irvine, Heidi Jacobs, Bena Kallick, Jamie Lewis, Ann Lieberman, Joe McDonald, Deborah Meier, Jerome Morris, Joe Nathan, Mary John O'Hair, Judith Preissle, Pedro Reyes, Jovita Ross-Gordon, Jim Scheurich, Paul Schwarz, Jack Shelton, Warren Simmons, Ted Sizer, Linda Skrla, Wilma Smith, Duncan Waite, Pat Wasley, and Margaret Wilder.

I have drawn material from literally hundreds of schools that I have had the pleasure to work directly with, including member schools from our school renewal network (the Georgia League of Professional Schools, established in 1988) and from other kinship school renewal networks, among them the Coalition of Essential Schools, the Annenberg Rural School and Community Trust, the Accelerated Schools, the School Development Program (Comer) Schools, the Oklahoma Network for Excellence in Education, the Southern Maine Partnership, Foxfire Foundation, and the National Center for Restructuring Schools and Teaching.

Recent examples of school sustainability and leadership were drawn from visits, observations, interviews, or readings from externally nominated schools. I have protected the confidentiality of particular people and schools where I spent time on site by altering their identity in the text. But I do want to acknowledge that the eighteen sample schools were drawn from these nominated schools:

Alternative Community School, Ithaca, New York

Belle Sherman Elementary School, Ithaca

Bethune Academy, Aldine Independent School District, Houston, Texas

Brown School, Louisville, Kentucky

Burrus Elementary School, Marietta, Georgia

Central Park East, New York City

Ella Baker School, New York City

Federal Hocking High School, Stewart, Ohio

Hahira Elementary School, Hahira, Georgia

Helms Community School, Houston

International High School, Long Island, New York

Katz-McMillan Cooperating Schools, Las Vegas

Landmark High School, New York City

Lanier Middle School, Houston

Madeiri Junior-Senior High School, Cincinnati

Madison Elementary School, Norman, Oklahoma

Minnesota New Country Charter School, Henderson, Minnesota

Noble High School, Berwick, Maine

R. L. Norton Elementary School, Snellville, Georgia

Phantom Lake Elementary School, Bellevue, Washington

Pierce School, Brookline, Massachusetts

Quest High School, Humble, Texas

Roosevelt Elementary School, Norman, Oklahoma

Salem High School, Conyers, Georgia

Santa Monica Alternative High School, Santa Monica, California

Souhegan High School, Amherst, New Hampshire

St. Paul Open School, St. Paul, Minnesota

Schools Without Walls, Rochester, New York

Williston Central Middle School, Williston, Vermont

I extend special appreciation to all my colleagues in the College of Education at Southwest Texas State University, to Ph.D. student Susan Maxey, who was of immense help in completing the final phase of this book, and to the generous support of the Mitte Foundation. Much appreciation goes to Donna Bell for her exemplary skills and competence in preparing this manuscript and her cheerfulness in working with me over the past twenty years. Thanks to Lesley Iura, editor, and the entire production staff who once again did an excellent job in preparing, editing, and producing my third book with Jossey-Bass. Lesley, I appreciate greatly your wisdom and guidance as we thought through this project from beginning to end.

I have again the wonderful fortune to express my love and devotion to my best friend and spouse, Sara Orton Glickman; our daughters, Jennifer Glickman Stapper and Rachel Glickman; our sons-in-law, Volker Stapper and Henry Zacchini; all their children and our grand grandkids, Lea, Noah, and newly arrived Amelia; my mom, Ruth, and my late dad, Harold; my brothers and sisters, Ernie and Lillian, Joy, Sherry and Michael, Randy and Cindi, and all our cousins; and my late father-in-law, Stu, mother-in-law, Jo, and her husband and our dear friend, Pete.

To all family and friends, whether by blood, by law, or by spirit, it makes little difference: I was raised in a family culture that believed that life could only be lived fully among others. I am so fortunate to live among so many caring humans. Now we all, once again, turn to the greatest and most satisfying task at hand: making a better life for all our children.

Carl D. Glickman
August 2002

Preface

The essays in *Holding Sacred Ground* reflect more than twenty-five years of writing about the real issues that practitioners must resolve in regard to school change; classroom improvement; public purpose; instructional leadership; teacher development; and policies for accountability, standards, and authority. Included are several essays written within the past two years and drawing from school visits to eighteen powerful examples of progressive education and sustainability.

In determining essays, I was guided by the question, "What must school leaders think about and practice if all students are to have a truly democratic education; an education that equips each student with the knowledge, skills, and applications to become a wise, caring, and participatory citizen of an improving democratic society?" A democratic education is conceived of as achieving *the necessary core academic learning* that allows each student to have greater opportunity for personal and professional advancement, and achieving *the necessary responsibilities of a valued and valuable citizen*, in using one's education to contribute now and in the future to building a better home, community, and society. This form of education balances individual pursuit with collective responsibility as the particular obligation of the public school. To develop and implement such an education for students at all grade levels takes thought, courage, and savvy leadership.

The National Commission for Service Learning, on which I recently served as a member, under the chairmanship of former astronaut and U.S. Sen. John Glenn, issued a stirring, bipartisan report on this needed form of education (www.servicelearningcommission.org). It stated that the great failure of American public schools is, ironically enough, the lack of a participatory education where every student sees the connection between academic achievement and contribution to a larger community. This collection of essays adds concrete evidence and examples of practice to the commission report. It is a guide to all those educators and community members who understand that the simultaneous issues of an academic achievement gap between poor and wealthy students and the dramatic decline in public participation and civic involvement among the last five generations of citizens in America are related to each other.

What follows are essays organized into six parts. The first, "Great Schools," helps define leadership, education, and public purpose. Part Two, "School Renewal: Ironies and Challenges," makes clear the necessary operational framework if a school is to weather the unpredictable obstacles ahead. Part Three, "Instructional Leadership," is about the particular leadership formats, approaches, and strategies for enhancing teacher thinking and collective action.

Part Four, "Teaching, Learning, and Service," offers examples of the inner world of curriculum, methods, and strategies for improving student achievement while building citizen capabilities. Part Five, "Standards, Policies, and Authority," is about the dichotomized times that educators live in today and the importance of protecting unique schools, those that forge their own way and can document success for students. It includes a policy paper that I was invited to write for legislative action on school-based accountability, authority, and flexibility. Part Six, "The Crux of Education, Democracy, and the Future of Our Place," is a candid appraisal of the relationships, controversies, and definitions of education, public interest, and democracy.

The final essay, Chapter Twenty-Two, completes this collection by noting the urgency of sustaining progressive schools over the long haul as the greatest hope for reinvigorating an informed and caring citizenry capable of making better homes and places for everyone. In the Appendices, I have placed two essays about my own struggles as a facilitator of school renewal, to respect the wisdom of experienced teachers and find areas of hope within a school to replenish the soul and keep momentum toward better possibilities.

Previously published essays were chosen from more than one hundred articles and twelve books appearing in print from 1977 to the present. Each essay was chosen according to my personal "gulp" and "emotive response" criteria. If I remembered gulping with apprehension before submitting a particular essay for publication, *and* if after publication I received spirited response from readers, then the essay made the final selection here. In addition, four new essays were written for this book to present vivid contemporary cases of school practice from some of the most successful and enduring progressive public schools in the United States. These cases give a clear illustration to central ideas of school leadership, courage, and endurance.

Occasionally, essays will have similar passages. The decision to keep similar passages was based on the internal coherence of each essay and its ability to stand alone. I would suggest that you use this book in any number of ways. One might be to review the Table of Contents and then read from beginning to end; another is to skip to an essay that piques your interest, or focus on a particular part. The essays can be used for in-school discussion among school faculty and aspiring or current school leaders; or as a text in a graduate seminar on leadership, sustainability, and progressive or democratic schools; or just as occasional late-night reading prior to sleep! Regardless of sequence and usage, I hope you bring your heart, mind, and soul into these central ideas of education, school, leadership, and the future of our place, and join in making such possibilities real for all our students.

The title of this book, *Holding Sacred Ground*, touches on the grand idea that democracy and progressive education rest on the learning of an entire populace. People learn more fully how to learn and live for themselves and with each other when accorded an education that allows everyone to participate in "the general diffusion of knowledge," "the marketplace of ideas," "freedom of expression," and "the pursuit of truth." In an open society, citizens make wiser, more deliberate, and more caring decisions for the betterment of all than kings, aristocrats, or other rulers could make for them. Thus democracy is as much an educational theory as a political theory; one rests upon the other. The task of holding sacred ground is only for the courageous educator who passionately believes in the connection between education, democracy, and schooling and is willing to go against the odds to serve as a beacon of what is indeed possible.

Carl D. Glickman
August 2002

Holding Sacred Ground

Part One

Great Schools

Chapter One

More Than a Donation

Education with Public Purpose

In a televised address to the U.S. Congress and the American people on January 29, 2002, President George W. Bush announced the commencement of the bombings of Afghanistan to root out the al Qaeda network and overthrow the Taliban government. He concluded his address by asking each American student to donate one dollar to help the children of Afghanistan. Bush made clear through this gesture that the U.S. war was against the terrorists and not the vulnerable people of the country. Though his leadership was steady during this tumultuous time, Bush unknowingly missed an unparalleled educational opportunity for students, teachers, parents, and local communities to connect school learning with participatory democracy. Now that monumental events, tragedies, and emotions have subsided, it is time to reflect upon what we mean by education with public purpose and how we narrow the huge disconnect between education, citizenship, and democracy.

The Purpose of an "American" Education

I am using this "American" case as illustrative of what might be a similar issue in other nations and ask readers of other countries to make their own applications. In the United States, the hope of universal, high-quality education for all as espoused through the centuries by Thomas Jefferson, Horace Mann, W.E.B. Du Bois, Martin Luther King, John Dewey, Benjamin Barber, Amy Gutmann, Cornel West, bell hooks, and others was to improve democracy for all by the rule of free citizens (Glickman, 1998b). Americans were to live in a "free-dom" rather than in a "king-dom," one where free men and women would rule the public domain.[1]

This conception of democracy does not determine what stance a citizen should take in terms of a political party, economic system, the environment, religion, welfare, sanctity of life, and so on.[2] Democracy is simply the belief that citizens have the capacity to educate and govern themselves through participatory problem solving, doing profoundly better than a king, oligarchy, or tyrant could do it for them. It is the belief that in a democracy the unfettered pursuit of truth is the best way to educate and to live. With an education guided by such public purpose, citizens would use their education to advance the ideals of life, liberty, and the pursuit of happiness for all.

The Rise of Generosity and the Abandonment of the Promise

Evidence of an accumulation of disinterest in American democracy as found in the studies of Robert Putnam (2000, 2002) should be a wake-up call about public purpose and the practice of education. The average adult American does not attend a single public, civic, or community meeting in a year. The decline in citizen engagement in community, neighborhood, and government affairs is more than 40 percent since the 1950s, and it continues with each generation. In many areas in America, the only place where citizens voluntarily see people different from their own group of friends, family, church or mosque or temple members, business acquaintances, or hobbyists is at the shopping mall—and the mall is a place to browse, shop, and walk past each other, not a place to talk or listen to people different from oneself. America increasingly has become a country of enclaves, separation, and private associations where only like-minded people band together according to the same professional, economic, religious, political, or recreational interests.

Outside of the current national crisis, keeping informed about local, state, or national affairs has continued to drop, and the simple act of voting in a national election is consistently an activity of less than the majority of Americans. In state and local elections, an embarrassingly low percentage of citizens determine the outcome. Please keeps in mind that voting is the most minimal form of citizenship, demanding nothing more than showing up and hopefully pulling a lever or connecting the lines.

To be sure, people become involved with occasional volatile town or city matters that directly affect their own property or taxes, but to be involved in public life as a core part of one's own life is not a common practice for Americans. The continuous practice of public discussion and decision making as to the benefits of the life of a larger community has been delegated by most Americans to career politicians, professionals, and special-interest or lobbyist groups. "We, the people" is greatly exaggerated; a more apt term would be "The few who decide for everyone else."

Yet volunteerism among the young in America has significantly risen—and definitely accelerated in generous and heartfelt ways since September 11 (Putnam, 2002). Charitable contributions are high, and paid membership in various nonprofit, public-focused organizations is at an all-time high. Volunteerism by American youth has been exceptional. But even as admirable and wonderful as volunteerism is, it is not democratic engagement. Volunteerism is a unilaterally controlled service provided by an individual or group to another (feeding the hungry, building homes for the poor, tutoring a young child, donating money, and so forth). The volunteer gives and the recipient receives. It is not a reciprocal relation of equals learning to solve issues together with no givers or takers, just problem-solving citizens who need to relate to, listen to, challenge, and understand each other and eventually find an acceptable working solution.

A story told by a prominent national leader about a meeting with student volunteers at a prestigious university is illustrative of the difference between democratic engagement and volunteerism.

These top students spend half a day per week offering help to children and families in a destitute neighborhood. The students describe the plight of the youth and families with whom they work, ranging from inadequate health care to scarce job opportunities or children without a home to return to after the school day. They recite the satisfaction and frustration of three years of volunteering in this neighborhood.

The students were asked if, after graduation, they would consider running for public office or serving as a citizen member on a neighborhood committee, commission, or board that could make policy for improving the conditions that they, as volunteers, are so much aware of. Of the forty students, only two said they would have any interest in such public, visible, and potentially contentious work. Most said they expected to continue to volunteer whatever they might eventually do in life or work, but to serve in any public group having the potential power to correct the shortcomings of a neighborhood was distasteful and not in their plans. Keep in mind that these students are America's brightest and most academically talented youths with a heart of gold, providing much-needed service. But to volunteer is one thing; to participate with others on solving a public issue is an entirely different matter to them.

The lack of youth involvement in public affairs is a legacy inherited from previous generations, particularly from their parents, and the earlier World War II baby boom generation who dramatically removed themselves from public affairs. But it shows us how far we have come from Alexis de Tocqueville's observation of America in the nineteenth century (de Tocqueville, 1948). As a foreigner, he was amazed by town life in America among all citizens. Financiers, farmers, and streetsweepers could sit down together without pretense to figure out what needed to be done to improve public life. He saw this egalitarian form of participation as uniquely American (Dewey later referred to it as "associative living"). Obviously, there was the searing hypocrisy of second-class citizenship of women and those enslaved and denied citizenship, but the idea that citizens could freely and willingly give of their minds and their time to work together to improve their community struck a chord with de Tocqueville. It is a chord that allows leaders of some of the most disenfranchised groups in America to continue to believe that the greatest hope for rectifying the severe injustice and inequities of race and class is through a participatory democracy (see West, 1993a and 1993b). It is a chord that resonates with most Americans, yet most rarely practice it.

America is on the cusp of a failed experiment—not a failure for corporations, individuals, or national wealth, and not a failure of military power or of being a world power, but a failure to improve education of all citizens so that "we the people" means just that, all of us, all of us having a stake in engaging with each other in building a better neighborhood, community, state, nation, and world. Tilting toward democratic vitality can only happen through the quality and nature of free public education provided for all our students, an education that prepares all students with the choices of democratic citizenry.

Reclaiming the "Public" in Education

In the past two years, I have spent time examining outstanding public schools and classrooms that reflect the diversity of ethnic populations, economic status, and geography throughout the United States. These schools have had at least ten years of documented student success. The students in these schools outperform those in comparable schools on such student indicators as graduation rate, achievement test scores, employment secured, postsecondary accomplishment, intact family, longer and healthier life, and active citizenship and leadership to their community.

What I was struck by on each visit—whether in a rural primary school in the South, an intermediate suburban school in the West, or a high school in the urban North—was the explicit commitment of each school to democratic values. Whether in displays of student work in the halls; service-learning activities in the neighborhood; words written in a school publication; or language used by students, faculty, and parents in discussing their schools, it was clear that curriculum, assessments, and promotion and graduation requirements reflected the belief that academic learning goals and contributions to the larger community are integral to each other.

These schools had expectations of what all students should be able to know and do at whatever age or grade level of the school, or prior to graduation. Students were expected to develop a public portfolio, exhibit, demonstration, or presentation that connected learning across academic subjects; used accurate skills of reading, writing, arithmetic, and speaking; integrated technology; and showed evidence of study, investigation, and problem solving. Most important, the project had to result in a concrete contribution to a real setting at school or in the home, community, state, nation, or world. Each student was guided by a format and assessment that specified a description of quality work worthy of earning school credit.

I saw kindergarten children using their prereading skills and learnings of geometric designs to develop illustrated books for families of preschoolers. I found eleven- and twelve-year-olds using the study of science, ecology, and habitats to protect wildlife in their local park. I saw middle schoolers using art, history, and English to develop breathtaking displays of the history of their town, which would remain in the local library. I found groups of secondary students working on a range of graduation projects: increasing census participation in their town, pursuing a new engineering design for a bike path around a restrictive highway, reducing economic and racial stratification in their neighborhood, devising economic development strategies for increasing work options among the unemployed, and conducting scientific experiments for ways to purify and conserve water.

Conclusion

To end where we began: instead of asking each student to donate a dollar, George W. Bush might have challenged American students, teachers, faculty, parents, and communities to use school learning to figure out concrete ways to improve the lives of Afghanistan children. He might have asked them to become better informed, wise, caring, and participatory democratic citizens by learning about the history, geography, life style, habitat, and physical conditions of Afghanistan, its people, and its children. This is a task much harder than sending a dollar, but the benefits and understanding gained across America by students about the impact their education could have on the larger world would have been awesome in imagination and contributions. His asking of a donation from school children is symptomatic of how we have come to view education and citizenship. Education is for learning academic skills and knowledge as measured on a high-stakes standardized test, and it is for the goals of individual advancement and economic productivity. Volunteering money and service is seen as separate from learning. The idea that learning can be enhanced academically, socially, and aesthetically by students contributing to issues of a larger world is not found in the practices, standards, and assessments of schools (see report of the National Commission on Service Learning, 2002).

We should be doing as the National Commission has urged. We should be asking schools to reshape school time, curriculum, and assessment to challenge students to demonstrate each year how they can use their education in real ways to serve society. This is the challenge of our time, not a challenge to George Bush alone but to all of us: to connect the ideals of democracy with the practices of education.

Notes

1. Citizenship and democracy were based on the belief that humans can best govern themselves. Such a democracy is predicated on respect for freedom of expression; general diffusion of knowledge; a free press; separation of church and state (which supports all religious, spiritual, and agnostic or atheist beliefs); participation of the citizen in government at local, state, and

national levels; the rule of the majority with responsiveness to minority opinions; a system of checks and balances whereby no person or authority can have unilateral control over determining the lives of others; and finally the rule of evolving laws that protect the rights of the individual to live as he or she chooses with the responsibility to ensure the same rights for others.

2. For an interesting set of ideas on democracy and public purpose, read the sequence of essays by Glickman (1998a), Scheurich (1998), and Glickman (1999). Chapter Twenty is a reprise of that sequence.

References

Glickman, C. D. "Educational Leadership for Democratic Purpose: What Do We Mean?" *International Journal of Leadership in Education*, 1998a, *1*(1), 47–53.

Glickman, C. D. *Revolutionizing America's Schools*. San Francisco: Jossey-Bass, 1998b.

Glickman, C. D. "Commentary: A Response to the Discourse on Democracy: A Dangerous Retreat." *International Journal of Leadership in Education*, 1999, *2*(1), 43–46.

National Commission on Service Learning. *Learning in Deed*. Battle Creek, Mich.: W. K. Kellogg Foundation and John Glenn Institute for Public Service, 2002. (To order report and video: www.servicelearningcommission.org)

Putnam, R. D. *Bowling Alone: The Collapse and Revival of American Communities*. New York: Simon & Schuster, 2000.

Putnam, R. D. "Bowling Together." *American Prospect*, 2002, *13*(3). [www.prospect.org/print/V13/3/Putnam].

Scheurich, J. J. "The Grave Dangers in the Discourse on Democracy." *International Journal of Leadership in Education*, 1998, *1*(1), 55–60.

de Tocqueville, A. *Democracy in America*, vols. 1 and 2. New York: Knopf, 1948.

West, C. *Beyond Eurocentrism and Multiculturalism*. Vol. 1: *Prophetic Thought in Postmodern Time*. Monroe, Me.: Common Courage, 1993a.

West, C. *Race Matters*. New York: Vintage, 1993b.

Chapter Two

Leadership for Navigating Great American Schools

In 1805, prior to beginning his presidential commission to explore and map the northwestern United States, Meriwether Lewis spent nearly a year in discussion with President Thomas Jefferson and in visiting experts in botany, geography, astronomy, native cultures, language, trade, and health and medicine. He knew how to navigate rivers, hunt, and live in the wilderness, but he was aware of what he would need to know to have a reasonable chance of discovering a route from St. Louis, Missouri, to the Pacific Ocean. He planned to the best of his ability what he would need, hired a select crew of twenty-five, and had a boat built to his specifications. It was made of metal, with great capacity for storage of food and supplies; it could be navigated by paddle, sail, or pole or carried over low water and dangerous currents. Lastly, he hired a senior person, Gen. William Clark, as co-commander and gave him equal authority on all matters of planning, traveling, supervising, and mediating encounters with native tribes and French, Spanish, and English fur traders.[1]

Whether you view Lewis and Clark's expedition as heroic or tragic depends on your vantage point, but there is no doubt that the expedition was a great success in accomplishing its purpose. For that to happen, Lewis knew that he needed first the right personnel, both strong and smart; second, the best resources of

Particular thanks go to the graduate students and faculty participating in the Southwest Texas State University Ph.D. Leadership Seminar of January 17, 2002, for their collective critique and refinement of this chapter.

information; third, the best interpersonal relations with influential people at home and with those he might meet en route; fourth, supplies for as many unanticipated occurrences as possible; and fifth, the ability to share and develop leaders among the crew to help the journey continue under changing conditions and seasons (Ambrose, 1996, chapter eleven).[2]

Lewis's story has commonality with stories about the beginning of successful schools imbued with public purpose, that is, "great American schools."[3] Certain people are mentioned and others are not. Usually the story is centered on the school leader (the principal, director, or head) and successful navigation of school events. But such a picture is too simplistic in explaining why a school ultimately succeeds and endures. A leader has many coleaders. Some might have more understated power and influence than the leader. It may be a parent who can contact a school board member to defuse a potential school controversy. It may be the school secretary or a custodian knowledgeable about the community who might communicate to citizens why it is important to support certain school changes. It may be student leaders who rally their parents or a teacher association representative whom others look to for direction.

In any success story about such a school, there are people widely known and others working quietly in the background that have much to do with navigating a school's successful expedition. The genius of formal leadership in a great American school is, as the trip begins, to immediately plug into this constellation of private relations and influential persons. The same, less visible people who might make a school successful can also be the greatest obstacle to change. They might protect their individual place in a mediocre school as being a higher priority than collectively creating the best education for all students. This is where the first testing of a school's commitment to academically challenging and democratic education for all children becomes so crucial to later school success.

Standing Firm on School Commitments

The examples that follow are not meant to single out any group as blockers and resisters of change, since there are many cases where parents, educators, and students, when given the opportunity to have exploratory and open discussion, visit other schools, participate in professional development activity, are given leadership responsibility for school planning, and have the support and time to reorganize their methods; they become the bedrock of support for lasting change in their school. However, the initial steps of planning and implementation include dealing first of all with controversy, to publicly test schoolwide commitment to deliver a better education for all students. Leaders need to know when and how to use moral authority and power to support the vision and congruent practices agreed to by the school community. Open discussion and dissenting opinions are all part of forging a school agreement, but once a decision is made, meeting the challenge from those who refuse to participate or resist is crucial for later success.

A middle school in the Midwest had a terrible prior record of poor achievement among students. A small percentage of staff led by the veteran guidance counselor refused to implement the new performance-based report cards or draw up the new flexible schedule of course time that had been agreed to by a majority of faculty to begin that next fall. The counselor, with the teacher association, was aggrieved over almost every decision that the principal and faculty made. The principal knew that there were many teachers, young and old, who believed strongly in the changes but were intimidated by the counselor. The principal discussed this situation in private with the superintendent of schools. Afterward, knowing that district support was secure for her to confront the counselor, she met with him and suggested that he support the school's decision, resign, or take early retirement. She would not tolerate his refusal and would closely document his performance for possible dismissal proceedings. In the interim, the counselor was removed from his duties and reassigned for the remainder of the year as her administrative assistant.

The rest of the school faculty, staff, and students gasped when the reassignment took place. After one more incident and meeting between the principal and counselor, the principal began formal termination proceedings. Then everyone in the school knew that the commitment to a new and better education was real. In the following three years, several more teachers, uncomfortable with the expectations of open collegiality, team planning, and peer coaching, and after several supervision cycles of conferences and observations to achieve professional goals, were asked to leave or else left of their own volition. Teachers enthusiastic about being part of the new program replaced them. This school later grew into one of the most highly accomplished examples of high-quality education in its state.

One high school in the South was almost stopped in its initial year by ten parents who objected to heterogeneous grouping of their students in core, interdisciplinary courses. The principal met with the parents and then asked them to bring their request to an ad hoc group of students, parents, and faculty. When the group heard the request, they listened, deliberated, and then explained to the parents their reasons for not acquiescing to a concern of a few parents that would disrupt the entire school plan. They did recommend that the parents, with their children, should sit down with their classroom teachers and develop more individualized activities that would go beyond the requirements of a class.

The parents were not happy with the recommendation. They wanted separate classes for their children, who they believed were particularly advanced and talented. The ad hoc group then met with the principal. Together they recommended to the superintendent that the school board hold a referendum, polling all the parents at the school on whether they were satisfied with the new education being provided. The superintendent and school board agreed. The principal and faculty were fairly confident that the majority of parents would approve the current program, but they were amazed when the results were tallied and 92 percent of the parents supported the school. The board then directed the dissenting parents to either keep their children in the school as structured or transfer to one of the two other high schools. The message to everyone, at this crucial time, was that the school was not to be turned back.

Preparation and Appraisal

Let's return to the Meriwether Lewis analogy. After staffing the crew and gathering supplies, he still delayed. His crew grew impatient, waiting on the banks of the Missouri River in St. Louis in ideal traveling weather for nearly six weeks. Lewis wanted to make sure that he had all the proper arrangements, including seeing that diplomacy was being served by having the Osage tribal chief meet in Washington, D.C., with President Jefferson. Further, he wanted to test and evaluate crewmembers for the various tasks ahead. As a result, he and Clark replaced several crewmembers with two multilingual scouts. He needed time to assign and establish working relations with junior officers. Finally, he would not depart until an additional shipment of nails and mosquito nets was on board.

This sense of preparation is typical of many great leaders, notably Martin Luther King, Nelson Mandela, Mother Jones, Sojourner Truth, and Mother Teresa. These leaders (and others, even my cousin Mary Jane, when she and her group of women plan and execute a successful one-week mountain trek each summer) minimize the chances of failure through extensive planning and thus, en route, are ready to respond and readjust to the many unanticipated day-to-day problems that occur.

To create a school with the integral purpose of producing academic excellence and an engaged citizenry is extremely difficult in most schools and districts in the United States. A school that moves toward creating and sustaining a great American education, where all students are expected to meet high academic learning goals with real application and contributions to the community, must have a sufficient number of educators, or at least a core group who are willing to challenge themselves, and who are curious, enthused, excited, and committed to expending time and energy. These human capacities can be developed and nurtured over time with virtually all faculty. But to create what I refer to as a great American school, the challenge is immediate. If a school must redesign in the fall, a number of faculty (tilting toward a majority) must be on board and ready. This often does not exist in most schools, so the strategy for change is quite different if in beginning a new school hiring and staffing can immediately place the right people for the voyage ahead.

In the same manner that most educators don't understand the necessity of an American education that links academics with student engagement in the real world, this is doubly true of most parents. Parents know schools as they experienced them; the notion of public demonstration and criteria for mastery are totally foreign to them. Thus any leader planning for change immediately meets confusion, skepticism, or outright hostility from some parents— particularly parents of students doing well under the current system. Any attempt to change the school might be seen as favoring the struggling students to the disadvantage of the "advanced" student.

One principal, in launching changes in his school, knew of such a group of parents and said, "One of my most important first jobs was reaching out to this group of students and parents and telling them that the changes would push everyone to new heights. I told them, 'We will guarantee that when your student leaves us, he will be better prepared for whatever he chooses to do next. This is our guarantee to you as we remake this school.'" Bold but necessary words, used to assure everyone that all would do better under the new school mantle of an American education.

Finally, and perhaps most important, there is the importance of including students, listening to them, and having them participate in the plan and design for change. As a principal, George Wood wrote about reinventing Federal Hocking High, in rural

Ohio, from a low-performing school to a stellar one involving students in capstone performance assessments: "We began with our students. We wanted to know how they experienced high school, what they should be like when they graduated, how we could make the school a place where teachers and students knew one another well enough to work together. . . . We wanted a community built around personal relationships; students working with and for teachers who they knew were committed to their best interests"(Wood, 1998, p. 35).

Building the Foundation

Leadership lays a foundation for internal stability and cohesiveness though developing a three-dimensional framework (Glickman, 1998):

1. A covenant of beliefs
2. A governance structure for schoolwide decisions
3. An action research process for continuous internal study

The covenant is developed through broad participation of stakeholders in defining a good education and what all students are expected to learn and demonstrate prior to exiting the school.

The governance structure is an operational scheme that makes clear where decision-making authority lies in bringing the covenant to life in practical matters of teaching methods, technology, curriculum development, staff development, schedules, grouping and placement practice, assessment and reporting of student learning, hiring and staffing, supervision, mentoring, peer coaching, evaluation, instructional materials, utilization of classroom and school space for instruction, community interlinks for student service learning and use of community persons and resources throughout the educational program, and allocation and expenditures of the school budget.

Action research is the ongoing study of what is possible on the basis of research as to what other schools have done successfully and a school's own continuous collection and analysis of how all students achieve against the school's indicators of quality performance.

In a previous book (Glickman, 1998), I explained at length the practical details of how these dimensions must be interconnected for a school to have a solid foundation for dealing with the skepticism or criticism that typically occurs in the beginning. Figure 2.1 is an illustration of these connections.[4]

To have one of these dimensions in place without the others leaves a school floundering. For example, having a smooth, agreed-upon governance process without a clear schoolwide covenant of beliefs can create much committee work for faculty, parents, and students without any sense of direction about desired educational achievements. This is in fact what many "site-based management" schools have become: people spending hours in deliberation about managerial and administrative matters without attending to the heart of a school—curriculum, instruction, and assessment. The same is true for a school that supports teachers doing action research in their own classroom, grade level, or department without a schoolwide covenant or governance structure. This can create much individual or small-group insight into how to improve learning but not yield an overall thrust to a school's collective efforts for all students. A school covenant without a schoolwide decision-making process to activate it and without action research to process the overall progress on student learning is simply a slogan, a product of intellectualizing with little in the practice of the school.

Successful American schools typically devote several years to developing an internal set of operations and beliefs that later establish a system of work standing above the influence or charisma of any one individual or group. These operations define the school.

If school members feel stuck on further implementation, they can immediately go to their action research process to learn from other schools and study why their own student work is not of the quality desired. The framework of covenant, governance, and

Figure 2.1. School Renewal Framework

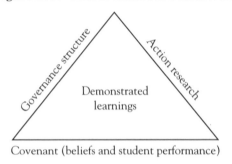

Covenant (beliefs and student performance)

action research remains a steady one for resolution and focus on further work. In turn, the framework substantiates that the school is an enduring institution, a community of purpose and activities not dependent on any individual or individuals.

Examples of Staying on Path

In one elementary school in the Northeast, during the school's second year of operations in 1975, a vocal parent challenged a student-designed mural being hung on a classroom wall and used by a classroom teacher. The parent went to the principal and complained, insisting the mural be taken down. The principal, instead of doing what many in authority normally do, did not play the role of knowing what is best for everyone else. Instead, she asked the parent if he understood the school's covenant, and if so why should there be disagreement with a classroom teacher using a mural designed and painted by the students that was in accordance with it. The school covenant clearly states that "education in a democracy must promote understanding and respect for all people."

The classroom mural was developed in a literature unit on the American family, depicting a range of American families. The mural includes gay and lesbian couples with their children. The principal told the parent that if he believed the school should change its covenant, then that would have to be done through the same governance process that created the beliefs and purposes; the parent could petition the School Improvement Team for doing so. If not, then the matter was resolved and the poster would remain.

Note that the principal did not impose her own beliefs or try to negotiate between parent and individual teacher to find a resolution that would satisfy or accommodate both. To do so would have undermined the collective operations of the school and sent a message that a democratic community at the school is not really important. The principal's handling of this incident during the beginnings of remaking this school left a lasting impression, an "institutional imprint" of how the school works. The imprint is still evident almost thirty years later, expressing what is valued in the school and how matters are to be handled.

A high school in a blue-collar community in the North redesigned itself in 1984. After five years of implementation, the first graduating class of students showed extraordinary accomplishment in increasing the graduation rate, performance on state examinations, and acceptance for postsecondary schools and scholarships. At this point, the principal decided to leave and pursue a position in another state. He was replaced through a hiring-and-staffing subcommittee of the governance process. The new person hired had more advanced curriculum and assessment skills than the predecessor, and the achievement and complexity of what students learned continued to improve.

In a large elementary school in the far West, the teachers were amazed to find themselves, in their second year of school change, at odds with their much admired, forceful, and charismatic principal about scheduling time for greater curriculum planning. They proposed canceling the monthly contracted half-days, wanting instead to meet every Wednesday for two hours. They would select volunteer parents to be trained as certified substitutes and have them conduct a weekly period of electives with students. This would free the staff for the last hour of school time so that, combined with the extra hour after school, they could have more continuous and frequent planning. The principal adamantly opposed the plan. He believed the school board and teacher's union would not allow a variance from the district contract; furthermore, even if approved, it would take too much time to prepare parents to be unpaid substitutes and establish an elective schedule and work out the placement of students.

At loggerheads with each other, teachers and principal agreed to take the issue to the larger school governing body, "the school team," which had been established the year before and comprised eleven members from among students, parents, teachers, staff, administrators, and community and business representatives. The school team listened to the proposal and the objections. Referring to the school covenant and the strong expression in it about "the school and community being partners in student learning" and parents being a child's first teacher," they considered how the plan would give teachers more frequent time for planning and students would have additional ways to pursue individual interests with community experts and resources. They deliberated and agreed by consensus to support the plan. The principal stated that, although still personally opposed, he "as a member of the council will of course support the team's decision and do all that can be done to make it happen." Through such action, the message was heard loud and wide that the school was to be a school, not a collection of individuals trying to outcontrol each other. The conclusion of this particular case was that the school board approved the proposal and the teacher union supported the waiver. Within three months, parents having a fine array of impressive educational talents and interests were certified as substitutes and began Wednesday afternoon electives. Seventeen years later, Wednesday afternoon community electives for students continue to thrive as a proud tradition of the school.

Conclusion

It might sound overly dramatic to say the planning of a great American school is akin to the leadership of Lewis, King, Gandhi, Jones, and Truth, but I don't think so. The idea of knowing when the time is right, when the staff, knowledge, and supplies are on hand to keep a school on the path to becoming a sacred institution of education must be carefully thought through. Leaders cannot know all the obstacles, but they certainly need to be aware of the large ones that have stopped other schools. Informal and formal political support must be lined up, and a core staff must be on hand that is tough, smart, and willing to take charge when controversy arises. Finally, those who lead need to use, with others, the moral authority and conferred power to keep to the path of a public education that unleashes the power of student learning to alter the world for the better.

Notes

1. Meriwether Lewis formed an expedition on the basis of planning for what was known at the time about the path to be taken; staffing and evaluating the best crew (including a Native American woman and an enslaved African American); sharing and delegating leadership with others; purchasing a variety of foods, supplies, and materials for all kinds of weather and geography; and finally using the talents of the crew to figure out what to do when the inevitable internal difficulties arose such as meeting hostile hunters or coming across unnavigable rivers or snowy peaked mountains too high and cold to climb. The expedition succeeded because of the initial planning and some very good luck. Without good planning, good luck would never have been a factor. They wouldn't have gone far enough on the journey to have had good fortune.

2. Lewis is not to be idolized. He was at times depressed, a few times punitive, and at the end his work furthered the horrible treatment of our first Americans by pushing them off their lands. What is significant about accomplishing any major purpose is to understand that success doesn't equate with what is right. There is a history of great success by leaders and groups who are successful in perpetuating harm to others.

3. What I define as great American schools are those in the progressive tradition of exemplary, public-spirited education for all students. This essay began after my colleagues and I had worked for a decade with schools of our Georgia League of Professional Schools, a school renewal network predicated on democratic educational values (see Glickman, 1993, 1998). I wondered why many of the schools that showed great promise in the first three to five years of effort were unable to carry out such change beyond the first school leaders and core faculty. Typically, when a new superintendent or principal was hired or a new school board elected, the school's focus on democratic education was eroded or lost. Some of our schools were able to sustain their efforts through economic, demographic, and political changes and through a succession of leaders and faculty, but clearly they were the exception.

When curiosity is piqued, one goes looking for explanations, if not answers to such questions. So I went exploring to find what I eventually defined as great American schools, those that had sustained their efforts with documented student results for ten to thirty years or more. I used four criteria in asking many prominent state and national education leaders to identify and provide insights about these schools. I was looking for (1) *sustainability* of ten to thirty years of education consistent with beginning, core values; (2) *progressive education*, characterized by activity-based and participatory learning; school-developed curriculum; team structures; equity emphasis on race, class, gender, disabilities, and ethnicity; linkage of education between school and community; performance-based assessment or student learning, and inclusive, heterogeneous (nontracked), mainstreaming emphasis on placement of students; (3) *regular schools* under the governance of a school district with the same funding and student enrollment conditions as other schools in the district, meaning not a magnet or elective alternative school; and (4) *documented student results* higher than comparable schools as measured by student test scores; student performance and demonstration; success in later life in jobs, family, health, and next level of education; civic and community participation; lower drop-out rate; higher promotion and graduation rate; and parent and student satisfaction.

With twenty schools identified, I could go about my exploration. (Obviously, there are many great schools in the country, but I found enough of them to begin.) I interviewed various students, teachers, parents, administrators, and other education and community leaders who had been part of each school at some time in its history. I followed up with classroom visits at fifteen of those schools, and I conducted more interviews and collected written case studies, newspaper accounts, internal memos, and other communications about significant historic happenings. I was not in the role of empirical researcher looking for causal predictions of generalizable factors; rather, I was trying to be a journalist observing and recording the story of each school.

Please note that in my writing I have altered the identity of persons and locations of a school to protect the confidentiality of most of them. Throughout my visits and interviews, I was amazed at how honest and penetrating people were in helping me uncover what is usually the hidden side of leadership, volatility, and schooling. I am most grateful for the explanations that I received about how certain progressive schools have continued to excel for ten to thirty years. Hopefully, the insights drawn from these K–12 schools, which represent the geographic, economic, and ethnic diversity of America, will be instructive to today's and tomorrow's educational leaders who believe strongly in the public purpose of education. I invite your thoughts, reactions, and comments.

4. Thanks to Partee Elementary School (Gwinnett, Georgia) students, faculty, administrators, and parents, who correctly redefined what must be in the center of the framework: demon-

stration of student learning as congruent with one's school covenant.

References

Ambrose, S. E. *Undaunted Courage: Meriwether Lewis, Thomas Jefferson, and the Opening of the American West.* New York: Touchstone, 1996.

Glickman, C. D. *Renewing America's Schools: A Guide for School-Based Action.* San Francisco: Jossey-Bass, 1993.

Glickman, C. D. *Revolutionizing America's Schools.* San Francisco: Jossey-Bass, 1998.

Wood, G. H. *A Time to Learn: The Story of One High School's Remarkable Transformation and the People Who Made It Happen.* New York: Dutton, 1998.

Chapter Three

Sustaining a "Sacred" Education

Symbols, Stories, and Ceremonies

When I enter a Jewish synagogue, even if it has been years since my last visit, I look first at the adults and children mingling and chanting. I then look straight ahead to the pulpit; my eyes lift to the embroidered curtains of the cabinet where the torahs (bibles) are stored, and then I slowly look up to the glow of the eternal light. At this moment, comforted with the familiarity of these symbols, ceremonies, and words, I know that part of me has returned to a place that remains a steadying influence on me as life evolves.

It is not so much the religion itself, as I have not participated much in any formal religion for most of my adult life, but it is the symbols that remind me of how my thinking has been shaped. This comforting assurance with sacred symbols is nearly as strong as when I visit other religious and spiritual places, or when walking in the woods and seeing the swoop of a redtail hawk, or looking out our rural road and glimpsing the red jacket of a kind neighbor who has traveled this road since childhood.

These figures, places, and images form a vision of home, what is of the past but continues to live in the hopes of the future. All of these places are sacred to me in that they signify continuity and effort to keep a way of life alive for further generations.

The "Sacred" and Schools

When we walk into most schools; there are few, if any, symbols of an education that will continue into the future. Yes, the American flag waves, and pledges are made, but these are symbols of a nation—not of education in this particular place we call school. Yes, many schools have their students wear a T-shirt, jacket, or other uniform proclaiming a slogan about what a great school X is. Or the school has its mascot, a prince or lion that promotes sports, band, and other extracurricular activities. But none of these mascots or slogans conveys the promise of education.

Let me contrast this lack of symbols, customs, and traditions with a visit to a school where I first encountered the word *sacredness* in reference to a school. I knew immediately that this school does connect with the heart and soul of generations of students, many of whom come back years later to lift their eyes and remember.

Yael, a fourteen-year-old, brown-skinned, bright-eyed female student, approaches me with grave concern. She says to me, "You haven't heard the entire story." Next to her walks an older woman. They both catch up and walk alongside me. We have just finished an hour-long meeting in which I interviewed a group of current and former students at this city high school. The school has been in existence for twenty-eight years and is one of the most highly accomplished, progressive public schools in America.

The school draws from all categories of students (by lottery) and has a large percentage of minority students (African American, Asian, and Hispanic), recent non-English-speaking immigrants, a higher percentage of special-needs students than most high schools, and many from a low socioeconomic population. It enrolls a range of students, from those who would be categorized as a failure or dropout at another high school to those who would be regarded as an academically very able student capable of doing extremely well in any conventional school. This school turns nearly all of them into purposeful students. Nearly all graduate in the normal time, state tests show that all students statistically grouped according to various ethnic and socioeconomic categories for comparison outperform their peers from other schools, and nearly 80 percent go on to postsecondary education while the remainder go directly into a vocation. Follow-up studies have shown that graduates of this school outpace their peers from other high schools in college graduation, job secured, intact family, active citizenship and leadership in their community, and longer and healthier life.

On the day I happened to be visiting, the annual three-week integrated semester was commencing, where classes of students, teachers, and parents were finishing academic projects involving extended activity often in a location outside of school. I was fortunate to be able to gather students and staff in between activities. My questions of them were to find out what they thought about their school, what makes it different from other schools, and why it has been in existence so long. Feeling quite satisfied by the details of their answers about curriculum, the schedule, courses, teachers, staff, and leadership, I was amused and surprised by the urgency of Yael and an older woman to speak to me further.

The older woman is the first to speak. She tells me she is Yael's mother, and that "I went to school here as a child and this school changed my life. I vowed that some day, I would volunteer here so that I could pay this school back. I am married, hold a good job, and now my oldest daughter, Yael, is here. This school allowed me to do more than I could ever have imagined." Yael listens quietly and then bends down and picks up a piece of paper litter off the school path. Yael tells me she needs to get to her seminar on ecology, but she wants me to know that "What we all told you in that meeting was what we do at this school, but that's not the most important part of our place."

Her mother adds, "It's hard to explain to others. When you attend this school, it never leaves you. It is with you forever." Yael interjects: "When you meet someone who went to school here, whether younger or twenty years older, there is a special closeness between us. It's not that we don't have times when school is a pain, but this school is always part of us." Her mom, listening intently, says to me quietly, with a welling of tears in her eyes, "What you need to know is that we are standing on sacred ground." Yael nods quietly, the two say good-bye, and the moment is gone.

What they leave me with is an impression that I have gathered in working with and visiting particularly powerful schools throughout America over the past thirty years. These places are not simply a compilation of classrooms, kind teachers, expansive hallways, and organized class schedules. The attitude, purpose, activities, rituals, and demonstration of student achievement have created an intergenerational institution of sacredness premised on democratic ideals. Within each of these schools, there are powerful symbols of the unique, progressive education that lives on in all who pass through.

Enduring Symbols

In Yael's school, every student, every day, begins homeroom in a morning circle with fourteen other students and a faculty member who is their advisor, mentor, and friend. Thirty-five minutes each day, they have this time to share the best of their work, conceive joint projects, assist each other in weathering a tough time at home or in school, or simply relax and enjoy the companionship of one another. The circle is not coerced, nor is it a therapy group; it is simply a way for faculty and students every day to pause and see, care, and learn from each other.

In another school, Jerold Middle School, every morning the entire membership of the school sits in a large open space in the center of the building for morning call—they hear the day's announcement, usually observe a student or faculty or community member's short recital, and participate in singing a student-written song, the anthem of what it means to be a Jerold student. Each graduating class adds additional lines to the musical; over twenty years, the Jerold song has grown into four versions.

In Padre Elementary School, one immediately notices what is hanging on the wall in the entrance: a huge and colorful quilt done by the first graduating class of students of a then-new education program begun decades before. In that first historic year, working with teachers and parents, each student stitched into the quilt her or his own patch describing the connection of the school to its community. One sees patches with scenes of barn raisings, fresh rivers flowing with fish, new industries being created, and small farms flourishing. Also on the quilt are patches that show the first schoolhouse for white students and a separate one for black students. There are patches depicting scenes of great turbulence during court-ordered integration years, patches of various community leaders, of Native American ancestors, and scenes of great conflict and reconciliation. Each patch contains the signature of the student. The quilted patches together make up a large story of community, place, and school and contain the hopes for a better future.

What is striking about this display (or other similar displays, such as the diverse urban high school where students landscaped and built outdoor walls and benches with ceramic tiles that invite students, faculty, and parents to sit and talk with each other) is not just what one sees in these great schools but also what one doesn't see. Most typical schools have on their walls a large plaque that praises the official planners of the building (the superintendent, school board members, city commissioners, and mayor), or there is an inscription about school honors bestowed by others (state and national blue ribbon awards), or a trophy case with team honors for sports or academics, or individual displays of student pictures, writing, or paintings. In great American schools, the featured displays are designed by each student as part of a larger scheme to be left for future students and educators to build upon. Each display beckons; it leaves an open space and invitation for each subsequent class of students to add their own contribution as a continuous line of ongoing work. From the first year of the school to the thirtieth, visitors know that student work is central to the appearance of the school; the school belongs to those who have walked, are walking, and will walk these halls.

In other ways, great schools signify the purpose and continuity of their beginnings. There are schools that open the day with a song or pledge created with students about what it means to be a learner. In others, there are annual events where students and community members identify a neighborhood need to work on together, or there is a school musical production created by and with all students to inform, entertain, and leave an aesthetic good to the larger neighborhood.

All of these displays, events, and rituals become the expected, annual sequence of ways to lock arms between school and community. Each display or event allows a generation of students, teachers, and parents to remember the events of their own time as they appreciate the work of the current generation. These great schools have camplike qualities, where academic, intellectual, and personal interactions between school and community are ritualized in special displays and moments that unite everyone in a common experience.

A nice example of such ritual is a small K–12 school in the Midwest that began in the early 1970s and continues to use a single graduation robe for its graduating seniors. The first class was composed of only a few students. Thirty years later, and now graduating thirty students at a time, the original graduation robe (heavily stitched and repaired) is still worn by each graduate. Each young person wears the robe and crosses the podium, and after receiving the diploma he or she lifts the robe and it is circled back over the head of the next graduate, and the cycle continues.

Creation Stories: A Peabody and Snowy Saturday

School success over time is never just one special event, meeting, or activity. Rather, it is, as Michael Fullan and others have noted, a journey of recursive decisions and actions. Yet I did find stories about particular events still shared among colleagues after decades, continuing to give direction to the school. These stories have become symbolic and ceremonial reminders of the core values of education of the school and the necessary commitment and ongoing vigilance to keep the work alive. For example, one middle school in a high- to moderate-income area of a midwestern city, a school justifiably well known for its inquiry-centered curriculum, has a simple phrase to remind everybody what the school is about. The words "Don't Do a Peabody" (which refers to the acceptance of a generous grant from a well-known foundation) capture the fight the faculty successfully exerted against a national school reform model they had originally applied for and received for a renewable three-year period. With it came significant grant dollars for teacher and staff development, travel, and computers for students.

After the first year of being trained and monitored by the school reform program staff developers, the faculty realized they had made a huge mistake. They found rigidity rather than flexibility in the training and forced application of external curriculum, sequenced lesson plans, and teaching and assessment methods. The program was at odds with the core of critical inquiry that had defined the school. Rather than accept this loss of core values, they met with their principal and parent group and decided to openly reject the model and return additional funds. In effect, they took their school back; now they realize how careful they must be in the future about acquiring additional programs, regardless of extra funds gained. Even today, sitting in on a school council meeting or a casual conversation in the teacher's lounge, one is still likely to hear, in any discussion of future efforts to improve the school, the caution of "Let's not do a Peabody again." Old-timers and new faculty all know what these words mean and the hard choices ahead to keep the school on course.

A similar case of sustaining core values through a significant event might be illustrated in the intermingling of education with another sacred story. I found myself sitting around a circular table in the staff lounge with a group of six teachers from a school in the Northeast. In that conversation, I learned about a blustery, snowy Saturday. Four of the teachers had been part of the beginning of their school twenty-five years before, and the other two were in their first and second year at the school. The newest member of the group asked the veterans to tell me the story. The story, she explained, would let me in on why this school is so different from the other three schools she had worked at. The town, twenty-five years earlier, had been racked by a no-win situation of closing a school from one part of the city and merging it with another. The change was due to financial reasons, and no one was happy about it. The school to be closed served mostly poor and minority students, and the school to remain was composed of mostly white and affluent students.

After a tough first year of merger and trying to fit one school into the other, discord among students, faculty, and parents grew. The principal invited all teachers, staff, and parents to forget about merging one school into the other and instead participate in creating a new school out of the two—a school that would be about harmony, diversity, democracy, high academic achievement, and active citizenry. The principal made it clear that the school as is, with two competing faculty, parent, and student factions, could no longer exist. He would leave if a unified and better school could not metaphorically be raised. The principal was an innovative and highly respected educator in the community, and his words were taken as sincere and heartfelt. But little did anyone imagine what was to come.

The principal set aside every faculty, parent, and community meeting and student council meeting for the remainder of the year to imagine a better, more "public" school. Separately, faculty met once a week before school to review samples of student work and discuss how such work could be improved. Saturday mornings were special sessions set aside by the principal at his home for volunteers to meet with him to coordinate and solidify the plans for the school. Through the principal's pushing, a new scheme emerged. It would include multiage grouping, individual education plans, descriptive report cards without grades, quarterly diagnosis of each student's learning with a conference with each student and his or her parent, and new forms of assessment linked to service to the community.

Current textbooks would be heaved, old classroom chairs and tables removed, new curriculum either purchased or developed by staff to recognize the contributions of all groups of Americans, and the physical organization of the school changed into cluster student teams staying with the same group of teacher and aides and parents for three years. Each class would no longer be identified with the name of a particular teacher; no more "Ms. Fernback's fifth grade classroom," but instead the "Charger Scholars," in room four of the Academic Inquisitor Cluster. Agreements were secured, some with great fight and some teachers and a librarian leaving the school. Teams planned new student assessments; full implementation would begin in the fall. Saturday morning meetings would continue through the upcoming, new school year to share information about progress.

After some initial confusion about how to assign students, inform parents, and choose cluster teachers and aides, the fall was off to a good start. By Thanksgiving, however, there were signs of frazzled and disenchanted staff, tired and working twelve-hour days, and feeling they couldn't keep up with everything.

Then came the Saturday morning meeting in January. It was a bitterly cold day, and everything exploded after the customary doughnuts, rolls, scrambled eggs, coffee and tea, and juice that the principal always personally prepared and served at these weekend sessions. He now sat with a group of fifteen teachers, staff, and parents around the living room next to the wood stove, some on sofas, chairs, or cushions, or on the floor.

One teacher forcefully spoke for the group: "We have to slow down. We can't change our classrooms. We can't change how we work with each other, and we can't change how we involve students at the same time we rewrite curriculum and fill out new record-keeping forms. We are killing each other with so many meetings. We just can't do it. It is impossible. We need to slow down."

The principal, obviously sympathetic, listened. Another teacher interjected that, at the beginning, this had been the most exciting year of her teaching career, but it would make life easier if they could just concentrate on the new curriculum, return to the old report cards, and get back into self-contained classrooms. Then more complaints and frustration were echoed, some remarking about uncaring students and know-everything parents; others were upset about the principal, and about themselves for not being up to the job.

The principal was silent for forty-five minutes and then said: "I hear you. We do need to consider how much we can give to the school and still have healthy lives, but we will not retreat to old ways. You are the professionals, and it is our job as professionals to figure out how to make this work."

Snow began to fall. It accumulated as the talk increased in intensity. Eventually the anger was spent, and an earnest discussion led to agreement about how to help each other, how outside help could be secured, and how they could stay on course. By noon, there was recommitment to the work ahead, but now that the meeting was over no one could leave! During the discussion, hardly anyone noticed the full-fledged blizzard that now literally had everyone snowed in. So the afternoon was spent in games, television, more food, music, laughter, and calls to family.

One teacher reminisced to me how the memories of the Saturday remain so strong today because it made clear that, despite the obstacles, the principal "was convinced that we were capable of educating students in ways that most people, including ourselves, had doubts about. He trusted us unconditionally and he wouldn't let us give up." It was a powerful lesson that, twenty-five years later, is clearly learned in the success of students, the buzz of activity, the still-twelve-hour work days, and the esteem that the community holds for these teachers. Admittedly, many educators would not choose to work at such a demanding place, but it is wonderful that there are educators who would work nowhere else.

The Viking Funeral

To end this treatise about sustaining great progressive schools with the aid of sacred symbols, ceremonies, and stories, I turn to Souhegan High School, in Amherst, New Hampshire, a large, progressive, and relatively affluent school that created a compatible tradition for faculty and staff, called the Viking Funeral. This is a ritual where the entire staff ends their last day of school by sharing with each other the memories of the year that they wish to note, speak of, and then release. They walk together to the river and, while standing on the bank, quietly put their notes into a small, cardboard "Viking boat," which then is pushed into the current and moves down stream: "'The Viking Funeral' is the place to say goodbye . . . many of us let go of fear and frustration. . . . Each year someone discards feelings of insecurity, of not being good enough or smart enough. . . . We have stated publicly that we were releasing anger, pain, rage, and sadness. We have used the occasion to mask the silly and the profound . . . it is our most sacred ritual" (Silva and Mackin, 2002, p. 128).

As the boat moves away, the year is over, elations and despairs are released, and the struggle to reach out to the future community of students, parents, and each other begins all over again.

Conclusion

Leadership in sustaining great American schools includes important symbols, traditions, and words and events that symbolize what is eternally important. These traditions signify that students and adults have used their education to make a better place for all. (See Smith, 2002; and the report of the National Commission on Service Learning for more examples of this work.) The traditions are not ornamental, but real; they demonstrate what students and adults learn, how it is recognized, and how it is left to the next generation to build upon.

References

National Commission on Service Learning. *Learning in Deed*. Battle Creek, Mich.: W. K. Kellogg Foundation, and John Glenn Institute for Public Service. (To order report and video: www.servicelearningcommission.org.)

Silva, P., and Mackin, R. A. *Standards of Mind and Heart: Creating the Good High School*. New York: Teachers College Press, 2002.

Smith, G. A. "Placed-Based Education: Learning to Be Where We Are." *Kappan*, Apr. 2002, pp. 584–600.

Part Two

School Renewal

Ironies and Challenges

Chapter Four

Good Schools and Effective Schools

What Do We Want?

In the past eighteen months I've had more than a dozen opportunities to react to the words *good* and *effective* as descriptors of schooling and teaching. In each case, I've been left confused and groping for the meaning of the terms. I share here four specific incidents that enabled me to clarify the terms in my own mind, because out of that clarification has arisen a basic issue that every professional educator needs to face.

The mother of a public school student in a distant state phoned to ask me for advice. She explained that her child's school had become involved in an "effective schools" program and that the outcomes included eliminating all recess periods; devoting more time to teacher-centered, total group instruction in reading and mathematics; relying on textbooks and mimeographed drill sheets; curtailing individual and small-group projects; closing classroom learning centers; and canceling field trips and free time for students. The mother quoted her child as saying that "school isn't fun any more; it's so serious, and we have to work all the time."

This mother phoned me because she and other concerned parents had decided to gather information from researchers about the relationship of children's play to cognitive development. They intended to present their findings to the superintendent, in the hope of altering their school system's commitment to this particular brand of supposedly effective schooling. As we ended our conversation, she said that the parent group expected a difficult battle, because students' test scores had risen under the new program, causing most observers to consider the approach effective. As far as she and the other parents in her group were concerned, however, the school "isn't good" anymore. Long after our conversation was over, her words—"effective but no good"—stayed with me.

Several months later another phone call came, this time from a secondary teacher who was gathering information in an attempt to block district implementation of an effective-schools and effective-teaching program. She had read an article that I wrote some years ago, criticizing a particular effective-teaching program (Glickman, 1979). I suggested to her that one cannot rationally reject the idea of effective teaching in general. My earlier criticism had to do with the application of one specific program in the schools. She then explained that teachers in her district were "being told what to teach, how to teach, and when to teach—it's being crammed down our throats, and we don't like it. It might be effective, but we don't like it." Déjà vu. Once again, I was hearing the words "effective but no good." (I later learned that the teachers in this school system cast a unanimous vote of no confidence in the superintendent, who left her position at the end of the year.)

At a state education convention last spring, a panel of speakers was convened that included the state department official in charge of evaluation and testing, a prominent representative of the business community, a member of the state board of education, and a university faculty member. Their task was to answer the question, What is an effective school? The prepared responses from the panel members included repeated reference to such matters as test scores, student attendance, and the dropout rate.

The moderator then asked each panelist to respond from personal experience to the question, How do you know that you are in a good school? The tone and content of these unrehearsed responses changed dramatically. The panelists mentioned the smiles on students' faces, the care and concern that teachers showed in talking with students, the excitement with which students engaged in activity, the openness with which students questioned one another. Just as numerical data predominated in the formal presentations, affective indicators predominated in these off-the-cuff responses. Remember that the affective responses came from some of the same people who had been (and still are) in the forefront of the movement for effective-teaching and effective-schools reforms predicated on improvement of test scores. Interesting, I thought, how changing the question, from what an effective school is to what a good school is, generated dichotomous responses.

During the last two years, I've been a member of a team of researchers studying schools and school systems labeled as "improving" (as defined by some of the criteria from the effective-schools research, adjusted for students' socioeconomic status). We visited these schools and interviewed teachers, administrators, and central office personnel. After every visit, we discussed what each of us had found out about the process of improvement in that particular school.

At the conclusion of one such debriefing session, a member of the research team commented that she would not want to teach in or send her own child to the school that we had just visited. Her comment prompted a serious discussion about whether this particular school was good or not. Unquestionably, the school was effective; after all, the test gains were impressive (not falsely manipulated), and they reflected changes in program and instructional approach, as well as hard work and commitment on the part of school personnel. Yet we argued among ourselves about whether the school was good or not. Those who judged it good claimed that the school was maintaining a strict academic focus, that the students were learning what they were taught, and that the school was giving youngsters the basic skills they needed to cope effectively in the real world. Those who judged the school "bad" claimed that it was too mechanical, too uniform, too teacher-directed; that the teaching lacked spontaneity; that everyone did the same thing at the same time; and that learning by discovery was missing. Once again, we did not question the school's effectiveness; we argued only about whether or not the school was good.

Many of the clarion calls for school reform cite findings from recent research on effective teaching and effective schools as an example of how schools and classrooms should change. The reformers, who speak from a formal distance, tell us that the goal of all schools should be effectiveness—as measured by such factors as student scores on a test of basic skills, their attendance rate, and their performance on the Scholastic Aptitude Test (SAT). The reformers emphasize that we ought to narrow the academic focus on the curriculum; test students more frequently; raise standards for promotion; and have teachers state specific, measurable objectives and follow a prescribed instructional approach (with large groups) that involves reviewing, explaining, demonstrating, guiding practice, checking for understanding, and summarizing. The findings of recent research on effective teaching and effective schools are treated as laws of science that apply to all teachers and all schools. (Ironically, many of the researchers who have studied effective schools have argued strongly against overgeneralizing their findings; see Hunter, 1985; Gage, 1986; Brandt, 1986; Rosenshine, 1986.)

The findings of the research on effective teaching and effective schools are too often equated with what is desirable or good. By failing to distinguish between *effectiveness* and *goodness*, we avoid two central questions in education. The first that schools and school systems must deal with is, What is good? Only after that question has been answered should they deal with the second: How do we become effective? The current fascination with findings from the research on effectiveness has blinded schools and school systems to the more basic question of goodness.

Do higher SAT scores justify labeling a school good if the price for the higher scores is an increase in the dropout rate? Are higher scores in reading and mathematics good if students gain them at the expense of time spent in studying science, social studies, art, or music? Is an average gain of eight points on a reading test score worth increasing allocation of time and resources to direct instruction in reading? Is this gain more desirable than maintaining the current achievement level in reading but devoting a greater proportion of class time to a whole-language approach that emphasizes creative writing or critical thinking?

The research on effective schools and effective teaching does not answer these questions for us. The research is neutral; it does not choose our goals but simply tells us how to accomplish certain things (which may or may not be among our goals). To be blunt, educators who care about the fate of all children must define *goodness* before they worry about *effectiveness*.

It has often been said that individual public schools must be accountable to both the community and the state. But the full truth goes beyond that statement; we educators must also be accountable to ourselves. What we see as worthy should mediate what we do. What are our educational goals for students? When do we draw the line and say, "Enough is enough"?

I am determined to draw my own line—now! I strongly believe that the effectiveness movement is unnecessarily restricting the curriculum, narrowing the teaching approach to direct instruction, and controlling teachers by judging them as being on task only when they are teaching to specific objectives. Many administrators seem determined to evaluate teachers on how well they stick to a tightly outlined sequence of instruction, geared to a specific objective.

A special education teacher recently told me that she had asked her supervisor for permission to take her students on a five-minute walk to a grocery store to observe transactions at the check-out counter. The supervisor immediately asked, "Which specific objectives will this walk accomplish?" The teacher replied, "I don't know. I simply want my students to see transactions involving real money. Besides, getting out of the classroom for a while would be fun." Responded the supervisor, "I'm sorry. If it's not one of our curriculum objectives, we don't do it!"

Where I draw the line—and where I believe that others (at least the parents and teachers who have phoned me) are drawing the line—is at the insistence that learning must always be tightly controlled, narrowly prescribed, and clearly specified. Some learning fits that pattern, of course. But we must always keep in mind the words of Jean Piaget: "The goal of intellectual education is not to know how to repeat or retain ready-made truths (a truth that is parroted is only a half-truth). It is in learning to master the truth by oneself at the risk of losing a lot of time and going through all the roundabout ways that are inherent in real activity" (1973, p. 106).

When we take an excursion into learning, we can choose to drive straight to our objective, keeping our eyes straight ahead, exerting steady pressure on the pedal, and stopping only when necessary. Or we can choose to make the drive part of the excursion, by slowing down to admire the scenery, visiting historical and cultural sites, and dining in restaurants situated off the beaten track. If we follow the second plan, we may not arrive at our objective as quickly—but we will have learned more and spent the time more pleasantly.

I neither can nor want to answer the question, "What is desirable for each school and each community?" In my opinion, teaching for specific academic achievement has much to commend it. But the question remains, At what expense? We are currently traveling more efficiently to a predetermined destination, but is it the *only* destination? An effective school can be a good school, and a good school must be an effective school—but the two are not necessarily the same.

References

Brandt, R. S. "On the Expert Teacher: A Conversation with David Berliner." *Educational Leadership*, 1986, *44*, 4–9.

Gage, N. L. "Does Process-Product Research Imply Non-Deliberation in Teacher Education?" Paper presented at the annual meeting of the American Educational Research Association, San Francisco, Apr. 1986.

Glickman, C. D. "Mastery Learning Stifles Individuality." *Educational Leadership*, 1979, *37*, 10–102.

Hunter, M. "What Wrong with Madeline Hunter?" *Educational Leadership*, 1985, *2*, 7–60.

Piaget, J. *To Understand Is to Invent: The Future of Education*. New York: Viking, 1973.

Rosenshine, B. "Teaching Content: A Critique of a Lesson on Federalist Paper No. 10." Paper presented at the annual meeting of the American Educational Research Association, San Francisco, Apr. 1986.

Chapter Five

Pretending Not to Know
What We Know

> The first task of restructuring—confronting our
> own professional knowledge—is not easy, but it is
> likely to produce the courage to improve, at least
> in a few good schools . . . [we] can't pretend to not
> know what is known.
>
> —*Joyce Carol Oates, "Excerpts from a Journal"*

Calls for "restructuring" schools raise a question as to what knowledge should guide our efforts. I've become aware, as a participant in an effort known as the Georgia League of Professional Schools, that restructuring needs to begin with confronting our own professional knowledge. For too long, professionals have gone about the business of teaching and operating schools in ways they privately admit are not in the best interest of students. The reasons for doing so are plentiful; we all live with district policies, state regulations, traditional school structures, mandated curriculum alignment, community pressures, and limited resources. Then too, we can, by pretending not to know what is known, live with dissonance between our internal values and our behavior (Festinger, 1957).

Today as we answer the call for restructuring, school faculty can begin by opening up their suppressed knowledge, thus creating debate and fostering their own value-driven enthusiasm for "doing the right thing" for students rather than simply for "doing things

---

This chapter is an adaptation of two previous presentations: the 1990 Johnnye V. Cox Distinguished Lecture, in Athens, Georgia; and the 1991 ASCD Annual Conference Assembly, in San Francisco.

right" (Sergiovanni, 1991). We have the opportunity to stop pretending not to know.

Let us spend the rest of this essay describing what we know,
summarized in eleven statements in three categories. (I admit of no
higher enlightenment than other educators, and I'm confident
there will be disagreement with my claims.) I conclude with a discussion about the need for "elite" schools, to pioneer a new era
of intellectual confrontation. If we don't confront what we know,
the rhetoric of innovation-for-its-own-sake will drive the underlying values away, and this reform movement will become another
fad, enduring for a few years only to be replaced by the next
(Slavin, 1989).

Teaching and Learning

Let's begin by looking at what we know about teaching and learning.

1. Tracking Students Does Not Help Students.

We know that the evidence shows no benefits are gained by tracking students into ability groups, as shown by Oakes (1985), Slavin
(1987, 1990), George (1987), and Garmoran and Berends (1987).
Higher-achieving students do not do better when together, and
lower-achieving students do much worse when together. Tracking
clearly discriminates and clearly perpetuates inequity among students; higher-track students tend to be white and wealthy, and from
a highly educated family; lower-track students tend to be black and
Hispanic, poor, and from a poorly educated family. Students tend
to be put into an ability group less for their academic ability and
more as a result of their socioeconomic status. Once assigned to a
low track, very few move into a higher one; their performance as
low achievers becomes self-perpetuating. Consequently, tracking
often results in segregation of students by socioeconomic status or
race. This may not be the intent, but it is the result.

In responding to these findings, some schools have eliminated
or dramatically reduced homogeneous grouping and ended separate

classroom programs (such as gifted and Title I). The San Diego schools, for example, no longer have remedial education. In British Columbia, a phased-in elimination of tracking, or "streaming" (through the eleventh year of schooling), has begun, leaving tracking for the last two years, when students specialize in a vocational or college-bound program.

But in many places tracking continues even when the evidence is overwhelmingly against it. Perhaps it benefits a few individual students and placates some parents; more often, tracking continues because it's easier to manage classrooms and schools when the range of ability is restricted rather than if they are expansive and students need to be taught in multiple ways. Recently, the National Education Association (1990) and the Quality Education for Minorities Network (Henry, 1990), as well as the National Governors Association (1990), have asked for elimination of ability grouping in the United States.

2. Retention Does Not Help Students.

In an update of his classic meta-analysis of studies comparing the education of students who were retained with students of comparable achievement and maturity who were promoted, Thomas Holmes concluded that in longitudinal studies "retained students were no better off in relation to their younger at-risk controls who went on immediately to the next grade" (1989, p. 28).

In the past fifteen years, study after study has shown rather convincingly that there is little benefit to retention (Shepard and Smith, 1989). Students retained one year have only a 50 percent chance of graduating, and students retained twice have little if any chance to graduate (Gastright, 1989). It stands to reason that a student who starts high school at the age of sixteen is not going to stay in school until he or she is twenty.

As Holmes (1989) concluded, "Those who continue to retain pupils at grade level do so *despite* [italics mine] the cumulative research evidence" (p. 78). The task of the school is not to sort and thwart students but instead to assist them to move along from year to year with the knowledge, concepts, and skills that allow them to graduate in twelve years with the prerequisites to be productive citizens.

3. Corporal Punishment Does Not Help Students.

As one who spent his earlier years as a researcher on the effects of various discipline approaches and who continues to keep up on this literature, I find no research that shows any long-term benefit from paddling students. In fact, there is research (see the "Fifteen Thousand Hours" study by Rutter and others, 1979) that shows the least successful schools are the most punitive. At its best, what corporal punishment does is make students comply out of fear, become subversive in their misbehavior, and learn the lesson that physical might is the way to resolve problems. At the worst, the students who are big enough simply rebel and physically counterattack.

Schools and states that eliminate corporal punishment are helping students to learn self-control. Still, thirty-one states allow corporal punishment, and more than 1.1 million paddlings are administered in a year (White, 1990). The United States remains one of the few countries in the world where corporal punishment is still practiced.

4. Students Learn from Real Activities.

In a century of public schools, little structural change has occurred in classroom teaching (Cuban, 1984). The majority of classroom time is spent on teachers lecturing, students listening, students reading textbooks, or students filling out work sheets. To observe a classroom now is to observe one fifty years ago: a teacher standing and talking, students sitting and daydreaming (Goodlad, 1984). Perhaps the last real structural change occurred when the desks were unbolted.

Yet we know that real projects, with primary sources, real problems to solve, and real discussion show dramatic and significant gains in student achievement and motivation (see Slavin and Madden's summary, 1989, of instructional approaches; and Brophy,

1987). Teachers need to learn multiple ways of teaching students so as to engage their minds, their bodies, and their souls (Joyce, 1990). Teachers need to reflect on how students think, listen to students describe what helps them learn, and share with their colleagues activities and method that get closer to active learning.

5. Effective Teaching Is Not a Set of Generic Practices.

Rather than generic practices, effective teaching is a set of context-driven decisions about teaching. Effective teachers do not use the same set of practices for every lesson (Porter and Brophy, 1988). They do not, like mindless automatons, review the previous day's lessons, state their objectives, present, demonstrate, model, check for understanding, provide guided practice, and use closure. Instead, what effective teachers do is constantly reflect on their work, observe whether students are learning or not, and then adjust their practice accordingly.

Effective teaching, then, is a set of decisions about the use of a variety of classroom materials and methods to achieve certain learning goals. Researchers and theorists from Madeline Hunter to Barak Rosenshine, David Berliner, and Jere Brophy have disclaimed any responsibility for application of their own research as a simple-minded prescription of uniform criteria for monitoring and evaluating teachers. Such prescription is driven by psychometricians looking for objectivity and reliability. The problem is that such concepts of tracing are divorced from reality and simply not valid (see Darling-Hammond, 1992).

6. There Is Nothing Inherently Sacred About Carnegie Units, Classroom Size, and Grade Levels!

A leading school reformer, Phil Schlechty (1990), has eloquently expressed what we know about this:

> There are, at present, a number of structural elements in schools that preclude flexibility in the allocation of human resources. Chief

among these are the concepts of school class, grade level, and the Carnegie unit in high school. . . . Arranging schools in classes, and classrooms, and grouping children by age or ability or sex or any other characteristic, represents only a few of the possibilities for grouping children for schoolwork. One could just as well group children according to the tasks that must be performed to carry out a particular piece of schoolwork or according to any of a number of other grouping arrangements one might conceive. The Carnegie unit is another convention. Invented primarily as a means of satisfying the interests of higher education in having a basis for judging college preparedness among youth, the Carnegie unit became a standard measure in American education just as the pound, the quart, and the inch are standard measures in American commerce.

The problem with these conventions is not that they exist. . . . The problem arises when upholding the convention becomes an end in itself [pp. 64–65].

Schlechty explains that alternatives to these conventions are not necessarily better, but they might be. The point is, we'll never know unless we try.

Teachers and Work Conditions

Now let's move on to what we know about teachers.

7. *Outstanding Teachers Do Not Teach for External Incentives.*

Incentives, a career ladder, and a merit pay plan are not inducements for a great teacher; the pleasure of seeing the effect of his or her decisions on students is. Garret Keizer (1988) wrote about receiving the Star Teacher of the Year award:

Last year my freshman student Jessica Davis took a first prize of a thousand dollars in the Honors Competition for Excellence in

Writing. I taught composition in Jessica's English class, and when we learned of her candidacy, I gave her extra coaching outside of class, which she graciously acknowledged in the newspaper articles about her. But the fact is, I did not make Jessica Davis a good writer. Somewhere on the scale of merit between me and God are at least eight elementary and middle school teachers. . . .

Another teacher, who works in a local elementary school, starts her summer by tearing up every note, exercise, and handout that she has used the preceding year. In the fall, she will begin from scratch. Just the thought that I might be forced by theft or fire to adopt this woman's standards makes me light-headed. How does one quantify that kind of integrity?

As I write, one of our first grade teachers is adjusting the last hem of the authentic Pilgrim costumes she has sewn for every student in her class. A girl so poor that she has on occasion come to school without underwear stands smoothing down the folds of her long dress in wonderment. "See my dress" she calls out to the visitor. It may be the cleanest, newest, handsomest thing she has ever worn—this garment of another age's austerity. How many hours this teacher must have spent at home behind a sewing machine— how many seconds will it take to punch her dedication into someone's business-model, performance-oriented, incentive-based, computerized version of how schools ought to run [pp. 117–119].

After interviewing and studying outstanding teachers of the past fifty years, Duval (1990) concluded that these teachers spent up to $2,000 a year out of their own pocket for supplies, materials, and trips for students: "This group of teachers spent their own money knowingly and for maximum effect. . . . Being able to secure materials, services, and other things of use . . . without having to go through a tiring, tedious bureaucratic process is something prized by all of the excellent teachers" (p. 192).

Eliot Wigginton, past Teacher of the Year in Georgia and founder of the renowned Foxfire program, wrote this:

I am a public high school English teacher. Occasionally, on gloomy nights, my mood shifts in subtle ways, and familiar questions rise in my throat; in social situations, confronted by those whose lives seem somehow more dramatic, an implication in the air is that I will have little of interest to contribute to the conversation; many people with fewer years of formal education make more money. Then the mood passes, for I know that surface appearance is deceitful and salary is a bogus yardstick of worth.

Actually, if the truth be told, it is only rarely that I wonder why I am still teaching. I know why. I teach because it is something I do well; it is a craft I enjoy and am intrigued by; there is room within its certain boundaries for infinite variety and flexibility of approach, and so if I become bored or my work becomes routine, I have no one to blame but myself; and unlike other jobs I could have, I sometimes receive indications that I am making a difference in the quality of people's lives. That, and one more thing; I genuinely enjoy daily contact with the majority of the people with whom I work [1985, Introduction].

So what do we know about what motivates excellent teachers? We know that it has to do with discretion and control over resources, time, instructional materials, and teaching strategies so as to make better educational decisions.

How have we responded to what we know, over the past seventeen years? It is amazing that currently, with the technology available to us, most teachers have to wait in line in the school office to make a phone call to a parent. What other professional is left without a phone in his or her workstation? At a time where personal computers are essential to almost every knowledgeable worker, teachers don't even have phones! Instead, 96 percent of teachers spend an average of $250 per year of their own money on teaching supplies because they lack control over the teaching budget. What's more, a recent Carnegie Foundation Study (1990) found more than 70 percent of all teachers in the United States are not involved deeply in decisions about curriculum, staff development, grouping of students, promotion and retention policies, or school budget.

School Improvement

Now let's look at what we know about improving schools.

8. Teacher Evaluation Does Not Relate to Schoolwide Instructional Improvement.

The evaluation boondoggle has been perhaps the greatest robbery of educational resources in our time. There is little research that establishes a clear link between the amount and type of teacher evaluation and attainment of schoolwide priorities. Yet policy makers have poured millions of dollars into evaluation systems while ignoring the daily support needs of teachers.

Blankenship and Irvine (1985) found, for example, that a majority of all experienced teachers in Georgia had never been observed, been given feedback, or had a conference focused on thinking critically about ways to improve teaching. Throughout their careers, all classroom visits by observers were for the purpose of judging and rating. Furthermore, 90 percent of teachers had never had a chance to observe a peer teacher and discuss what they could learn from each other. The lack of helpful and supportive assistance has been underscored by conclusions of the Fifteen Thousand Hours study: "It was striking, however, that in the less successful schools teachers were often left completely alone to plan what to teach, with little guidance or supervision from their . . . colleagues and little coordination with other teachers to ensure a coherent course from year-to-year" (Rutter and others, 1979, p. 136).

Uniform systems of teacher evaluation have cost millions of dollars and millions of hours—and for what? To rid the profession of fewer than 2 percent of our teachers. Imagine what could happen if the bulk of that money and time were reshifted to help competent teachers become even more thoughtful and skillful in the craft and art of teaching, through peer coaching, group problem-solving sessions, curriculum work, staff development, and clinical supervision.

Teacher evaluation may be a necessary control function of an organization; but it improves a school only when the majority of people border on incompetence—they either shape up or get out. Most of our schools do not employ a majority of incompetent people; rather, we employ people who could use more help and assistance to think through the long-term and short-term decisions they are making on behalf of students.

9. The Principal Is Not the Instructional Leader But the Coordinator of Instructional Leaders.

The arrogance with which the education community has embraced the concept of "principal as instructional leader" is mind-boggling. We really want to believe—as my friend Ed Pajak (1985) suggests—in the principal as Rambo, leading a school up the path of glory. This concept—the principal as all-knowing, all-wise, and transcendent in vision, who can lead the staff development council and the curriculum council; be an expert on group facilitation and organizational change; spend 50 percent of his or her time in the classroom with uncanny analytical and conferencing abilities; deal with all manner of students, staff, parents, and communities, plus fill out all necessary forms, run all the schedules, and take care of maintaining the air conditioner and furnace—this is an incomprehensible idea for supporting school reform.

Let me express what we all know about powerful, successful schools. In such a school, the people who are seen as most credible and having the greatest expertise about teaching and learning are the teachers themselves. There are teachers in our schools who are beyond those of us in a formal leadership position in their knowledge, skills, and application of curriculum and instruction. In successful schools, principals aren't threatened by the wisdom of others; instead, they cherish it by distributing leadership. The principal of a successful school is not the instructional leader but the educational leader who mobilizes the expertise, talent, and care of others. He or she is the person who symbolizes, supports, distributes, and coordinates the work of the teacher as instructional leader (see Chubb and Moe, 1990).

10. Successful Schools Work from Professional Judgment, Not Prescriptive Lists!

In his 1990 book *Improving Schools from Within*, Roland Barth says:

> Our public schools have come to be dominated and driven by a conception of educational improvement that might be called *list logic*. The assumption of many outside of schools seems to be that if they can create lists of desirable school characteristics, if they can only be clear enough about directives and regulations, then these things will happen in schools. . . . The vivid lack of congruence between the way schools are and the way others' lists would have them causes most school people to feel overwhelmed, insulted, and inadequate— hardly building blocks for improving schools or professional relationships. . . . Moreover, I doubt that we would find that many teachers, principals, and students in high-achieving schools comply closely with anybody's list. As Ronald Edmonds often said, we know far more about the features that characterize an effective school than we know about how a school becomes effective in the first place. Why, then, do we try to force schools we do not like to resemble those we do like by employing means that have little to do with the evolution of the kind of schools we like? [pp. 37–40].

11. The Measure of School Worth Is Not How Students Score.

What counts is not scores on a standardized achievement test but rather the learning students can display in an authentic or real setting.

The fixation with test scores has recently come under a storm of criticism. George Hanford, past president of the College Board (which is the developer of the Scholastic Aptitude Test), wrote that the scores produced by tests exude "an aura of precision out of proportion to their significance, which in turn fosters an unsuitable reliance on them, to the exclusion or neglect of other indicators that are equally important and useful" (1986, p. 9).

It is not that standardized tests are useless. They are a source of information about what a group of students know. How much weight should be put on that source of knowledge, rather than other sources of knowledge, is the issue of dispute. Wise (1988) warns us that "many schools no longer teach reading, they teach reading skills; no longer do they teach important reading skills; instead, they teach only reading skills measured on the achievement tests."

The task force on education of the National Governors Association states that "the present system requires too many teachers who focus largely on the mastery of discrete, low-level skills and isolated facts. . . . By doing so . . . the system denies opportunities for students to master subject matter in depth, learn more complex problem solving skills, or apply the skills they do learn" (Henry, 1990, p. 1A).

The task force goes on to say that top priority must be given "to developing new tools for assessing student performance" and "that portfolios, essays, or other open-ended problems that require students to synthesize, integrate, and apply knowledge and data need to be developed as alternatives to the exclusive use of conventional multiple-choice tests" (Henry, 1990, p. 8A).

This indeed is the rationale for why states and provinces (California, Connecticut, Utah, Vermont, and British Columbia) and school districts (such as Dade County, Florida; and Rochester, New York) have employed teams of teachers to develop alternative assessments (Wiggins, 1989) and have moved to eliminate or severely reduce the use of standardized tests. This also is the reason that as part of the Coalition of Essential Schools, many public high schools are developing new performance exhibits to replace Carnegie units and basic skill tests for graduation requirements.

What Do We Do with What We Know?

These eleven statements are *my* views of what we know; a school might develop different statements. My point is that we must confront our knowledge and use it to guide our efforts; then we must operate our schools in different ways, using our knowledge. We ask our districts and states to pilot new teacher evaluation and supervision systems. We ask to develop new assessment measures, create new curriculum, new grading and grouping organizations, new discipline and management systems, and our own staff development plans. We ask that teachers be given equal voice in all decisions about teaching and learning, and we include parents and students as participants in such discussions. Above all, we ask that the school be the center for professional decisions, where teachers and administrators control the priorities and means of helping students to learn.

Beginning now, we ask that existing resources be reallocated to the school level to assist us. In a district or state where schools are being given the power to change themselves, most of the money that previously went into centralized and controlling functions is now being reallocated to the local school. Instead of having a curriculum specialist at the central office, the teacher is given an extended contract to do curriculum work. Instead of having a central office supervisor, teachers are given released time to function in the role of master, mentor, and coach. Instead of staff developers, teachers and administrators are given time to plan their own staff development. Instead of following a state or district formula of funding per classroom size, faculty can rethink the roles of teacher, counselor, administrator, and specialist. (For example, rather than hire another teacher for twenty-five students, a school might hire three paraprofessionals; rather than replace an assistant principal, a school might spend the money for a part-time bookkeeper and use the balance for specialized group work for students.)

Basically, the idea is to flatten and streamline the centralized bureaucracy and redistribute the curriculum, staff development, personnel, and administrative budgets to the schools. In Dade County, as site-based management and shared governance increased to more than one hundred schools in three years, the central office has been dramatically reduced, with salary and budget reallocation to the local school. Thus, a decentralized school-based initiative can expect to expend no greater amount of money but to increase the amount of state and district money going directly into a school to support instructional services to faculty and students.

In many cases where the district is small, we are not going to reduce our central office positions. Instead, central office spending has to be rethought. The point is, if we are serious about the school being the unit of change, and if we are serious that the time has come for teachers to make decisions about their professional work of teaching and learning, then the current organization of centralized control, monitoring, and distribution of money must be changed. This is why initially we need to think of this reform movement as one dealing with elite schools only.

The Elite: A Few Good Schools

The decentralization, deregulation, site-based, empowerment movement is on the right track because it uses what we know. But ultimately it will be right only if the quality of education improves, and the quality of education will not improve if we don't first move with "elite" schools.

By elite, I don't mean a school that is necessarily rich or poor, suburban, urban, or rural. I don't mean a school where all students have a high IQ or all teachers have an advanced degree. Instead, an elite school is a place where central office people, building administrators, and teachers trust each other to share in decisions about teaching and learning. An elite school is a place where those with formal leadership responsibility know, as Schlechty has remarked, that "in democratic environments power is achieved by giving it away rather than struggling for more" (1990).

So, an elite school is one where the faculty wants to share in the choice and responsibility of schoolwide decisions and where administrators and supervisors likewise want them to share—my caution is that there are few such schools in the nation, perhaps 10–20 percent. In most places, each party is suspicious of the other, and people fight to protect their own domain. The leaders think that to empower teachers will lead to anarchy and evil, and most of the teachers think that administrators and supervisors who talk about empowerment are giving paternalistic lip service to listening to their suggestions rather than truly sitting with them as co-equals in real decisions.

Consequently, teachers, schools, and central offices who don't see this chance to deregulate and decentralize as an opportunity for students but instead see it as a threat to current jobs—and it is a threat to many of our jobs as we currently function—should not get involved, nor should they be forced to operate in such a manner. All of our current legislation and centralized monitoring should continue to direct them. These schools and districts should sit on the sidelines and watch what an elite school can do for and with kids. Only then will we discover whether those schools willing to use what they know can usher in a far better future for students, educators, and public education.

References

Barth, R. S. *Improving Schools from Within: Teachers, Parents, and Principals Can Make a Difference.* San Francisco: Jossey-Bass, 1990.

Blankenship, G., Jr., and Irvine, J. "Georgia Teachers' Perceptions of Prescriptive and Descriptive Observations of Teaching by Instructional Supervisors." *Georgia Educational Leadership,* 1985, 1(1), 7–10.

Brophy, J. "Synthesis of Research on Strategies for Motivating Students to Learn." *Educational Leadership,* 1987, 45(2), 40–48.

Carnegie Foundation for the Advancement of Teaching. *The Conditions of Teaching: A State by State Analysis.* Princeton, N.J.: Carnegie Foundation for the Advancement of Teaching, 1990.

Chubb, J. E., and Moe, J. M. *Politics, Markets, and America's Schools.* Washington, D.C.: Brookings Institution, 1990.

Cuban, L. *How Teachers Taught: Constancy and Change in American Classrooms.* White Plains, N.Y.: Longman, 1984.

Darling-Hammond, L. "Supervision and Policy." In C. Glickman (ed.), *Supervision in Transition: 1991 ASCD Yearbook.* Alexandria, Va.: Association for Supervision and Curriculum Development, 1992.

Duval, J. H. "Dedication/Commitment: A Study of Their Relationship to Teaching Excellence." Doctoral dissertation, University of Vermont, 1990.

Festinger, L. *A Theory of Cognitive Dissonance.* Palo Alto, Calif.: Stanford University Press, 1957.

Garmoran, A., and Berends, M. "The Effects of Stratification in Secondary Schools." *Review of Educational Research,* 1987, *57,* 415–435.

Gastright, J. F. "Don't Base Your Dropout Program on Somebody Else's Program." *Research Bulletin,* Apr. 1989, vol. 8.

George, P. S. *What's the Truth About Tracking and Ability Grouping? An Explanation for Teachers and Parents.* Gainesville, Fla.: Teacher Education Resource, 1987.

Goodlad, J. I. *A Place Called School: Prospects for the Future.* New York: McGraw-Hill, 1984.

Hanford, G. H. "The SAT and Statewide Assessment: Sorting the Uses and Caveats." In *Commentaries on Testing.* Princeton, N.J.: College Entrance Examination Board, 1986.

Henry, T. "Governors Access Education: Report Asks States to Redesign System." (Associated Press) *Burlington Free Press,* July 29, 1990, p. 1E.

Holmes, C. T. "Grade Level Retention Effects: A Meta-Analysis of Research Studies." In L. A. Shepard and M. L. Smith (eds.), *Flunking Grades: Research and Policies on Retention.* New York: Falmer Press, 1989.

Joyce, B. (ed.). *Changing School Culture Through Staff Development: 1990 ASCD Yearbook.* Alexandria, Va.: Association for Supervision and Curriculum Development, 1990.

Keizer, G. *No Place But Here: A Teacher's Vocation in a Rural Community.* New York: Viking Penguin, 1988.

National Education Association. *Academic Tracking.* Washington, D.C.: National Education Association, 1990.

National Governors' Association. *Educating America: State Strategies for Achieving the National Education Goals.* Washington, D.C.: National Governors' Association, 1990.

Oakes, J. *Keeping Track: How Schools Structure Inequality.* New Haven: Yale University Press, 1985.

Oates, J. C. "Excerpts from a Journal." *Georgia Review, 1989, 14*(1 and 2), 121–134.

Pajak, E. F. "Implications of the Education Reform Movement for School-Based Instructional Leadership." Presentation at the Alabama Association for Supervision and Curriculum Development, Birmingham, 1985.

Porter, A. C., and Brophy, J. "Synthesis of Research on Good Teaching Insights from the Work of the Institute for Research on Teaching." *Educational Leadership*, 1988, 45(8), 74–85.

Rutter, M., and others. *Fifteen Thousand Hours: Secondary Schools and Their Effects on Children*. Cambridge, Mass.: Harvard University Press, 1979.

Schlechty, P. S. *Schools for the Twenty-First Century*. San Francisco: Jossey-Bass, 1990.

Sergiovanni, T. J. "The Dark Side of Professionalism in Educational Administration." *Kappan*, 1991, 72(7), 524.

Shepard, L. A., and Smith, M. L. *Flunking Grades: Research and Policies on Retention*. London: Falmer Press, 1989.

Slavin, R. E. "Ability Grouping and Student Achievement in Elementary Schools: A Best-Evidence Synthesis." *Review of Educational Research*, 1987, 57, 293–336.

Slavin, R. E. "PET and the Pendulum: Faddism in Education and How to Stop It." *Phi Delta Kappan*, 1989, 70(10), 752–758.

Slavin, R. E. "Achievement Effects of Ability Grouping in Secondary Schools: A Best-Evidence Synthesis." *Review of Educational Research*, 1990, 60, 471–499.

Slavin, R. E., and Madden, N. A. "What Works for Students at Risk: A Research Synthesis." *Educational Leadership*, 1989, 46(5), 4–13.

White, B. "School Paddlers Say They Could Do Without It." *Atlanta Journal and Constitution*, Feb. 4, 1990, p. 5.

Wiggins, G. "Teaching to the (Authentic) Test." *Educational Leadership*, 1989, 46(8), 41–47.

Wigginton, E. *Sometimes a Shining Moment: The Foxfire Experience*. Garden City, N.Y.: Anchor Press/Doubleday, 1985.

Wise, A. "Restructuring Schools." Presentation to the Annual Georgia Leadership Institute, Athens, Georgia, June 1988.

Chapter Six

Pushing School Reform to a New Edge

The Seven Ironies of School Empowerment

There is a line from a blues classic by Memphis Slim that can aptly be applied to the current rhetoric about school restructuring: "Everybody wants to go to heaven, but nobody wants to die." Heaven can be construed as school empowerment, the decentralization of educational decision making, school-based staff development, and site-based management. Having worked closely for many years with schools engaged in these activities, I'm wary of school people's impulse to jump on the restructuring bandwagon without assessing their own readiness to take on the pain and confront the conflict involved—and without realizing the extraordinary courage necessary to sustain such change.

Let me be clear, I'm a firm believer in the benefits to education of the move from legislative, externally developed regulations to site-based, shared-governance initiatives. But I'm afraid that if schools move too quickly and without a clear picture of the issues at stake, they will fail to improve education for students. Legislators will perceive that failure as another example of why teachers and schools need to be controlled and monitored more strictly than ever. With decentralization, the stakes are high. Education as a profession has much to gain, but it also has much to lose.

The banner work of the restructuring movement is *empowerment,* and it places the school at the center of inquiry, raising questions about the conventional structure of schooling. There is a headiness to this movement, which arose in reaction to the heavy-handed legislative reform of the past. It has become clear that improving education is more complex than merely finding the correct mix of external rewards and punishments to ensure compliance from the teacher. Instead, the issue of how the educators are treated within their own school walls must be resolved if we are to have lasting, significant change in schools. In essence, educators will be given greater latitude over curricular and instructional decisions as long as those decisions recognize the dual objectives of equal access to knowledge for all students and accountability to the public for results (Glickman, 1990a, 1990b).

The time to release ourselves from any simplistic and ineffective prescription has passed; the time to dream is upon us. How we handle the next three to five years has grave consequences for the future of public education and for the future of teaching as a profession. As John Gardner noted: "In times of crises, individuals discover unsuspected strengths and reveal capacity for bravery, endurance, generosity and loyalty beyond all expectations. . . . Sometimes capabilities remain hidden simply because the circumstances of life do not evoke them . . . but sometimes the gifts have been buried by early defeats and harsh treatment, or layered over by cynicism, or held inactive by self-doubt. . . . The battles we wage . . . are not just exercises in compassion. They are battles for the release of human talent and energy" (quoted in Baldwin, 1989, p. 37).

Indeed, this continues to be a time of crisis in public education. The results of a 1989 Gallup/Phi Delta Kappa poll of the public's attitude toward the public schools indicate that the public is ready for "tradition-shattering change" and is willing to pay for it through higher taxes" (Parents Network, 1989, p. 11). (I'm confident about the public's readiness for the first but less confident about prospects for the second.) Teacher unions and associations, state departments of education, private educational foundations, universities, and many local school districts are responding to the challenge to initiate change by piloting demonstration schools. These schools are being controlled mainly by school professionals with varying input from parents and students. Examples of such experiments are

Schools for the Twenty-First Century in Washington State; the Carnegie Schools in Massachusetts; the schools in Dade County, Florida; the schools in Jefferson County, Kentucky; the National Education Association's Mastery in Learning Project; the Teachers as Leaders Project of the American Federation of Teachers; the Coalition of Essential Schools; the Relearn Network; and two projects that I direct for the University of Georgia, the demonstration schools and the League of Professional Schools.

Almost daily, we read about another district whose school board has approved a decentralized, site-based management plan. Many schools are in the midst of serious restructuring effort. People are scrambling, trying to define and operationalize the concept of empowerment. In simplified form, the theory of professional empowerment is that, when given collective responsibility to make educational decisions in an information-rich environment, educators will work harder and smarter on behalf of their clients: students and their parents (Glickman, 1989, 1990b).

But thus far the results of restructuring efforts have been more rhetorical than real. Most schools that have been involved in empowerment reform don't look much different from schools that have not been involved. We hear recurrent questions from those standing on the sidelines: Where is the substance of decentralization and empowerment? What is being restructured? How is education for students in this restructured school any better than it was before?

These are tough questions. I'd like to try to answer them with insights from our own efforts in Georgia and from other similar efforts at school improvement. Even when we look at a documented success, we discover irony and vulnerability. Therefore, in this chapter I address the contradictions of empowerment—not as a critic of empowerment, but as a proponent. I truly believe that the movement to improve schools through empowerment may be for many of us the last chance in our lifetime to make of the school an institution worthy of public confidence and professional respect.

University of Georgia Projects

The first project of the University of Georgia's Program for School Improvement (PSI) currently has five demonstration sites. Our demonstration schools have a high percentage of students from a low socioeconomic background. Neither the school nor its district is likely to have a surplus of time or money. Furthermore, the PSI demonstration schools operate in a heavily legislated state. We assist these demonstration schools with planning, and we collaborate with them in setting schoolwide instructional goals, in implementing plans, and in conducting research on the effect a program has on students. All our schools make decisions via a process of shared governance in which teachers and administrator are equals; no individual has veto power over the others.

In the winter of 1989–90, the PSI began a second project, the League of Professional Schools in Georgia. This association is now open to any public school that wishes to participate. We offer planning workshops for school teams of teachers and administrators, an information retrieval system to keep schools up-to-date on the most recent research and case studies, follow-up meetings for revising plans, conferences to discuss innovation with staff members from other schools, and help in planning action research. We also design methods of evaluation and provide consultation to help schools assess their programs toward their goals. To date, sixteen elementary schools, three middle schools, and six high schools have become members of the League of Professional Schools.

In 1983, Oglethorpe County High School began working with the PSI to develop a participatory decision-making process led by teachers at the school. In the intervening years the school has, among other things, increased instructional time, improved student achievement, and decreased its dropout rate. The efforts to improve the school have resulted in programs that give students more personal attention, including an interdisciplinary, team-taught school-within-a-school. By spring 1989, the school had reduced its dropout rate by 50 percent, and the proportion of students who passed the state's test of basic skills had increased from 67 to 90 percent.

Another school, Fowler Drive Elementary School in Clarke County, began an arrangement with the University of Georgia in the fall of 1986. The current goal of its professional staff is total reorganization of the school into what is called the Community of Learners for Advancing Student Success (CLASS). The project involves grouping teachers, students, aides, and parents across grade levels into nuclear and extended families, arranging courses thematically, and offering accelerated language tutorials. Faculty members have participated in staff development activities focused on cognitive monitoring, peer coaching, and whole language. By the end of the 1988–89 school year, the school was experiencing an 80 percent increase in the student success rate, a gain in teachers' conceptual thinking, and greater internal locus of control among students. The school has received state and national awards for its effort in language education and staff development.

Morgan County Primary School entered our program in 1988. In 1989, the school set goals to ameliorate the climate, boost students' self-concept, and improve their attitude toward learning. A task force drew up recommendations that have led to the use of team planning and establishment of a schoolwide instructional council. Preliminary results over two years have included statistically significant improvement in the climate of the school and a decrease in the number of students in the lowest quartile on tests of achievement.

Clarke County School District has implemented the Twenty-First Century Project, a bold districtwide partnership focused on strategic planning to improve curriculum, instruction, staff development, and program evaluation. Teachers have majority representation on the project's task forces and equal representation with administrators, community members, and university personnel on an overall review board. In 1988–89, the project accomplished several things: (1) coordination of social and support services for students and parents, (2) creation of transitional ninth grade programs for overage students, (3) implementation of staff development pro-grams focusing on integrative language and reading activities, and (4) establishment of middle school parent-teacher conferences. Task forces are currently turning their attention to special instruc-tional programs, to support services for students and families in all grades, and to the Twenty-First Century Institute, a nontraditional secondary school for students in grades nine through twelve.

Recently, our school projects have undergone several external evaluations, and the findings have been positive. The demonstra-tion sites have shown evidence of a positive and significant effect on students and faculty members. The good news is that, over time, a school can use a process of shared governance to control its own destiny and reorganize itself creatively to help students and teach-ers become more successful.

The work of these schools, though, is characterized by high excitement and high anxiety. The results suggest that we're on to something, but there is also the feeling that the floor could fall through at any moment. Even in the high school, where the empowerment operation has been in effect for more than six years, there is no assurance of permanence or stability. We're only as good as we were yesterday, and every day we feel the pressure first to maintain and then to go beyond our current success.

Such change is not easy. I'm convinced it will never be easy—and that's the rub. Are we willing to work in a world in which uncertainty, rather than routine and habit, is the norm? Can we stand the ambiguity of such a world? Can those of us who are part of the old system consciously help to create a new system? I think we can, but to do so we must understand what it's like to push school reform to a new edge.

The Seven Ironies

C. Vann Woodward noted that there is deep irony inherent in any major public success: "All these grim and paradoxical sequels to a noble cause will have to be incorporated before our . . . story [is] brought up to date" (quoted in Leuchtenburg, 1989, p. 129). I would argue that, where school empowerment is concerned, we must be aware of and manage the "grim and paradoxical sequels" before sustained school success can occur. When a school pushes reform to a new edge, it finds itself looking out over the abyss. I'd like to suggest seven ironies of empowerment that I speculate come with the territory of "a noble cause."

Empowerment and Improvement

The first irony is that *the more an empowered school improves, the more apparent it is that there's more to be improved.* In his classic study of effective schools, Wilbur Brookover found that faculty members in schools that were undergoing improvement had a higher level of dissatisfaction with their teaching than faculty members in schools that were not successful and not improving (Brookover and others, 1979). The conclusion rings true in every one of the PSI demonstration schools. When teachers are involved as equals with their administrators in setting instructional goals, and when those goals come out of an expanded arena of knowledge, then teachers must confront many factors that previously seemed unimportant.

Knowledge can make us dissatisfied with what we are currently doing. When a school examines itself, when it looks hard at what students are and are not learning, when school people look at their lofty philosophy and goals—and then ask themselves if their resources, curriculum, and teaching strategies are consistent with their espoused beliefs—dissatisfaction invariably creeps in. When school people examine the level of achievement of various student subpopulations, they uncover information that is difficult to handle. The ordinary school is busy convincing itself and others how excellent it is; a great school knows that it is not as good as it can be. As a school is empowered to study itself and begin to achieve success, it becomes increasingly aware of the awesome challenge still ahead. Eventually, those in an empowered school come to understand that education is a humbling enterprise that can never be perfected.

Empowerment and the Nonempowered School

The second irony is that *the more an empowered school is recognized for its success, the more nonempowered schools criticize it.* When the staff of an individual school take the lead in redistributing power, plan their own staff development, and spend untold hours organizing instruction and curriculum in a new way, the school is at best tolerated by others in the same district. When the school demonstrates evidence of success and gains attention, it often comes under siege. In a moment of public frustration, a superintendent once remarked to his board, "I'll be damned if I'm going to let other schools torpedo this demonstration school. These teachers and administrators have put their blood and guts into their school. What they receive in return is not appreciation but hostility from other schools. This school will lead us out of our educational mess—if only other schools will try to understand rather than criticize what it is doing."

There are at least three ways of explaining this irony. First, hard-working people in a school that is not receiving public recognition may feel some natural jealousy toward the one attracting attention. Second, the effort of one school may call into question the lack of similar effort in another. Third, there are legitimate questions about whether real change occurs in a demonstration school.

Criticism of the empowered school is understandable in light of the first and third explanations. However, I believe that many an attack on an innovative school stems from the second situation: one school's willingness to risk and succeed calls attention to the lack of effort by others. Teachers and administrators in the unimproved schools may feel they are being pressured to change. Individually and collectively, they may not be ready to participate in shared decision making. Since teachers in the same district talk with one another, supervisors might be confronted with such unsettling questions as, "Why are teachers in that school so involved in making decisions while in our school we're not involved at all?" On the other hand, teachers might see the amount of effort that colleagues in the empowered school are expending and worry they will be forced to increase their own workload. What they do not understand is that the staff people working longer and harder have chosen that lot.

When administrators or teachers feel threatened by the efforts of an empowered school, there is a natural tendency to attack; the best defense is a good offense. Although a school practicing empowerment might receive praise for its effort, it might also be criticized and ostracized. A blessing for many an empowered school is benign neglect.

Collective Empowerment and Individual Differences

The third irony is that *the more an empowered school works collectively, the more individual differences and tension among the staff become obvious.* If a school wants the faculty to be truly involved in decision making, then previously submerged tension and factionalism rise to the surface and must be dealt with in the public arena. In a nonempowered school, business gets done by giving in to the vocal and the powerful. By playing one side against the other and keeping parts of a problem obscured, an administrator can suppress a potentially volatile issue. The strategy of divide and conquer and the exercise of top-down power are the conventional approach to the issue of school change. With empowerment, tension becomes visible, and the opponents see one another clearly. Nel Ward, in an excellent case study of an empowered high school, supports this point; increased involvement resulted in increased polarization between those faculty members who have developed collegiality and the past leaders (Ward, 1989).

The notion that a school using a process of shared governance is a utopia of people holding hands and dancing on rose petals is quite misleading. Shared governance brings differences to the surface, it gives everyone equal rights and responsibilities to influence schoolwide decisions, and it intensifies ideological debate.

Is it worth it? In the high school that Ward studied, the answer was clearly yes: "Despite the 'frustration and inner turmoil' resulting from a departure from personal comfort zones, teachers expressed intense pleasure . . ., believing that 'future years will profit from this turbulent one.' One teacher said that she would hate to return to the 'static feeling of the past'" (1989, p. 14).

The Impracticality of Generalizing the Empowerment Model

The fourth irony is that *the more an empowered school becomes a model of success, the less the school becomes a practical model to be imitated by others.* One PSI demonstration school has developed an exemplary dropout prevention program. Another has been awarded for its school-based staff development program. Some visitors travel thousands of miles to observe these schools. Educators looking for solutions to the problems of their own schools record in detail each program subcomponent. Unfortunately, although the schools are demonstration sites, their programs are to a large degree *not exportable.*

People have to understand that these programs work not because they are so meticulously crafted and engineered but because the faculty will not let them fail. They developed these programs, and they are determined to make them work. Why? Simply because the responsibility for the success of a program lies with them and no one else. They do not wish to be seen as people making stupid decisions!

Therefore, when an empowered school succeeds, it establishes curricular and instructional programs that are unique to its own staff, students, and history. The *process* of how a school came to such a decision is more transferable than the program. I shudder when I think of a superintendent or principal trying to implement in a top-down manner a program developed through grassroots participation. To do so merely repeats the mistakes made with "teacher-proof" curricula. It is only the general notion of informed, representative decision making that can be easily transported. Even the specific decision-making model of a particular school should not be seen as prescriptive.

Across the country, we are now seeing districts and states mandating shared governance. The American tendency to package, simplify, and sell has invaded the empowerment movement. The contradiction should be obvious. If a school's instructional priorities, goals, and actions are to be derived from the collective wisdom of the faculty, then the process of governance must also be derived from their collective wisdom. Mandating a uniform mode of decision making for all schools makes a mockery of the notion of professional wisdom. Instead, we should articulate and define the concept of an empowered school, offer examples of empowerment, and leave the process and substance to each school. Our objective should not be to transfer programs but to develop the knowledge that leads to full use of professional and collective wisdom.

Empowerment and Hesitation

The fifth irony is that *the more a school becomes empowered, the more it hesitates to act*. Confidence in one's power is, ironically, often accompanied by wariness about what one proposes to do. It's easier to complain that our school can't be better because our perceived enemies are holding us back or not letting us improve than it is to act when we have the power. The historian William Reid (1987) has stated that those who operate within the system often do not try to change it, even though they complain about it. The reason is they know how they fit into the current operation. They know their status, and they know their lives are secure. What we complain about today, we complained about yesterday, and we'll complain about it again tomorrow.

Life is simpler when we have an enemy to circumscribe our actions. Life becomes much more difficult when there is no enemy out there; if there is an enemy in empowered schools, the enemy is ourselves. No one tells us what we can't do; instead they're asking us what we wish to do. The resources aren't infinite, and boundaries still exist, but the message is that it's all right to dream and to act on our dreams. This situation can be frightening.

I vividly remember the case of Fowler Drive Elementary School, which for two years had made small, satisfying changes in teaching methods and staff development. In the third year, the principal asked staff members—experienced in schoolwide decision making—to meet in cross-grade groups and come up with their version of a dream school for students. The teachers eagerly took on the challenge and discussed how they would alter grouping patterns, change grade-level placement, replace basal readers with real books, and revamp remedial programs. They talked about how they would change the school from grade-level teams to cross-grade-level families. After several meetings, a committee was formed to develop specific ways to make the dream school a reality.

Unexpectedly, the faculty members began to wonder whether they wanted their dreams to come true. They would be in different classrooms (some had been in a classroom for a decade or more). They would use new teaching materials, and they would work with a wider range of students. In effect, each person's life would be changed from the known and the comfortable to the unknown and the less comfortable as the school moved toward its goal. No one was telling the faculty members they couldn't do it; yet the faculty hesitated between an easy dream and the hard reality of action. For six weeks, faculty members reviewed, backpedaled, and hesitated. Finally, when it came time to act, they unanimously agreed to open their dream school in the fall.

Such hesitation is similar to what happens when you step on the gas pedal of a car to move into the passing lane. You put the pedal to the floor, but the car hesitates for a moment. You must decide whether to keep the pedal down and pass or ease up on the pedal and return to the cruising lane. An empowered school eventually learns that it has a vehicle for accelerating change, yet with this realization comes the knowledge that they can move at a speed and in a direction that could change lives. Secure roles and routines must be abandoned, and risk is certainly involved. The hesitancy comes in thinking through the risk, and this gives a school a chance to ponder the path it is to take—to dream and then act, or to dream, dream, and dream some more.

What Is to Be Gained and Lost in Empowerment

The sixth irony is that *the more an empowered school has to gain, the more it has to lose.* It has been my experience that the early stages of a school's efforts at empowerment can bring about immediate, short-term gain for students—perhaps a new staff development program, a change in instructional scheduling, or a bolstering of particular elements of the curriculum. Student attitudes improve, and achievement rises. The changes lead to satisfaction among staff members, but then the pressure increases for the school to become bolder in its innovation and demonstrate more dramatic student gains and accomplishment. The external pressure to show others can begin to replace the original intent of showing ourselves what we can do for our students. Public relations and projection of a positive image of the school can become the overriding concern. Real and wise changes for students can become less important.

Why does this happen? I think it is largely because educators have bought the notion that developing school effectiveness is a linear and progressive process. To fit what Jean Piaget characterized as the American idea of improvement, a good school needs to become better each year than it was the year before. Our students must perform better, accomplish more, participate more, and exhibit more—year after year. The push for short-term yearly gain is a downfall. By always focusing on short-term accomplishment, we trivialize and deny the value of the process of arriving at what is most important, enduring, and significant. Education is a long-term proposition. We can afford false starts, missteps, and ragged progress, and we should anticipate them as we plan for the future.

It is often the case that a school that quickly achieves some indicators of success feels it must do better the next year. This is a self-destructive myth that we should abandon. No corporation, government, society, community, or school can have an unbroken string of successes. Instead, as in the natural rhythms of life, there are good days and bad days, good years and bad years. Much of our research on effective schools consists of one-year snapshots that tell us nothing about sustained effort. Even if a school improves on some measures one year, we do not know whether the gains are worth the effort until we see what the following years bring. Similarly, the lack of obvious, immediate signs of improvement for one or two years might be insignificant when the fruits of sustained labor become apparent in the third and fourth years.

It is important to realize that school success is neither linear nor uniform. Larry Cuban makes the case that, for some schools, just maintaining student accomplishment in a time of dramatic upheaval should be interpreted as a sign of success. What we should be striving for is attainment of those educational goals that are most important for our students and that account for the ebb and flow of our purposeful school life. We should think of the school as a community of students, educators, and parents working together for many years. What should drive the efforts of an empowered school are patterns of improved learning. Thus any change in a particular measure of achievement can be explained either as a redirection of energy to more important things or as a signal that revived attention is needed. Over the course of a single year, isolated examples of improved learning often mean little. A short-term gain or drop in any measure is not an indication of success or failure, unless a school has no long-term goals. Without long-term goals, a school will focus on the immediate, the expedient, and often the superficial. It succumbs to the pressure of mortgaging the future for the present.

Empowerment and Democracy

The seventh irony is that *the more an empowered school resembles a democracy, the more it must justify its own existence to the most vocal proponents of democracy.* This irony is a baffling one. Schools that are overtly democratic in their decision making are somehow seen as flawed by the individual who is unwaveringly loyal to democracy in the larger society.

At a state conference of superintendents, the principal of one PSI school explained how his vote on the instructional council carries no more weight than the vote of any other member. The school has operated in this fashion for many years, with notable instructional success. A highly visible and powerful superintendent asked, "But you do have veto power over the council's decision, don't you?" The principal answered, "No, I have the same vote, the same rights, and the same responsibilities as everyone else." The superintendent was left speechless and sat down with a shrug of disbelief.

At another meeting, this time with school principals, the same person was challenged by another principal, who asked, "Aren't you the legal authority in your school? Aren't you the captain of the ship? How can you be one vote on a council?" Our principal replied, "Yes, I'm the legal authority, but decisions about school-wide educational improvements are the prerogative of all professional educators. I'll sink or swim based on the decisions of a body of intelligent people." The roomful of participants was stunned that a school principal would operate in such a manner.

I'd like to dwell on this issue of democracy in the schools. I find it easy to explain, yet difficult for many school people to accept. They seem to be afraid that a school run democratically will be out of control—afraid of bad decisions compounded one after the other until the school ultimately falls apart. But, to paraphrase Thomas Jefferson, when citizens in a democracy make an unwise decision, the solution is not to abandon democracy but rather to further educate citizens so that they will be wiser in their next decision.

We citizens of the United States believe that democracy is the proper form of governance to improve society. Indeed, in our constitutional democracy no one individual or office has ultimate control over the will of the governed. The president of the United States, our chief executive officer, does not have absolute veto power. He can use a veto to delay a decision, but that veto can be overridden. We Americans believe so strongly in the rightness of the rule of the governed that we have gone to war on many occasions to defend our democratic way of life when we perceived it was threatened. We believe that, in a democracy, varying perspectives about the common good result in the best decisions possible. We applaud the democratization of other countries because we believe that government of the people, by the people, and for the people is an expression of human freedom and dignity.

Now, if we believe all of this, let's carry the argument a step further. Public schools are the *only* tax-supported institutions that have as their main purpose educating students to become citizens of a democratic society. Virtually no one questions the benefit of democratic governance of our larger society. Virtually no one questions that the purpose of a school is to provide an education that is appropriate to a democratic society. Yet we do not make the connection that it is legitimate, correct, and ethical for professional educators in a school to operate according to democratic principles.

Why should a principal of a school have absolute veto power over schoolwide decisions when the president of our nation does not have an absolute veto over governmental decisions that affect all of society? Why do we believe that society's decisions should be made through the collective wisdom of the people but that a school's instructional decisions should be made by the principal, the central office staff, and the superintendent? Why are we willing to fight to protect our democratic form of government, while we refuse to recognize the same form of government as a legitimate way of operating a school?

I understand why such entities as corporations (whose purpose is profit) and other public institutions, such as the postal service (whose purpose is service), do not need to operate democratically. However, I do not understand how we intend to promote the values of democratic citizenship in our students when they are a model of authoritarian rule. It is inconsistent to endorse democracy in society but to be skeptical of shared governance in our schools.

Schools that plan to embark on a program of reform based on empowerment must understand the irony of having to defend use of a democratic process within a democratic society. The querulous questions should be directed at those schools that operate non-democratically. Why should teachers not have equal say with administrators about the professional work of teaching and learning?

Having addressed seven ironies of empowerment, I wish to conclude with what it means to push school reform to a new edge. Those involved in reform that is based on empowerment must deal with its ultimate effects. A friendly and supportive critic of mine often chides me with the comment that our demonstration schools and our professional schools are focused on the process of school improvement (decision-making procedures for setting goals, developing action plans, and assessing effects) and not on the radical or innovative substance of change. I can point to a significant decline in the dropout rate, improved student achievement on a test and in writing samples, a higher student promotion rate, and improved scores on measures of student self-reliance. Likewise, I can cite a significant gain in teachers' critical thinking, an improved school climate, and increased teacher participation. Yet my friend is not impressed with such results. I know that, although our claims are documented, they are not always uniform or consistent. Furthermore, I'm aware that one could cite other, competing explanations for why the schools have improved.

Although there's little doubt that an empowered school fosters a better educational environment than it did before beginning the empowerment process, such evidence still does not amount to what my friendly critic refers to as "substantial change." I believe what he has in mind are easily observable, technological changes that would "blow your socks off." Perhaps he is thinking of the latest computer and interactive video instruction, of students traveling to and studying all the corners of the community and the world, of old notions of testing being replaced by sophisticated naturalistic assessment, of teachers communicating through electronic bulletin boards, of grade levels gone and letter grades done away with, and of teaching in every classroom that is incessantly inspirational and constantly up-to-date.

Although some of our schools are breaking out of conventional mode and moving into areas that involve substantial change, to most onlookers they still look like an ordinary school. The students are doing better, the teachers and administrators take pride in what they've accomplished (and what they've suffered), and there is a strong sense of community among staff and students. We could have shared our restructuring effort with schools that were already interested in building a capsule simulating a voyage to Mars. Instead, we chose ordinary schools sharing the belief that the most significant structural change for the future of public education would be not quick adoption of an innovation but a change in how teachers view their work.

I've written many times about how some of our best and brightest teachers have left the public schools because of their lack of influence in decision making (see, for instance, Glickman, 1989 and 1990b, or in this book Chapters Nine and Eleven and Appendix A). These teachers became increasingly dissatisfied with their careers because no one was interested in their ideas about how to improve education. Of course, not all the best and the brightest have left. Many have stayed the course, working under conditions that a less self-motivated person would flee from or surrender to (Brandt, 1989). The empowerment movement has put a light back into the eyes of the talented, experienced teacher—a light that is clearly visible to intellectually alive young adults who are contemplating education as a career. The empowerment movement sends the message that teaching no longer has to be routinized, isolated, individual, and mindless. Rather, teaching can be a career in which a community of professionals working on behalf of students can engage in critical inquiry and collective dialogue.

In 1776, this nation developed a form of governance that was based on civil participation, not as a means to a higher end but as an end unto itself. As we watched authoritarian governments in Eastern Europe crumble and be replaced by more democratic systems of governance, we surely recognized that the substance of the changes lies in the new order itself, in the ensuing changes in relationships, hierarchy, and power. What remains is the work to fulfill the spirit of the new character.

Where the empowered school is concerned, then, we answer the question of substance in this way: an empowered school is better because of how teachers, administrators, and students treat one another. Over time, the empowered school achieves many of its goals. Equally important, how people work together in an empowered school is a sign of what is possible for the next generation of student and educators. In the end, education comes down to what happens between teachers and their students. We have to find ways to encourage teachers to combine the latest in research and technology with their own contextual knowledge of students—and from that mixture to make education decisions for, and ultimately with, their students.

Let me return to my chapter title. We teach a new edge through empowerment, site-based management, and shared governance. Standing at this new edge, however, forces us to confront irony. When students succeed, a school calls attention to itself and can become a subject of criticism, which can bring on defensiveness. When students fail, educators might be accused of being incapable of professional thought and then "legislated" to the point of automation.

The fundamental issue is democracy—how it should function in a school to prepare students for democratic citizenship and what happens when educators practice democracy to make educational decisions. Democracy is not an efficient mechanism, and at times it produces horrendous decisions. But democracy is the core belief that unites us as a people.

Most critics of public education say that our schools will never change; they suffer from too much inertia, too much bureaucracy, too much tradition, and too much structural control. Certainly our schools are not more bureaucratically and structurally controlled than were the governments of Eastern Europe. Yet those countries created new systems of governance almost overnight.

The empowerment movement in the United States has a kinship with the democratization movement across the world. Discontent over the disenfranchisement of educators—at times simmering beneath the surface—has now reached the boiling point. The movement toward restructuring and site-based management could be the key to producing truly literate, educated citizens. If we have enough schools supporting and challenging one another, we just might revolutionize the face of education and leave the schools a better place for this generation and future ones.

Empowered schools must contend with contradiction and assist one another as they move along a path characterized by high excitement and high anxiety. But as the tightrope artist Karl Wallenda said, "Being on the tightrope is living. Everything else is waiting" (quoted in McCall, 1988, p. 41). Many schools and educators have stopped waiting and have taken up the challenge of pushing school reform to the edge. Once there, they face the distinct danger of falling off. But they also know what it is to feel alive.

References

Baldwin, D. "John Gardner, the Serious Optimist." *Common Cause*, Sept./Oct. 1989, p. 37.

Brandt, R. "On Liberal Education for Tomorrow's World: A Conversation with Douglas Heath." *Educational Leadership*, Sept. 1989, pp. 37–40.

Brookover, W., and others. *School Social Systems and Students' Achievement: Schools Can Make a Difference.* New York: Praeger, 1979.

Glickman, C. D. "Has Sam and Samantha's Time Come at Last?" *Educational Leadership*, May 1989, pp. 4–9.

Glickman, C. D. "Open Accountability for the Nineties: Between the Pillars." *Educational Leadership,* Apr. 1990a, pp. 38–42.

Glickman, C. D. *Supervision of Instruction: A Developmental Approach.* Boston: Allyn and Bacon, 1990).

Leuchtenburg, W. "The Compliant Historian." *Atlantic,* Nov. 1989, p. 129.

McCall, J. R. *The Provident Principal* (rev. ed.). Chapel Hill: Institute of Government, University of North Carolina, 1988, p. 41.

Parents Network. "Tradition-Shattering Changes in Public Schools Are Favored." *Network News,* 1989, *15,* 11.

Reid, W. A. "Institutions and Practice: Professional Education Reports and the Language of Reform." *Educational Researcher,* Nov. 1987, pp. 10–15.

Ward, N. "Case Study: A High School Faculty Develops Collegiality Around the Knowledge Based on Teaching and Learning." Paper presented at the annual meeting of the American Educational Research Association, San Francisco, Mar. 1989.

Chapter Seven

Unlocking School Reform

Uncertainty as a Condition of Professionalism

Just when it appears that policy makers have locked up the reform of schools and teaching by prescribing the what and how of improvement, many researchers and practitioners point out that reform isn't quite so simple. The result is open and growing turbulence within the education profession. As one reform gathers momentum and becomes prevalent, a countermovement begins to create an intense undercurrent.

Legislation on the reform of secondary schools begins to peak, for example, and attention shifts instead to preschool and early childhood intervention. States implement higher graduation standards and core curricula, and attention focuses on the alarming high school dropout rate and the need for greater flexibility in programs. Research data on effective teaching are translated wholesale into teacher evaluation programs, and then researchers object adamantly to misuse of their findings. No sooner do scores on basic skill tests come to the fore as a measure of student achievement (and thus of school effectiveness) than critical thinking and cooperative learning emerge as more desirable educational goals. The notion of the principal as instructional leader reaches its zenith, and then some studies suggest that teachers, central office staff members, and other professionals can be equally effective in the role. And as states begin to implement merit pay plans for teachers, pay plans based on differentiated responsibility attract renewed attention.

Such turbulence and uncertainty seem reason enough for educators to feel helpless, dependent, and full of despair. But I would argue instead that uncertainty is power-inducing; it puts research findings and knowledge of instructional improvement into proper perspective.

With uncertainty as a given, we must rely on informed human judgment to drive future reform efforts. In accepting uncertainty, we acknowledge that we must learn from others as we develop our own course of action. In accepting uncertainty, we embrace improvement effort as a way of exploring, rather than controlling, the unknown. We open ourselves to risk, and we take responsibility for what our schools and our students become. I believe that, as we plan and implement school reform, we are beginning to understand the difference between knowledge and certainty.

An example from geometry illustrates this difference. In answer to the question, "How long is the coast of Britain?" the geometrician Benoit Mandelbrot noted that the coast has no real length apart from human judgment (Hardison, 1986). If we use a measurement scale of one hundred miles to an inch to draw the British coastline, we see that the coastline has large bays and capes. If we use a scale of ten miles to an inch, then new inlets and promontories appear. The coast becomes longer or shorter, depending on the scale used. Furthermore, what happens when measurement of the coast begins at a particular time? Each incoming wave reduces the coast, and each outgoing wave lengthens. Therefore, how do we find the length of the British coast? By agreeing on the purpose, perspective, and unit of measurement, as well as the particular time at which the measurement is to be made, only then can the question be answered. The length of the coast is a mathematical fiction created for us humans to find a representation that accomplishes our purpose.

In measuring school reform, as in measuring the coast of Britain, there is no independent certainty about how to arrive at an answer. How does a school improve? The answer at first seems simple. A school improves by having schoolwide instructional goals that teachers and administrators work together to accomplish. No great uncertainty here. But let's watch this new "coast" unravel, as we become specific about the change process and the instructional method.

In a recent study of three improving school districts (as measured by scores on criterion-referenced achievement tests), we found no common approach to change (Glickman and Pajak, 1987). District A took a top-down approach; decisions about curricula, time allocation, and lesson planning emanated from the central office and were directed to teachers by way of the principal. District B took a democracy-in-action approach, enjoining representative groups of teachers from each school to assess the need of students in the district and to decide which changes should be made. The central office helped the process along by coordinating meeting schedules, expediting clerical tasks, and establishing deadlines. District C took a decentralized, top-down and bottom-up approach. The central office made clear the three general goals of school improvement (higher achievement, better school climate, and more community involvement) and asked each school to establish its own objectives and strategies. The central office then made appropriate resources available to help the school reach its goals.

Upon completion of this study, we scratched our heads in amazement at how differently three improving school districts could implement change. We found no single answer to the question of how to change, but we did find alternative approaches aimed at the same instructional outcomes. (Of course, there were other outcomes too, among them teachers' long-term acceptance of the change, their feeling of pressure and stress, and the efficiency with which they used their time.) From the study, we found knowledge of change, but we could find no one correct approach to recommend to other school districts.

Next question: Who should lead change efforts? In a population of fifteen elementary and middle schools, we found little data suggesting that the principal was the sole or even primary instructional leader in terms of directly assisting teachers or carrying out curriculum development, staff development, or action research.

These tasks more often fell to teachers, or the lead teacher, or department head, or assistant principal, or a supervisor from the central office. The principal tended to function as a source of encouragement and support, allocating instructional leadership to others instead of serving as the all-knowing, ever-present instructional expert whom we often read about in the literature. Our findings reaffirmed Judith Little's conclusion (1982): when it comes to instructional improvement, in many cases the principal is more properly thought of as a "gatekeeper" than as a "doer."

As Phillip Hallinger and Joseph Murphy have noted, depending on the community the principal's role with regard to successful school instruction varies considerably (1987). Indeed, in some schools the principal attends mainly to such noninstructional tasks as public relations and parent contact, to free other individuals to observe in the classroom and provide feedback, confer with teachers, or lead a faculty group engaged in action research. (We know of one substitute teacher who initiated and implemented a major school reform.) Clearly, there is no certainty regarding which individuals in which positions should be vested with time, training, and resources to bring about school reform.

Continuing to demonstrate the difference between knowledge and certainty, let us examine instructional practices. Surely we know by now what effective instruction and effective teaching are. But read carefully the words of three of the most prominent leaders in the area of effective teaching. According to Madeline Hunter, "Teaching . . . is a relativistic, situational profession where *there are no absolutes*" (1986, p. 70; italics in original). Barak Rosenshine (1986) has noted that "it is difficult to apply many of the major elements from the teaching of skills to the teaching of content." Meanwhile, David Berliner, a pioneer in the study of time-on-task, used these words to comment on a new study of exemplary science teachers: "All our correlations are based on the notion of stability of teacher characteristics—but every time we do reliability checks we know we're in trouble, because we keep finding the behavior of these expert teachers unstable from day to day and year to year" (*see* Brandt, 1986).

To summarize, successful teaching is context- and classroom-specific. Teaching behaviors and the sequence of instruction vary, depending on the learning goal (acquisition of basic skills, understanding of content, cooperative learning, discovery, critical thinking, and so on) and on the prior competence of students (Ross and Kyle, 1986).

Accepting the idea that knowledge of instructional improvement is different from certainty liberates us from dependence on an expert and assures us that it is proper to make our own informed decision. A recent study by Kathryn Floyd (1986) showed that outstanding education supervisors consciously use the ambiguity, fragmentation, and inconsistency that characterize their work as an advantage, not a disadvantage. Freed of dogma and restriction regarding the right way to proceed, they see themselves as in control of making decisions with others that lead to instructional improvement.

Likewise, we should view the ambiguity surrounding school reform as an advantageous situation that enables us to control our own destiny. When we accept the existence of unknowns, we turn to others to help us make a decision. If we are to explore an unfamiliar cave, for example, we gather all the available knowledge about caves, we read about similar expeditions and talk to other spelunkers about their experience, and we review our own previous experiences in exploring caves. Before entering the unfamiliar cave, we use our knowledge to equip ourselves appropriately, rope ourselves together, and distribute equitably the load to be carried. Then, with confidence and competence, we duck our heads and step into the darkness. As we move forward, we make decisions on the basis of our expertise and experience, and of our confidence in one another. The consequences of each decision along our route into the unknown give us additional information to be used in making the next one.

The same thing is true when we step into the cave of instructional improvement. No one else has been in this particular cave, so we acquire as much knowledge as we can about similar school improvement efforts, and then we act. If we make a poor decision, we find out quickly enough. Rather than stop us from proceeding, a poor decision gives us more information to use in making the next decision.

When we believe with certainty that someone else can decide for us or that we can control what happens, we lose the capacity to receive and use information to educate and correct ourselves. Instructional improvement is a constant cycle of decision, discovery, and further decisions, as we explore the unknown. In accepting uncertainty, we unlock school reform and enter a new phase of professionalism.

References

Brandt, R. S. "On the Expert Teacher: A Conversation with David Berliner." *Educational Leadership*, Oct. 1986, pp. 4–9.

Floyd, K. "Meanings That Outstanding Central Office Instructional Supervisor Associate with Their Role." Doctoral dissertation, University of Georgia, 1986.

Glickman, C. D., and Pajak, E. F. "Concepts of Change in Improving School Districts." Paper presented at the annual meeting of the American Educational Research Association, New Orleans, Mar. 1987.

Hallinger, P., and Murphy, J. "Instructional Leadership in the School Context." In W. Greenfield (ed.), *Instructional Leadership: Concepts, Issues, and Controversies*. Newton, Mass.: Allyn and Bacon, 1987, pp. 179–203.

Hardison, O. B., Jr. "A Tree, a Streamlined Fish, and a Self-Squared Dragon: Science as a Form of Culture." *Georgia Review*, Summer 1986, pp. 394–403.

Hunter, M. "To Be or Not to Be—Hunterized." *Tennessee Educational Leadership*, 1986, *12*, 70.

Little, J. W. "Norms of Collegiality and Experimentation: Workplace Conditions of School Success." *American Educational Research Journal*, 1982, *19*(3), 325–340.

Rosenshine, B. "Unsolved Issues in Teaching Content: A Critique of a Lesson on Federalist Paper No. 10." Paper presented at the annual meeting of the American Educational Research Association, San Francisco, Apr. 1986.

Ross, D. D., and Kyle, D. W. "Developing a Framework for Presenting Teacher Effectiveness Research to Preservice Teachers." Paper presented at the annual meeting of the American Educational Research Association, San Francisco, Apr. 1986.

Part Three

Instructional Leadership

Chapter Eight

The Essence of School Renewal

The Prose Has Begun

The pressure of exhilarating events, which until
then had aroused in me a surprising level of energy,
abruptly vanished. . . . Many of my colleagues felt
the same way. We realized that the poetry was over
and the prose was beginning; that the county fair
had ended. . . . It was only then that we realized
how challenging and in many ways unrewarding
was the work that lay ahead.

—*Vaclav Havel, upon the ascendancy of
elected government in Czechoslovakia*

The quest for school empowerment flourished for a time as a countermovement to monolithic bureaucracy bent on control and standardization. As we built our network of democratic schools from
two to sixty-one, my colleagues and I experienced a headiness
about being in the vanguard of site-based control, shared governance, schoolwide instructional innovation, and action research.
The institutions in our League of Professional Schools were knowingly going against the grain, receiving recognition for their fight,
and gaining tolerance from most policy makers.

This study was supported in part by grants from the University of Georgia, BellSouth
Foundation, the Georgia State Department of Education, and the U.S. Department of
Education (84-073A). The views are those of the author, and no official support by spon-
sors is intended or should be implied.

Now the current shift in reform has generated feelings of exhilaration and fear in many of us. After a decade of legislated reform without the expected results, policy makers have actively turned to our schools (and others like them) as examples of a new way to improve education. Our state is a microcosm of the shifting reform agenda throughout the United States. Prior reforms are being dismantled, replaced with policies providing for deregulation and return of control to the local school. External agencies are being reorganized to support locally designed answers.

These sudden changes have left many of us who fought for such changes in a fearful predicament. I think of the words of Havel and wonder: *Can a countermovement now succeed as a dominant movement?* Are we—teacher, principal, central office staff person, superintendent, university personnel, professional association member, and local school board member—up to the task? Now that many of us have the freedom to decide how to educate, do we have sustainable ideas of our own? Ultimately, can the masses of practitioners in schools achieve massive change through decentralization?

I fear the bandwagon. I fear the proselytizers. I feel the rush of excitement. Ultimately I fear that we will blow it unless we strip this reform to its essential principles, lay the tracks for its accomplishment, and allow schools to learn from one another. What must be done *over time* to make the site-based change movement an enduring and sensible way to improve education? Let's address our collective fear and replace it with confidence based on how we might proceed.

A Super Vision

For a school to be educationally successful, it must be a community of professionals working together toward a vision of teaching and learning that transcends the individual classroom, grade level, and department. The entire school community must develop a set of principles, not simply as an exercise but to establish a covenant to guide future decisions about goals, staffing, scheduling, materials, assessment, curriculum, staff development, and resource allocation.

Here are six examples of such principles, derived from a cross section of educators, community, and business members, in answer to the question, "What should learning look like in an optimal educational environment?"

1. *Learning should be an active process* that demands full student participation in pedagogically valid work. Students need to make choices, accept responsibility, and become self-directed.

2. *Learning should be both an individual and a cooperative venture*, where students work at their own pace and performance level and also have the opportunity to work with other students on solving problems.

3. *Learning should be goal-oriented and connected to the real world* so that students understand the application of what they learn inside the school to their outside life and community.

4. *Learning should be personalized* to allow students, with their teachers, to set learning goals that are realistic and attainable but challenging and pertinent to their future aspirations.

5. *Learning should be documentable, diagnostic, and reflective*, providing continuous feedback to students and parents to encourage students and train them in self-evaluation. Assessment should be seen as a tool to develop further teaching and learning strategies.

6. *Learning should be in a comfortable and attractive physical environment and in an atmosphere of support and respect*, where the student's own life experience is affirmed and valued and where mistakes are analyzed constructively as a natural step in acquiring knowledge and understanding.

By developing such principles, a school creates for itself a guide to compare current practices and explore how it can act to reflect the principles more clearly and powerfully (Teaching and Learning Task Force, 1991).

A Process and a Commitment

Concurrently, the school needs to activate its covenant by determining the decision-making processes it will follow. How are schoolwide matters, such as approval of, and funding for, activities and materials, decided upon? Are there to be advisory groups? Shared decision-making groups? Do some people hold veto power? Are there direct referendums? elected representatives? Ultimately, who is responsible for which decisions? Simply put, a school needs a constitution, which clearly explains the path to be followed for resolving schoolwide instructional decisions.

For example, schools in the league make shared decisions according to a democratic process (League of Professional Schools, 1989). No one person or position carries greater weight in a decision than anyone else. The actual procedures of league schools vary from consensus to majority vote; from representation including only teachers and administrators to representation that includes central office, students, parents, paraprofessionals, and other community and business groups; from a narrow school focus on staff development and curriculum to a wide focus on total site-based resources (including the entire budget, and hiring and evaluating personnel). Once a constitution is proposed, revised, and agreed to by those it represents, the tracks are laid for their "school renewal train" to run.

A vision of learning (the *covenant*) with a concomitant decision-making process (the constitution) needs approval by those it will affect. Superintendents, school boards, and district personnel need to understand, approve, work with, and support the school's vision and operating plan, as well as provide technical assistance and resources for the work ahead. As important, the principal and teaching staff need to publicly commit themselves to the integrity of the process for an agreed-upon time. Commitment to principles and a governance process does not mean that every individual pledges to be actively involved in all decisions; rather, it is a commitment to how the school will operate. Individuals are agreeing to support the process and implement the decisions that come from it. With a vision, a process, and a commitment, the implementation work can begin.

Assessment and Information Seeking

Teachers and school-based administrators often groan when assessment is mentioned. Most practitioners are action-oriented; stopping to collect data seems to them a fact-finding effort that simply slows a school down. Unfortunately, site-based innovation means nothing if a school cannot determine whether the effort has had an effect on students. Most schools move from innovation to innovation ("we are doing whole language, or cooperative learning, or curriculum integration") and define success as implementation of the latest one. To be blunt, this is nonsense. What difference does any innovation make if a school cannot determine the effect on kids?

Effect does not necessarily mean test scores. It might mean an exhibit, a video of student work, a portfolio, an attitude and thought sample, the attendance rate, a transition to the next level of school and work, and so forth. The school must ask itself what data currently exist or could be collected to assess the results of current teaching practices for students, as well as what information could be collected at a later time to assess the progress of new efforts.

To determine equity of learning, data should be disaggregated by socioeconomic class, race or ethnicity, gender, and grade. The student too should not be overlooked as a data collector, interviewer, surveyor, synthesizer, analyzer, or reporter. For example, students might conduct a study to earn credit for a class in government, science, language, civics, mathematics, and so on. If teachers, students, and administrators are to have the information necessary for further decisions as they move toward goal attainment, the school has to be a center of action research.

Goal Setting and Prioritizing

After assessing current effects, a school must establish and clarify its most important learning goals. Does the assessment suggest goals such as developing skills and attitudes for responsible citizenship, acquiring appreciation for and facility with multiple forms of literacy, using science as critical inquiry across subject areas, and graduating with the prerequisites for employment and continuing education?

Such goal setting should be thought of pragmatically. What is most worth spending time and money on? Should a school take on multiple goals with corresponding assessments, or should it focus on one or two and branch out from there? For a school where a need is glaring and urgent, it is important to choose narrow goals—for example, improving mathematics performance, or reducing the retention rate. On the other hand, some schools will want to forge out, pursuing multiple goals under their guiding principles. The result is to change the entire educational experience and environment of the school. The question is one of evolution versus revolution.

Resources Must Reflect Priorities

Depending on the district and state policies, a school may have a varying degree of control over *time* (meeting, planning days, research), *money* (from staff development to the total school budget), and *educational designs* (curriculum, scheduling, assessment, grading, staffing, grouping, reporting). In our experience, for a school to begin site-based change it must have control over at least staff development time and money and at least some matters of curriculum. Staff development money and time should be used to plan and learn together those pedagogical methods, procedures, and skills needed to accomplish the school's goals. Curriculum should be planned and implemented, learning should be assessed, and the school should be organized in a way that reflects those goals.

Again, the issue is whether to seek improvement by working within the current structure (curriculum, schedules, tests) or by trying to transform it into new structures. This decision depends on the covenant of principles, the readiness and history of staff in prior accomplishment, and the support of the district and community.

Seduction and Distraction

As educators struggle with these issues, the national publicity around restructuring can become a distraction to the most important strides a school can make toward long-term development. In other writings, I have outlined how it is that many educators are mentally locked into dated conceptions of schooling (Glickman, 1991). Some of these conceptions are that (1) a school is a set of individual classrooms, (2) with twenty-five to thirty students per teacher, (3) where teaching is for set periods of time within a fixed school day and calendar year, (4) textbooks are the materials, (5) uniform curriculum is essential, and (6) students have to be in grades and be assessed by grade-level standardized tests.

Such a view of schooling has created an impossible burden for teachers and administrators to provide the best education for all students. The deep structures of the school press teachers to make the classroom routine and repetitive, with great emphasis on controlling rather than finding ways to motivate students (McNeil, 1986).

Ultimately, an optimal environment must spring from unconventional notions of schooling, such as allowing for longer blocks of time for students and teachers to be together, continuity of small communities of students and teachers, interactive materials and technology, interdisciplinary curriculum, extended school days and years, nongraded grouping, flexibility for differentiating staff, new assessments of learning, and built-in planning time for teachers through reallocation of instructional time and extended contracts.

The current problem with the national rhetoric about restructuring is that schools can be induced to try to make these changes without a thorough understanding of why it is necessary and why the change is worth the inevitable confusion and conflict that ensue. A particular innovation, rather than teachers' professional and moral knowledge about what's right for their school, can easily become the litmus test of being "pedagogically correct."[1]

To prevent that from happening, schools must restructure their vision and decision-making process first "as the necessary but not sufficient condition" for dealing with other structural changes (see Sarason, 1990). Otherwise, if not derived from the deliberate, democratic discourse of the schools, such current innovations as whole language, interdisciplinary curriculum, cooperative learning, interactive technology, nongraded schools, heterogeneity, and authentic assessments are doomed to burn bright for a few years and then fade away—to reappear in the next cycle following another "back to basics" movement.

Getting the Point

The League of Professional Schools is premised first and foremost on bringing teachers and administrators to the table, where they can view themselves (and others) as caring, committed individuals who want to do right. A community of professionals with a spectrum of personal values and ideologies, they struggle as a school for independence from external answers and authority figures. They laugh and cry together as they learn to be responsible stewards for the vision of their institution (Goodlad, 1991). In time, they learn that the independence from hierarchical authority they have achieved has to be reflected in their relationships and activities with students. This is the only way educators can come to understand democratic participation as an educative process for all who live in schools.

Note

1. Schoolteacher and spouse Sara Orton Glickman coined the term *pedagogically correct*.

References

Glickman, C. D. "Pretending Not to Know What We Know." *Educational Leadership*, 1991, *48*(8), 4–10.

Goodlad, J. I. "The Moral Imperative in Education: The Lawrence Kohlberg Distinguished Lecture." Delivered at Annual Conference of the Association for Moral Education, Athens, Ga., Nov. 9, 1991.

Havel, V. "The Velvet Hangover." *Harper's*, 1990, *281*(1685), 18–21.

League of Professional Schools. "Orientation and Planning Manual." (Unpublished manuscript.) Athens, Ga.: Program for School Improvement, 1989.

McNeil, L. M. *Contradictions of Control: School Structure and Knowledge.* New York: Methuen/Routledge and Kegan Paul, 1986.

Sarason, S. *The Predictable Failure of Educational Reform.* San Francisco: Jossey-Bass, 1990.

Teaching and Learning Task Force. "Report on Learning." (Unpublished manuscript.) Atlanta: Georgia Partnership for Excellence in Education, 1991.

Chapter Nine

Developing Teacher Thought

I believe that the development of teachers' ability to think about what they do should be the aim of staff development. As teachers are challenged with new and divergent information, possibilities to improve emerge and the classroom becomes a better place for students.

I do not subscribe to the prevalent view that teachers need to be trained in prescribed "effective" behaviors; allocation of teaching time; and a recipe for curriculum, management, and discipline practices. Indeed, though most teachers can do what they are told, their ability to think for themselves diminishes and they become apathetic about their own teaching. Bluntly put, prescription controls action and may in the short run achieve the intended results. But prescription does not promote teacher thought, and I believe that teachers who do not think for themselves are not able to help students think for themselves.

Research is fairly conclusive that the successful teacher is a thoughtful teacher. When classroom problems occur, this teacher can stand back from current practice and choose new practices that are likely to succeed (see, for example, Hunt and Joyce, 1967). Furthermore, the research is clear that thoughtful teachers stimulate their students to be thoughtful. For instance, a study of fifty-two teachers by Calhoun (1985) found that teachers of high conceptual thought provided more corrective feedback to students, gave

Much of this chapter is adapted from the author's *Supervision of Instruction: A Developmental Approach* (1985). The author would like to acknowledge Edward Pajak and Kathryn Floyd for their critiques of prior drafts of this chapter.

more praise, and were less negative and punitive. These teachers were more varied in their instructional strategies and were able to elicit more higher-order conceptual responses from their students than teachers of a moderate or lower level of conceptual thought. Harvey (1967) found that high-concept teachers produce higher-achieving students who were more cooperative and involved in their work. Witherell and Erickson (1978) found that teachers with the highest level of ego development demonstrated greater complexity and commitment to the individual student; greater generation and use of data in teaching; and greater understanding of practices relating to rules, authority, and moral development.

It is one matter to explain why the aim of staff development should be to improve teacher thinking. It's another matter to outline what staff developers have to know about both schools and cognitive learning to actually promote greater thought in a faculty. In this chapter, I explain some of the blocks to teacher thought inherent in the work environment. I also show how a cognitive adult learning theory can be combined with research on instructional improvement in four types of staff development activity: (1) direct assistance to teacher, (2) curriculum development, (3) in-service training, and (4) action research. Each can be used to promote an effective classroom and school environment.

The Difficulties

It is easy to document that the teacher's work environment is less than optimal. Lieberman and Miller (1984), in their book *Teachers, Their World, and Their Work,* update the work of Lortie (1975), Jackson (1968), and Sarason (1971) with five workplace factors that inhibit a teacher's professional growth:

1. *The legacy of the one-room schoolhouse.* The vestige of pioneer times when most schools had one teacher and one group of students within one confined area is still evident in schools today. In many cases, we have the one-room schoolhouse repeated every

few yards down the school corridor. Many teachers believe that "this is *my* classroom, *my* students, *my* materials, and *my* professional world, and others should leave me alone." In contrast, Little (1982) demonstrated that teachers in successful schools spoke of *our* students, *our* materials, *our* goals, and what *we* are trying to do.

2. *Inverse beginner responsibilities.* Too often, experienced teachers protect their own turf and pass the leftovers on to new teachers. A teacher resigns, and the other instructors in the school descend upon the classroom to remove materials, equipment, and furniture of value and replace it with their discards. The new teacher enters a classroom equipped with what no one else wants. Unfortunately, administrators often place the most difficult and lowest-achieving students with the new teacher. New teachers are therefore often left with the most demanding students and a picked-over classroom. The message to the beginning teacher is, "Welcome to teaching. Let's see if you can make it."

3. *Invisibility and isolation.* Blankenship and Irvine (1985) found that approximately 50 percent of all experienced teachers have never been observed for purposes of instructional improvement, and 76 percent of all experienced teachers have never been observed by another teacher in their school.

4. *Lack of professional dialogue.* Since most classrooms are closed off from one another, teachers rarely talk together as professionals. DeSanctis and Blumberg (1979) found that professional talk among teachers usually lasts less than two minutes per day. Teachers spend an overwhelming amount of their time talking to students and socializing with each other, but not solving instructional problems together.

5. *Restricted choices.* Teachers' working lives are often bureaucratic and restricted. They have few choices (Lortie, 1975). Schedules are set and they are told what and when to teach. Minimum competency, mandated curricula, and externally developed policy further restrict their choices. Goodlad (1984) found in his national sample that teachers have virtually no involvement in schoolwide decisions.

Teacher Cognition

Piaget viewed assimilation and accommodation as the twin processes of cognition. You must have some familiarity with a new idea to process it (assimilation), but then, as you process the idea, your mental organization changes to incorporate the new idea into a larger concept (accommodation). Piaget's theories have important implications for the professional development of teachers. Staff development must *identify* the teacher's present mental structures of organization, whether they be concrete or symbolic, and gradually introduce new information in a way that the teacher can group and act upon. When new information is presented over time, teachers can alter their previous ways of thinking about instructional problems and begin to act in a new way.

Table 9.1 describes three levels of teacher thought: low, high, and medium abstraction. Abstraction is the ability to distance oneself cognitively from immediate concrete experience, identify present actions that help and impede student learning, and determine future actions that are likely to succeed. Fortunately, such reflective and critical thought can be increased over time. Consequently, teachers must be challenged to discuss the whys and hows of what they do. They must be aware of others' performance. They must be given graduated experience with any new strategy. They must have some choice over how they will improve. Such alteration of the work environment creates a school that is intellectually alive and characterized by a "social ethos" in which people are purposefully and professionally engaged with each other (Rutter and others, 1979).

How should new teaching practices be introduced to teachers at each level? A teacher who thinks unilaterally and concretely (low abstraction) should be introduced to relatively few new practices. These practices must be explained and demonstrated before the teacher can decide whether it will improve instruction. On the other hand, a teacher whose thinking is of moderate abstraction can deal with new ideas at the verbal level and, with actual trial,

Table 9.1. Levels of Teacher Thought

Low Abstraction	Moderate Abstraction	High Abstraction
Confused about instructional problems	Identifies instructional problems by focusing on one dimension of the problem but does not use multiple sources of the information	Identifies instructional problems from various sources of information
Lacks ideas about what can be done	Generates one to three ideas about what can be done	Seeks and generates multiple sources of ideas about what can be done
Often asks to be shown habitual and unilateral responses to varying situations	Needs assistance from authority or expert in weighing consequences of action	Visualizes and verbalizes consequences of various actions
Depends on authority or expert to make change	Needs assistance from authority or expert in planning how to implement the change	Chooses for oneself the action(s) most likely to improve the situation and plans implementation Makes own change

determine the fit of the new idea with his or her already established approach. The teacher whose thinking is of high abstraction can process new ideas with mental imagery and determine in his or her mind what actions will lead to greater student success.

The reader might ask: "How does a staff developer assess the cognitive level of the individual teacher or a school staff person?" Staff developers should use the best assessment tools known: their eyes, ears, and informed judgment. The verbal and behavioral responses of a teacher are indicators of the level of mental operation and can be used to make a judgment regarding the appropriate entry point in working with an individual (or group of teachers). This means that staff developers must talk to the people they work with before launching a program. Staff developers can use four vehicles to increase abstract thought: a direct assistance program, a curriculum development project, in-service training, and an action research group. Table 9.2 may be helpful in relating the three levels of abstraction in thought to the four staff development approaches.

Developing Thought Via Direct Assistance to Teachers

Staff developers can provide several types of direct assistance to teachers (Glickman, 1981, 1985). They may coach or train peer teachers, supervisors, and administrators in conferencing techniques. When a staff developer, teacher, or supervisor works one-on-one with a teacher to improve instruction, he or she may use three conferencing approaches: directive, collaborative, and nondirective.

In the directive approach, the source of problem identification and solution comes primarily from the coach or supervisor. With a collaborative approach, there is an exchange of perceptions about the problem, generation of possible actions by the coach or supervisor and the teacher, and negotiated agreement (or a contract) about what changes should be forthcoming. In a nondirective approach, the coach or supervisor helps the teacher clarify instructional concerns by questioning the teacher about what he or she might do, helping the teacher think about consequences, and asking the teacher to choose a plan or course of action.

The conference approach should be matched to the teacher's level of thought (see Table 9.2). A low-abstract teacher is appropriately matched with a directive conference approach, a moderate-abstract teacher with a collaborative approach, and a high-abstract teacher with a nondirective approach.

Follow-up conferences should gradually move from directive to collaborative to nondirective, giving increased responsibility to the teacher to plan for himself or herself (see Gordon and Glickman, 1984, for full explanation of this process). For example, a teacher who is confused about what to do to improve instruction and is

Table 9.2. Teacher Abstraction and Types of Staff Development

Four Categories of Staff Development	Level of Abstraction		
	Low	Moderate	High
Direct assistance	Directive conference	Collaborative conference	Nondirective conference
Curriculum development	Initiative: externally developed and prescribed to faculty	Mediative: altered by faculty to fit local conditions	Generative: created by faculty
In-service training: (1) lecture and explanation (2) demon- stration (3) role play and feedback (4) classroom trial (5) peer discussion and obser- vation	More time spent on (1) lecture and explanation (2) demonstration	More time needed on (2) demon- stration (3) role play and feedback (4) classroom trial	More time needed on (4) classroom trial (5) peer discussion and observation
Action research (situational leadership of groups)	Staff developer controls group process and limits range of decisions	Staff developer facilitates group process; group makes own decision	Group has own leadership; staff developer is a member of group

dependent on authority might be asked to choose from a few specific activities proposed by the coach or supervisor. During the next
conference, the teacher might be asked to propose an idea to add
to the coach's or supervisor's ideas before making a decision as to
which ones to use.

Developing Thought Via Curriculum Planning

Staff developers are often asked to work with teachers on curriculum development. Such work can be viewed as an opportunity to promote teacher thought through nonthreatening intellectual engagement. Teachers who develop curriculum need knowledge of the content of the discipline as well as of the scope, sequence, and balance of that content (see Doll, 1982). Furthermore, the teacher needs skills in planning a curriculum (goals, objectives, activities, resources, evaluation, formats of curriculum writing, webbing, unit plans, cognitive mapping, and so on; Glickman, 1985).

Staff developers should determine the current knowledge and skills of group members by reviewing academic preparation, curriculum training, and work on previous curriculum committees. It is also important to observe how a teacher currently uses the curriculum guide in the classrooms and with what results. Additionally, staff developers have to determine the motivation and abstraction that the teacher brings to discussion about curriculum.

If we think of teachers along a continuum of three stages of abstraction, Tanner and Tanner's work (1980) on levels of curriculum development makes much sense. They speak of imitative, meditative, and generative curriculum. An *imitative* curriculum is developed outside of the school and prescribes what each teacher teaches, when to teach it, what activities to follow, and which tests to give. The imitative curriculum is a complete package that every teacher is expected to use in the same way. In the 1960s, this type of curriculum was (infelicitously) referred to as "teacher proof." Many of our textbooks, guides, and curriculum kits are intended to be used, not thought about.

The second level of curriculum development, *meditative*, refers to an externally developed curriculum revised by practitioners to match their local conditions. Teachers are asked to make modifications, change sequences, and substitute topics and activities according to the needs of their students. The meditative curriculum gives teachers an established structure to work within, but at the same time it demands that they improve.

The highest level of curriculum development, according to the Tanners, is *generative*, in which a faculty creates its own curriculum. Teachers first establish objectives for students and then either search out existing texts, kits, and guides that fit those objectives or make their own materials and activities if suitable ones do not exist.

Again, the initial match of curriculum development to level of abstract thought can be made by first determining the teacher's level of abstraction (see Table 9.2). Imitative curricula are initially appropriate for a group of low-abstract teachers who have little experience with curriculum. Meditative curricula are initially appropriate for moderate-abstract teachers who question the suitability of packaged curricula. Generative curricula are appropriate for high-abstract teachers who can do a better job in identifying need, objectives, activities, and materials than outside experts can.

Many schools vary considerably in the abstraction of their teachers' thought. In such a situation, splitting faculty into "bluebird," "robin," and "scarecrow" curriculum-development groups is not advocated. Instead, heterogeneous groups should be established with curriculum development matched to the highest abstract reasoning of the majority of the staff. Moral reasoning research (Kohlberg and Mayer, 1972) has shown that individual students and the group as a whole are pulled to a higher order of thinking when the majority of persons are not at the lowest stages. Staff developers can assess the abstract functioning of a school staff and determine the initial matching. Then, over time, as teachers gain more insight and experience with curriculum, they will benefit from greater opportunity for curriculum generation. If we believe enhancement of teacher thought is the major aim of staff development, then curriculum development is a potentially powerful vehicle.

Developing Thought Via In-Service Training

In discussing how training can be designed to extend teachers' thinking, the work of Hall and his associates (Hall, Wallace, and Dossett, 1973; Hall and Loucks, 1978), Harris (1980), Joyce and

Showers (1983), and Sparks (1983) is particularly helpful. Training is defined here as the formal learning activities provided by the individual school or school system for the purpose of improving teacher instruction. It is fairly well established that successful training includes a series of activities:

1. Lecture and explanation
2. Demonstration
3. Role playing and feedback
4. Classroom trial and feedback
5. Peer discussion (possibly with peer observation)

Hall and colleagues (Hall, Wallace, and Dossett, 1973; Hall and Loucks, 1978) have shown that teachers think about innovation in their classroom and school with a number of levels of concern. Those levels can be simplified into (1) orientation concerns ("What is the innovation, and why should I do it?"), (2) integration concerns ("I'm interested in new ideas and know something about them, but how do I do them?"), and (3) refinement concerns ("I'm doing them and want to make them better").

Hall and associates have shown that staff developers can plan training to match a teacher's particular stage of concern. Teachers with *orientation* concerns are best matched with a program focusing on expert testimonial, information about what other teachers have found to be useful about the innovation, and a demonstration by an expert on how the new skills and activities are used.

Teachers with *integration* concerns are best matched with training that emphasizes the doing part of the innovation in their own classroom. Therefore, integration teachers benefit most from demonstration, role playing, and feedback within the workshop setting, followed by using the innovation in their own classroom with trainer observation and feedback.

Teachers with *refinement* concerns benefit most when they share their own experience in using the innovation, are engaged in peer observation, and meet regularly to brainstorm on how they can help improve and strengthen each other's skills.

A mismatch occurs when integration teachers who are already knowledgeable and using the practices attend programs that are primarily lecture and demonstration, or when orientation teachers who have reservations about a new practice receive training that primarily focuses on trying out the new practice.

Staff developers can use the level of abstraction to plan a program appropriate to teachers' concerns. For example, a teacher with orientation concerns and a high level of abstraction can move quickly from lecture and demonstration to role playing and classroom trial and then to peer observation, sharing, and brainstorming. On the other hand, a teacher with similar orientation concerns but a low level of abstraction must spend more time with lecture and demonstration. Staff developers also might think of ways to cross-fertilize training sessions by using teachers with integration concerns to work with others who have refinement concerns, or by pairing teachers with refinement concerns with those who have orientation concerns.

Because school staff is likely to be mixed regarding the teachers' level of abstraction, a basic sequence of activities can be provided for everyone, with small-group or individual activities for those teachers who are behind or ahead of the group (see Table 9.2). For example, a group might meet every two or three weeks during a school year, beginning with explanation and demonstrating and moving to workshop practice and feedback, to classroom practice and feedback, to peer discussions and group refinement. Within that sequence, there are small-group and individual options for attending more presentations, viewing a film, reading, listening, or watching teachers who have implemented the practice. Some individuals may need more lecture and demonstration, more classroom practice with trainer feedback, more peer observation, or more time for group problem solving. Even though all teachers are involved in a similar sequence of training, options can be tailored according to individual needs.

Can this really be done? Well, teachers are asked to provide enriching activity for students who are behind or ahead. Why should staff developers not do the same for teachers? Such tailored training has a high probability of stretching teacher thought. As training moves from lecture and demonstration to doing and discussing, so does thought move from low to high abstraction.

Developing Thought Via Action Research

In action research, teachers identify an instructional problem, determine what current evidence is available about solving the problem, propose changes that might be successful, implement the change, and finally judge the success of their endeavor (see Watts, 1985; and Westbrook and others, 1985). Action research does not pretend to find results that are generalizable to other classrooms. Instead, it answers the question of whether the student and teachers in that one classroom or school are better off doing something different today than what they did yesterday.

Action research may go under various names: quality circles, organizational development (school improvement), or problem-solving groups. It can be conducted at the grade, department, or school level. The name is not important. What is important, however, is that a group of teachers be given the opportunity and the skills to take responsibility for instructional improvement. Fullan (1985) has noted that in nearly every successful school improvement program there was a data-based action plan developed by or with teachers.

As teachers work in groups to make instructional changes, they need both knowledge and group process skills. Staff developers must prepare teachers in these skills as they work through instructional problems. Successful groups have both task and human-satisfaction dimensions (Bales, 1953). There should be attention given to the sequence of decision making (problem identification, gathering information about the problem, exploring alternatives, weighing them, prioritizing action, distributing responsibility, setting a time line, and evaluation), decision-making rules (consensus, majority vote, or advisory vote), encouraging conflict of ideas (Hare, 1976, 1982), and building cohesion (Johnson and Johnson, 1982).

Staff developers can engage a faculty group in action research as a vehicle for extending teacher thought by using the tenets of situational leadership, or "life-cycle leadership" (Hersey and Blanchard, 1969, 1977). Leadership moves from an external agent controlling the content, structure, and procedures of a group to having the group assume responsibility for its own deliberation and action. For instance, teachers who are not used to working together and are low in abstraction when identifying and solving an instructional problem should be given a limited and well-defined topic. The staff developer would take an active role in structuring these meetings. A group of teachers with a moderate level of abstraction should have a leader who encourages members to share with the leader clarifying and facilitating group procedures. The leader of a group of teachers with a high level of abstraction should emerge from the group, with the staff developer simply acting as an individual group member with the same (or fewer) rights and responsibilities as any other member.

The way to develop teacher thought, autonomy, and collective action is by gradually increasing the choices for the individual or group and allowing people to function in a more participative and democratic way. For example, a staff that has just begun to work in decision-making groups might begin by tackling issues that deal with limited change (such as in the teachers' lounge). As they experience success, the topics addressed should become more schoolwide (say, increasing instructional time throughout the school, or planning a schoolwide discipline approach).

Conclusion

Developing teacher thought should be the aim of staff development in the same manner that Kohlberg and Mayer (1972) argued that developing student thought should be the aim of education.

You can't have one without the other. How staff developers work with teachers becomes the model for how teachers work with students.

There are currently many staff development programs being presented as the answer to all instructional problems. Researchers have not found the answers to all instructional problems. They have not even found the answers to effective classroom practice or successful schools (see Doyle, 1984; Stodolsky, 1984; and Fullan, 1985). Instead, what they have found are variables and relationships that teachers and administrators can use to make decisions about their unique situation. Staff development programs that tell administrators, supervisors, and teachers what they should do end up bypassing the valuable thoughts of those who are expected to act. To say that teachers must teach in a certain way is to use research to create mindlessness in the classroom and school.

A dramatic example of the use of "research as prescription," as opposed to "research as information," is an experimental study conducted by Deci and others (1982). One group of teachers had standards imposed by its supervisor. The other group was given information without prescription. The prescribed group of teachers were significantly more controlling toward students, dominated teacher-student talk, and frequently used words such as "you should" and "must." When educators attempt to control teacher behavior, teachers tend to control student behavior. The capability of both teachers and students to think is the primary loss.

I'd like to end on a personal note. I am suggesting a way to understand and organize the world of school and instruction. Unfortunately, such clarity does not exist in the real world of action, people, and schools. Solutions to real problems depend on the context, have no one right solution, and are often complicated and messy (Sternberg, 1985). Please resist with me the idea that research or researchers can solve our problems. Please resist what Dewey (1929) spoke of as "the tendency . . . to convert scientific findings into recipes to be followed" (p. 44). Scientific explanations are instead, in Dewey's words, "sources to be used, through the medium of the minds of educators, to make educational functions more intelligent" (pp. 32–22).

I hope you will consider my belief that the aim of staff development should be enhancement of teacher thought. My position is one source of information among competing sources about staff development. By considering all these competing notions, staff developers have the opportunity to think and plan for themselves. That is the aim!

References

Bales, R. F. "The Equilibrium Problem in Small Groups." In T. Parsons, R. F. Bales, and E. A. Shils (eds.), *Working Papers in the Theory of Action*. Glencoe, Ill.: Free Press, 1953.

Blankenship, G., Jr., and Irvine, J. I. "Georgia Teachers' Perceptions of Prescriptive and Descriptive Observations of Teaching by Instructional Supervisors." *Georgia Educational Leadership*, 1985, *1*, 3–7.

Calhoun, E. F. "Relationship of Teachers' Conceptual Level to the Utilization of Supervisory Services and to a Description of the Classroom Instructional Improvement." Paper presented at the annual meeting of the American Educational Research Association, Chicago, Apr. 1985.

Deci, E. L., and others. "The Effects of Performance Standards on Teaching Style: The Behavior of Controlling Teachers." *Journal of Educational Psychology*, 1982, *74*, 852–859.

DeSanctis, M., and Blumberg, A. "An Exploratory Study into the Nature of Teacher Interactions with Other Adults in the Schools." Paper presented at the annual meeting of the American Educational Research Association, San Francisco, Apr. 1979.

Dewey, J. *The Sources of a Science of Education*. New York: Horace Liveright, 1929.

Doll, R. C. *Curriculum Improvement: Decision-Making and Process*. (5th ed.) Needham Heights, Mass.: Allyn and Bacon, 1982.

Doyle, W. *Effective Teaching and the Concept of Master Teacher*. Austin: Research and Development Center for Teacher Education, University of Texas, 1984.

Fullan, M. "Change Processes and Strategies at the Local Level." *Elementary School Journal*, 1985, *85*, 391–421.

Glickman, C. D. *Developmental Supervision: Alternative Approaches for Helping Teachers to Improve Instruction*. Alexandria, Va.: Association for Supervision and Curriculum Development, 1981.

Glickman, C. D. *Supervision of Instruction: A Developmental Approach*. Needham Heights, Mass.: Allyn and Bacon, 1985.

Goodlad, J. I. *A Place Called School: Prospects for the Future*. New York: McGraw-Hill, 1984.

Gordon, S. P., and Glickman, C. D. "Applying Developmental Supervision: Tactical and Strategic Dimensions." *Thresholds in Education*, 1984, *10*, 24–26.

Hall, G. E., and Loucks, S. "Teacher Concerns as a Basis for Facilitating and Personalizing Staff Development." *Teachers College Record*, Sept. 1978, pp. 36–53.

Hall, G. E., Wallace, R. C., Jr., and Dossett, W. A. *A Developmental Conceptualization of the Adoption Process Within Educational Institutions*. Austin: Research and Development Center for Teacher Education, University of Texas, 1973.

Hare, A. P. *Handbook of Small Group Research*. (2nd ed.) New York: Free Press, 1976.

Hare, A. P. *Creativity in Small Groups*. Thousand Oaks, Calif.: Sage, 1982.

Harris, B. M. *Improving Staff Performance Through Inservice Education*. Needham Heights, Mass.: Allyn and Bacon, 1980.

Harvey, O. J. "Conceptual Systems and Attitude Change." In C. Sheriff and M. Sheriff (eds.), *Attitude, Ego, Involvement, and Change*. New York: Wiley, 1967.

Hersey, P., and Blanchard, K. H. "Life-Cycle Theory of Leadership." *Training and Development Journal*, 1969, *23*, 26–34.

Hersey, P., and Blanchard, K. H. *Management of Organizational Behavior: Utilizing Human Resources*. Upper Saddle River, N.J.: Prentice Hall, 1977.

Hunt, D. E., and Joyce, B. R. "Teacher Trainee Personality and Initial Teaching Style." *American Educational Research Journal*, 1967, *4*, 253–255.

Jackson, P. W. *Life in Classrooms*. New York: Holt, Rinehart and Winston, 1968.

Johnson, D. W., and Johnson, R. P. *Joining Together: Group Theory and Group Skills*. Upper Saddle River, N.J.: Prentice Hall, 1982.

Joyce, B. R., and Showers, B. *Power in Staff Development Through Research on Training*. Alexandria, Va.: Association for Supervision and Curriculum Development, 1983.

Kohlberg, L., and Mayer, R. "Development as the Aim of Education." *Harvard Educational Review*, 1972, *42*, 449–496.

Lieberman, A., and Miller, L. *Teachers, Their World, and Their Work*. Alexandria, Va.: Association for Supervision and Curriculum Development, 1984.

Little, J. W. "Norms of Collegiality and Experimentation: Workplace Conditions of School Success." *American Educational Research Journal*, 1982, *19*, 325–340.

Lortie, D. *School Teacher*. Chicago: University of Chicago Press, 1975.

Rutter, M., Maughan, B., Mortimore, P., Oustn, J., and Smith, A. *Fifteen Thousand Hours: Secondary Schools and Their Effects on Children*. Cambridge, MA: Harvard University Press, 1979.

Sarason, S. *The Culture of the School and the Problem of Change*. Needham Heights, Mass.: Allyn and Bacon, 1971.

Sparks, G. M. "Synthesis of Research on Staff Development for Effective Teaching." *Educational Leadership*, Nov. 1983.

Sternberg, R. J. "Teaching Critical Thinking: Are We Making Critical Mistakes?" *Kappan*, 1985, *67*, 194–198.

Stodolsky, S. S. "Teacher Evaluation: The Limits of Looking." *Educational Researcher*, 1984, *13*, 11–18.

Tanner, D., and Tanner, L. N. *Curriculum Development Theory into Practice*. (2nd ed.) New York: Macmillan, 1980.

Watts, H. "When Teachers Are Researchers, Teaching Improves." *Journal of Staff Development*, 1985, 6, 118–127.

Westbrook, C., and others. "Classroom Research: A Promising Model for Staff Development." *Journal of Staff Development*, 1985, 6, 128–132.

Witherell, C. S., and Erickson, V. L. "Teacher Education as Adult Development." *Theory into Practice*, June 1978, pp. 229–238.

Chapter Ten

Looking at
Classroom Teaching and Learning

Look around. Listen to the noisy swarm of students become suddenly quiet as students and teachers move into classrooms and doors close. What's happening behind those doors? What are students learning? How are teachers teaching? Should you open the doors and enter, or stay away? How often should you visit? What should you do, once you enter? How do you discover what is really going on between teacher and students? What recognition can you give to teachers who are already excelling, and what assistance can you give to those who are floundering or who are simply making it through the year? What can you do, as only one person, with responsibility for a teaching staff of 225, or 25, or 7 in a school? As a school leader, you are bombarded with so many student needs, parent concerns, teacher concerns, and district and state requirements and paperwork that it seems futile to think of improving the teaching of every teacher. What indeed can you, as only one person, do?

This scenario depicts common concerns from those who have schoolwide responsibility for an array of classrooms and teachers as they contemplate making frequent visits to every classroom for the purpose of improving learning for all students. It seems like a pipe dream for many in a supervisory or instructional leadership role, but in the most successful schools in the United States this level of support is the day-to-day reality (Glickman, 1993; Glickman, Gordon, and Ross-Gordon, 2001). These successful schools typically have no more time or resources than those where the scenario is wishful thinking. But the difference is how time, focus, and structure are used; how staff development, school improvement, personnel evaluation, and classroom assistance are used together; and how instructional leadership is defined and employed.

Whenever one person defines himself or herself as the sole leader, provider, and catalyst for improved classroom learning, any school with more than fifteen teaching faculty immediately confronts a lack of schoolwide instructional focus and assistance. Successful schools understand that direct improvement of teaching and learning in every classroom comes via a constellation of individuals and groups who undertake myriad activities and initiatives affording continuous reflection and change in classroom practice guided by the educational aspirations of the school.

Much has happened in education in the past decade. Among the changes are new standards and assessments of learning; new accountability schemes; new roles and responsibilities for teachers; and new forms of observation, feedback, and critique. We have much more knowledge about powerful teaching and learning. We also have separate, additional knowledge about teaching and learning for the continuous improvement of schools in varying geographic contexts (rural, urban, suburban) and community contexts (socioeconomic class, race, ethnicity, and gender).

So before we move into explanation and application, let's dwell on the first questions. Who is the person in the opening paragraph of this chapter? Who are you as a professional and as a person? Are you a student, a principal, a beginning teacher, an experienced teacher, a grade or department head, a mentor, an instructional lead teacher, an assistant principal, a central office supervisor, a curriculum or staff development director, an associate superintendent, or a superintendent? You may hold a single role or have a combination of many. For now, let's just say that your role has degrees of expectation, assumptions, status, influence, and authority that may be helpful or harmful in finding out what really is going on behind the classroom door.

Another way of asking who you are is in terms of personal identity: female or male; gay or straight; Christian, Muslim, Jewish, Hindu, Buddhist, agnostic, atheist, or of another spiritual or religious persuasion; southerner, northerner, midwesterner, westerner, internationalist; descendent of Europeans, Africans, Asians, Hispanics and Latinos, Native Americans, and so on; first-generation, third-generation, twelfth-generation; from wealth or from poverty. These personal identities are not absolutes—they may seem irrelevant for a book on leadership for improving classroom teaching— but such identity of self and how that identity influences the perspectives of others can have a powerful impact on your effort to open the classroom door, possibly determining which teachers you really have access to and what understanding and priorities you wish to see practiced behind the classroom door.

Lastly, who are you as a knower, practitioner, and communicator of excellent classroom learning? Are you certain of what good teaching is; what it looks like in action; and how students should interact, respond, and shine? Certainty can become arrogance and dogmatism, but uncertainty can become permissiveness and acceptance of all teaching as having equal merit. Understanding your own beliefs about good learning—whether inductive or deductive, individual or group, cooperative or competitive, paper-and-pencil test or performance-based, core knowledge or multicultural—is another element that can lower or raise barriers between you and what teachers do in the privacy of their own classroom.

So think about who you are as we first look at ways of structuring, observing, and improving individual teaching. "Know thyself," said Socrates. Through the ages, knowing oneself has served as a prelude to and foundation for relating well to others.

What you read here is useful to your immediate school world and should raise new possibilities of what every student deserves: teachers in every classroom of a school who are the greatest learners of their own practice, and an intellectually challenging and relevant education.

How Do Teaching and Learning Improve?

How do teaching and learning improve? Consider the statement in Exhibit 10.1. This is no mystery. It's as simple as this: I cannot improve my craft in isolation from others. To improve, I must have formats, structures, and plans for reflecting on, changing, and assessing my practice.

The typical and infrequent drop-in visit by an evaluator a few times a year without continuous discussion, critiquing, and planning with others leads to deadening and routinizing practice and diminishment of teaching as a profession. By definition, a *profession* is the work of persons who possess a body of knowledge, skills, and practices that must be constantly tested and upgraded with colleagues. A professional field, as opposed to a technical one, is one

Exhibit 10.1. If as a Teacher

If, as a teacher,

- I present the same lessons in the same manner that I have done in the past;
- I seek no feedback from my students;
- I do not analyze and evaluate their work in a manner that changes my own emphasis, repertoire, and timing;
- I do not visit or observe other adults as they teach;
- I do not share the work of my students with colleagues for feedback, suggestions, and critique;
- I do not visit other schools or attend particular workshops or seminars or read professional literature on aspects of my teaching;
- I do not welcome visitors with experience and expertise to observe and provide feedback to me on my classroom practice;
- I have no yearly individualized professional development plan focused on my classroom changes to improve student learning; and finally,
- I have no systemic evaluation of my teaching tied to individual, grade or department, and schoolwide goals

Then I have absolutely no way to become better as a teacher.

that prizes perpetual dissatisfaction with one's own practice with current clients as the core to better service for clients in the future. Research has found that faculty in successful schools always question existing instructional practice and do not blame lack of student achievement on external causes. Faculty in schools that have high intellectual standards and educate virtually all their students well work collegially and critically with each other, clearly knowing what they want of all students and striving to close the gap between the rhetoric of education aims and the hard, professional work of practice. The successful school stands in great contrast to the mediocre or low-performing school, where faculty work apart from each other, without common purpose, and with self-centered beliefs that they are doing the best they can. The source of the problem in the ordinary schools is always someone else: the students, the parents and caretakers, the school board, and so on (Glickman, 1993).

We have now a substantial professional knowledge base on how schools succeed, how great teaching is accomplished, and how students learn well. The challenge is to use more fully what we have learned from this knowledge base. As Ron Edmonds (1979) points out in his seminal work on effective schools, "We can, whenever and wherever we choose, successfully teach all children whose schooling is of interest to us. . . . We already know more than we need to know to accomplish this task" (p. 22). Without cultivating dissatisfaction and critique, without being clear about our purpose, and without using a knowledge base in practice, we have no education and no profession.

Organizing the Quest

To improve classroom learning for all students—preschool, elementary, middle, secondary, or postsecondary—we use the organization of professional knowledge referred to in Figure 10.1.

Student learning, the bull's-eye, is the focus of all that we do in the classroom and school—the standards we set, the expectations

Figure 10.1. Elements That Influence Student Learning in Renewing a School or Classroom

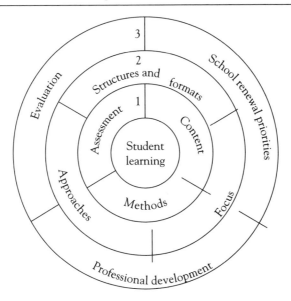

Student Learning—The focus of all we do in schools

1. Elements that directly influence student learning
     Content of what is taught
     Method used for teaching
     Assessment of student learning

2. Elements that organize the instructional leader's work with teachers
     Focus for observations and use of data
     Approaches to working with teachers
     Structures and formats for organizing instructional improvement efforts

3. Elements that provide the overarching context for instructional improvement
     School renewal priorities that convey the school vision
     Professional development plans and resources
     Evaluation of how and what students are learning
     Assessment of student learning

we have, and the common mastery we expect of students in each classroom. Student learning is directly influenced by the first concentric circle: the *content* (or curriculum) of what is taught, the teaching *methods* used, and the diagnostic *assessments* of student learning employed. To improve classroom instruction, educational leaders have the tools in the second concentric circle: *focus* on what to attend to in improving teaching, observing classrooms, using achievement data, and considering samples of student work; the human relations *approaches* for use in improving reflection, problem solving, and practice on the part of the teacher; and the *structures and formats* of various ways to work individually or in a group with teachers. To have a powerful school effect, all of this work has to be imbedded in the overarching third concentric circle: the overall vision and *renewal priorities* of the school; the *professional development* plans, resources, and time that the school and district make available; and *evaluation* of how and what students are learning and how to use the resulting data to guide further school priorities.

Here, let's attend to the bull's-eye of improved student learning by concentrating on circles two and three, and then conclude with how to embed this work into the entire school renewal process.

Structures for Classroom Assistance

"I can't do it. I don't have the time. It can't be done." If you, as a principal, assistant principal, lead teacher, department head, supervisor, or curriculum director responsible for more than fifteen teachers, believe that you are the sole instructional leader, then you can't do what this book is about. However, if you understand the use of multiple structures with multiple leaders for assisting, focusing, and improving classroom teaching and learning, then continuous improvement can become an ongoing reality. These are some of the structures for classroom assistance that are most useful in a school:

- Clinical supervision
- Peer coaching
- Critical friends
- A classroom action research team or study group

Clinical Supervision

The best known, oldest, and most widely used structure for working directly with classroom teachers is clinical supervision (see Cogan, 1973; Costa and Garmston, 1994; Goldhammer, 1969; Pajak, 2000). It is most often used in some type of line relationship, such as supervisor to supervisee, principal to assistant principal, department head to teacher, mentor teacher to mentee, cooperating teacher to student teacher, master teacher to intern, and so on. The explanation here is derived mainly from Glickman, Gordon, and Ross-Gordon (2001).

The structure of clinical supervision can be simplified into five sequential steps.

Step One: Preconference with Teacher

At the preconference, the supervisor sits with the teacher and determines (1) the reason for and purpose of the observation, (2) the focus of the observation, (3) the method and form of observation to be used, (4) the time of the observation, and (5) the time of the postconference. These determinations are made before the actual observation, so that both supervisor and teacher are clear about what is to transpire. The purpose of the observation determines the criteria for the remaining decisions on focus, method, and time of observation.

Step Two: Observation of Classroom Instruction

The next step, observation, is the time to follow through with the understanding of the preconference. The observer might use any one observation or combination thereof. The observer should keep in mind the difference between a *description* of an event and *interpretation* of it. Description is the actual event that occurs and is recorded. Interpretation is the meaning inferred from the event.

Step Three: Analysis and Approach

Analysis and *interpretation* of the observation and determination of approach are now possible. The supervisor leaves the classroom with the recorded observations and seeks solitude in an office or a corner to study the information. Regardless of the instrument, questionnaire, or open-ended form used, the supervisor must make sense of a large mass of information. Exhibit 10.2 is a form that can be used to organize this task.

The last determination for the supervisor to make in step three of the clinical structure is to select an interpersonal approach for use with the teacher in the postconference. Should the supervisor use a directive approach by presenting observations and interpretations, asking for teacher input, setting a goal, and either telling the teacher what action to take (directive-control) or providing the teacher with alternative actions to choose from (directive-informational)? Should the supervisor be collaborative by sharing the observations, allowing the teacher to present his or her own interpretation, and negotiating a mutual contract for future improvement? Should the supervisor be nondirective by explaining the observations and encouraging the teacher to analyze, interpret, and make his or her own plan? Some supervisors give the teacher the observation data prior to the postconference. This allows the teacher to review the data in advance and bring his or her own preliminary interpretation to the postconference.

Step Four: Postconference with Teacher

With the completed observation form, completed analysis and interpretation form, and the chosen interpersonal approach, the supervisor is ready to meet with the teacher in a *postconference*. It

Exhibit 10.2. Worksheet for Analysis and Interpretation of Observation Data

Analysis: Write the major findings of your observation. Write down only what has been taken directly from your observation.

1.

2.

3.

4.

5.

Interpretations: Write what you believe is desirable or not desirable about the major findings.

1.

2.

3.

4.

5.

is held to discuss the analysis of the observation and finally, if needed, to produce a plan for instructional improvement.

The first order of business is to let the teacher in on the recorded notes and impressions from the observation—to reflect back to the teacher what was seen. Then the supervisor can follow the chosen approach (directive-controlling, directive-informational, collaborative, or nondirective). The responsibility for developing a future plan may reside with the supervisor, be equally shared, or belong to the teacher. The conference ends with a plan for further improvement. Exhibit 10.3 can be used to develop such a plan.

Step Five: Critique of Previous Four Steps

The *critique* of the previous four steps is a time for reviewing whether the format and procedures from preconference through postconference were satisfactory and whether revision might be needed before repeating the sequence. The critique can be held at the end of the postconference, or in a separate conference after a few days. It need not be a formal session but instead a brief discussion, consisting of just a few questions ("What was valuable in what we have been doing? What was of little value? What changes could be suggested?"). The critique has both symbolic and functional value. It indicates that the supervisor is involved in an improvement effort in the same way as the supervisee. Furthermore, the feedback from the teacher gives the supervisor a chance to decide which practices to continue, revise, or change when working with the teacher in the future.

The five steps are now complete, and the teacher has a tangible plan of action. The supervisor is prepared to review the plan in the next preconference and reestablish the focus and method of observation.

Peer Coaching

Peer coaching is a structure whereby fellow teachers, as one another's colleagues, conduct a cycle of clinical supervision with

Exhibit 10.3. Plan for Instructional Improvement

Postconference date: _____

Time: _____

Observed teacher: _____

Clinical supervisor: _____

Objective to be worked on:

Activities to be undertaken to achieve objectives:

Resources needed:

Time and date for next preconference:

each other with overall coordination by a facilitator/leader (see Glickman, Gordon, and Ross-Gordon, 2001).

The first step is a meeting with teachers to discuss how a proposed peer-coaching program would fit into the instructional goals of the school or district, and then to decide on the specific purposes of the program. For example, if the purpose is simply to acquaint teachers with others' teaching strategies, less preparation is needed than if the purpose is to provide teachers with feedback on their teaching of a particular subject, or set of methods, or progress toward learning standards and then to assist them in developing a congruent action plan.

Before implementing this structure, teacher preparation includes training on (1) understanding the purpose and procedures of peer coaching, (2) conducting a preconference to determine the focus of observation, (3) conducting and analyzing an observation to distinguish between observing and interpreting classroom events, and (4) conducting two postconferences with different approaches for developing an action plan (such as using a nondirective and a collaborative approach).

Preparation should include a review of a standard form for writing instructional improvement plans in the postconference. The form should be simple and easy to fill out. Each peer member should understand that a completed plan is the object of the first four clinical steps and the basis for beginning the next round of coaching. See Exhibit 10.3 for a sample form.

Scheduling for peer coaching should take into consideration that a teacher will be less enthusiastic about the project if it means increasing the amount of personal time and energy expended beyond an already full day. A teacher is more likely to participate if time for peer coaching can be scheduled during the school day. For example, having teachers place themselves in teams that share the same planning time or lunch period allows preconference and postconference during the school day. Hiring a few substitutes for two days twice a year allows teachers to be relieved of class duties so that they can observe their peers. One substitute can relieve six classroom teachers for one period at a time during a six-period schedule. The principal, assistant principal, or central office supervisor can occasionally substitute in the classroom so that one teacher can coach another for a class period; this is a practice that not only permits relief but also shows great support for coaching.

A second way of freeing time for peer observation is for teachers to release each other by periodically scheduling a videotape, lecture, or some other large-group instruction so that one teacher can teach two classes. Whatever the actual schedule used to release teachers for peer coaching, the structure requires preplanning on the part of the instructional leader and teachers to ensure that teachers can participate without great personal sacrifice.

Another issue is arranging teams of teachers. As with most issues in education, no hard and fast rules apply. Generally, teachers should be grouped with each other so that they are comfortable together but not necessarily at an identical level of experience or competence. It may be useful to put experienced teachers with new ones, superior teachers with adequate ones, or adequate teachers with struggling ones. Team members should share some degree of understanding and comfort to begin with. Hence, it is undesirable to match people who think too much alike; nor is it desirable to match those who think too differently. The goal is to match people who are different but still can respect and communicate easily with each other.

In a number of schools, teachers present to the facilitator or leader a confidential list of colleagues they would like to work with. The facilitator/leader then matches up preferences and creates the team. This represents a practical approach; an ideal approach matches people on the basis of cognitive growth. For example, a teacher with great expertise in classroom management can be matched with a teacher who has had recent experience with student assessment. Each teacher then has cognitive skills in an area that matches the needs of the other. In creating a team, the choice is between an ideal way that matches people according to cognitive concerns and a practical way that matches them on the basis of their need for security with a new program. The practical match might be better when starting the program; after peer coaching becomes a familiar ongoing activity, the facilitator can rearrange the team with the goal of greater cognitive matching.

An additional, important component of a peer coaching program is close monitoring of peer progress. A peer coaching leader/facilitator should be available to the peer team as a resource person. For example, what happens when the preconference concludes with an agreement to observe a teacher's verbal interaction in the classroom, and the peer coach is at a loss about where to find such an observation instrument? The training program should answer such questions, but an orientation meeting cannot cover all possible needs. A leader/facilitator should monitor the needs of the peer team, answer questions, offer resources, and step in to help, as needed.

An elaborate monitoring system is not necessary, however. The leader/facilitator might simply check with peer coaches every few weeks. At a periodic faculty meeting, he or she might ask peer coaches to write a note on their team progress. The leader/facilitator should be sure that books, films, tapes, instruments on clinical supervision, and methods or instruments for observation are catalogued and available to teachers in the professional library.

Critical Friends

The concept of the critical-friends group was developed by the Annenberg Institute for School Reform at Brown University in conjunction with school-based renewal efforts in K–12 schools throughout the nation. The structure was first derived from the Coalition of Essential Schools and then complemented by other school networks, such as Accelerated Schools, the Georgia League of Professional Schools, the Southern Maine Partnership, and the Annenberg Challenge Urban and Rural School Initiatives. Critical-friends strategies offer a way to build a purposeful group of teachers (generally five to eight) who, together with a facilitator (internal or external), look at samples of student work or instructional problems and concerns over the course of a school year or longer. For example, each teacher might bring samples of student work (as indicators of high-, average-, or low-quality work) to a prearranged meeting, explain the concern with the work, and then listen carefully as colleagues analyze and suggest possible improvement. A critical-friends group typically includes a peer coaching component for teachers to become familiar with each other's classrooms and to follow up on a particular classroom change that an individual teacher has committed to accomplish. A "tuning protocol," developed by Joseph McDonald and David Allen (Allen, 1998), is often used to keep the group meetings focused and within a specific time limit (Exhibit 10.4).

A tuning protocol is a preestablished structured agenda with time limits and specific roles for members to follow in organizing discussion involving information, feedback, and learnings about how to improve instruction. Tuning may be thought of in the sense of piano tuning or a tuning fork, as a way to work through a sequence of conversations thoroughly and efficiently to find how to help put a teacher's instruction into harmony and congruence with that person's purposes and concerns. The idea behind the protocol is that if everyone understands the structured guide to be used, the facilitator and the members can keep the conversation from straying from the instructional goal, and the conversation yields both "warm" feedback (suggestions about what the teacher is doing well and should continue) and "cool" feedback (ideas and critiques about inconsistency and areas for change). By determining who speaks when (see, for example, step two of Exhibit 10.4), the protocol ensures that only the teacher who is seeking feedback on his or her instruction and student work is allowed to speak, sharing all the necessary background information and specifying questions that he or she wants the group to answer. During the time for feedback (step six in Exhibit 10.4), only group members speak; the teacher listens. This is all done to prevent entanglement, tangents, defensiveness, and confusion. Everyone in the group knows that if the group stays within the directions and time line, the meeting

Exhibit 10.4. Schedule for the Tuning Protocol Developed by Joseph McDonald and David Allen

I. Introduction   10 minutes
  - Facilitator briefly introduces protocol goals, guidelines, and schedule.
  - Participants briefly introduce themselves.

II. Teacher presentation   20 minutes
  - Teacher/presenter describes the context for student work (assignment, scoring, rubric, etc.).
  - Teacher/presenter poses her focusing question for feedback.
  - Participants are silent.

III. Clarifying questions   5 minutes maximum
  - Participants ask clarifying questions.
  - Facilitator judges which questions properly belong in warm and cool feedback (questions that involve more than a brief, factual answer).

IV. Examination of student work samples   15 minutes
  - Samples of student work might be original, photocopies of written work, or video clips of a presentation.

V. Pause to reflect on warm and cool feedback   2–3 minutes maximum
  - Participants may take a couple of minutes to reflect silently on what they would like to contribute to the feedback session.

VI. Warm and cool feedback   5 minutes
  - Participants share feedback while teacher/presenter is silent.
  - Facilitator may remind participants of teacher/presenter's focusing question (step II).

VII. Reflection   15 minutes
  - Teacher/presenter speaks to those comments or questions he or she chooses.
  - Facilitator may intervene to focus, clarify, etc.
  - Participants are silent.

VIII. Debrief   10 minutes
  - Facilitator leads an open discussion of the tuning experience the group has shared: What was effective? What concerns did the process raise?

will be completed in ninety minutes and the desired results accomplished. A school using such a protocol—or adjusting the model to create its own—might find initial meetings somewhat awkward (people might be used to jumping into a conversation whenever they wish, or straying into noninstructional areas), but after a few instances of employing the format they find it becomes comfortable and extremely helpful.

A number of other formats for looking at student work have been developed or described by Blythe, Allen, and Powell (1991) and McDonald (1996, 2001). But the key is to use a prescribed set of group tuning protocol steps monitored by a group facilitator/gatekeeper to ensure that there is a chance for the teacher to explain his or her instructional issue, time for colleagues to ask questions and gather more information about the issue, and ample opportunity for the teacher to listen carefully rather than defend or react to suggestions from colleagues before a plan of action is made. (The Annenberg Institute's *Looking at Student Work: A Window in the Classroom,* 1991, is an excellent short video that shows actual school teams using the critical-friends format.)

Classroom Action Research Teams or Study Groups

Use of an action research team or study group in a school can be tailored more specifically to the needs and issues in that school than can clinical supervision, peer coaching, or a critical-friends group. The format for an action research team or study group can be adapted from an external example or developed internally. In one school, as part of everyone's school-based staff development, each faculty member is expected to join and attend one study group for an entire school year, focused on a schoolwide instructional priority applied to his or her own classroom. Faculty meetings, faculty planning days, or team planning times are set aside for the members of the team to accomplish:

- Review of their common goals
- Their own research agenda, where they study a student learn-

ing goal (a reading, visiting a classroom in another school, team teaching, joint curriculum planning, attending a conference or meeting, videotaping their own classroom or another, and so on)

- Their own individual classroom action plan, consisting of changes in current teaching, assessment, and activity along with the needed resources or assistance from other study group members
- Collection of ongoing student learning data to determine the progress being made
- Progress reports on individual work, to the study group and the school as a whole

Another way to create a study group tailored to a school is to have each faculty member establish his or her own individual learning goal early in the year and then form a study group with others working toward a similar learning goal. Afterward, the same type of change, action, research, and reflection process is used.

In both cases, the study group members must focus on improvements to learning in *their own* classrooms and follow (or modify) a generic, action research sequence:

- Problem identification phase and data collection

    What is (are) the student learning goal(s) of highest priority?

    What else do we need to know about how our students are currently performing related to this goal?

    What do we now have as baseline data on student learning that can be used for later comparison?

- Planning and implementation phase

    What changes in our classrooms will we make?

    What assistance do we need from each other?

    What are actions and completion dates for changes in our own teaching and learning?

- Evaluation and reflection phase

> After the implementation period, what data do we gather to determine progress (or lack thereof) and use for any further action research cycle?

> How do we improve upon the process of action research next time?

It is important to separate the problem identification phase from the planning and implementation phase. The group has to be clear on instructional priorities and baseline data before taking action. A common mistake many faculties make is to simply choose a priority on the basis of feelings (the so-called cardiac approach to evaluation: "In my heart, I think we need to do better in these areas"). To be effective, each action research team requires data to support a common focus on improvement in certain areas of standards or achievement, such as writing, critical thinking skills, and so on. The team then develops a plan of action, including how to assist each other and what information to collect on student performance that demonstrates concrete evidence of progress.

A brief example might be helpful. In one school, action research groups were formed according to multigrade interdisciplinary teams. The team reviewed the previous year's state assessments of science proficiency and found that a majority of students were scoring low on certain objectives. Digging deeper into the objectives made the problem obvious: the team simply was not covering the content and its application tested by the proficiency exam. The group, not wishing to abandon its interdisciplinary work, instead developed a plan for incorporating the missing objectives in thematic units of science, technology, and the environment. They observed, coached, and reviewed samples of student work during the year that were related to the common instructional focus. The results from the state assessments a year later found more than 90 percent of students performing at a mastery level.

Conclusion

What is important is that there be user-friendly structures supported by time and resources and congruent with school goals and priorities. The structures may involve mostly one-to-one interaction (clinical supervision or peer coaching) or group interaction (action research team or study group), or a combination of both (critical friends). The structures for professional interaction must have a focus on what to observe and share about teaching and student learning.

More examples, case studies, and illustrations of the structures can be found in *Leadership for Learning* (Glickman, 2002). For now, simply think about which structures for continuous instructional improvement are in place in your own school and what further needs and possibilities might be contemplated.

References

Allen, D. "The Tuning Protocol: Opening to Reflection." In D. Allen (ed.), *Assessing Student Learning: From Grading to Understanding*. New York: Teachers College Press, 1998.

Annenberg Institute for School Reform. *Looking at Student Work: A Window into the Classroom*. New York: Teachers College Press, 1991. Videotape [28 minutes].

Blythe, T., Allen, D., and Powell, B. S. *Looking Together at Student Work: A Companion Guide to Assessing Student Learning*. New York: Teachers College Press, 1991.

Cogan, M. *Clinical Supervision*. Boston: Houghton Mifflin, 1973.

Costa, A., and Garmston, R. J. *Cognitive Coaching: A Foundation for Renaissance Schools:* Norwood, Mass.: Christopher-Gordon, 1994.

Edmonds, R. "Effective Schools for the Urban Poor." *Educational Leadership*, 1979, *37*(1), 15–24.

Glickman, C. D. *Renewing America's Schools: A Guide for School-Based Action*. San Francisco: Jossey-Bass, 1993.

Glickman, C. D., Gordon, S. P., and Ross-Gordon, J. M. *SuperVision and Instructional Leadership: A Developmental Approach*. (5th ed.). Needham Heights, Mass.: Allyn & Bacon, 2001.

Goldhammer, R. *Clinical Supervision: Special Methods for the Supervision of Teachers*. New York: Holt, 1969.

McDonald, J. P. *Redesigning School: Lessons for the Twenty-First Century.* San Francisco: Jossey-Bass, 1996.

McDonald, J. P. "Students' Work and Teachers' Learning." In A. Lieberman and L. Miller (eds.), *Teachers Caught in the Action: Professional Development That Works.* New York: Teachers College Press, 2001.

Pajak, F. *Approaches to Clinical Supervision: Alternatives for Improving Instruction.* (2nd ed.). Norwood, Mass.: Christopher-Gordon, 2000.

Chapter Eleven

The Supervisor's Challenge

Changing the Teacher's Work Environment

Many state legislatures are in the midst of proposing or implementing such reforms as higher educational standards for prospective teachers, salaries that are competitive with industry, eleven-month contracts, career ladders, and incentives such as grants and loans to attract outstanding students to teaching.

All of these reforms are worthy in that they strive to reward teachers with career advancement and a higher salary and status. Yet simply to attract and reward the capable and sensitive teacher by improving external conditions is not enough. Those of us who are familiar with the everyday life of teachers and schools know that unless the "place called school" becomes a professional work environment for the teacher, we probably will not improve the situation. We will continue to lose good teachers, and those who remain will still have little incentive to excel.

Supervisors, department heads, instructional lead teachers, and principals must take on the difficult task of changing those characteristics of the teaching environment that stifle improvement of instruction. Their best resource in this effort is our rapidly accumulating knowledge about the characteristics of schools that are effective.

A Cause Beyond Oneself

The research on effective schools is well known. Instead of recapitulating the specific findings of each study, let's look at what they have in common. They all refer to a particular type of social organization. Edmonds (1979) referred to a climate of expectations; Brookover and others (1979) to teacher expectations that students can learn; Little (1982) to collective action and common terminology used by teachers in discussing problems; Goodlad (1983) to goal participation and agreement; and Rutter and others (1979) to a "concept of ethos . . . the well-nigh universal tendency for individuals in common circumstances to form social groups with their own rules, values, and standards of behavior" (p. 184). Where an ethos develops around a clear educational purpose, an effective school emerges.

It should be emphasized that the more successful schools are not unduly regimented. Rather, they are characterized by good morale and the routine of people working harmoniously together as part of an efficient system that offers both supervision and support to teachers (Rutter and others, 1979).

Every major research study on effective schools has noted the organizational phenomenon of collective action, agreed-upon purpose, and belief in attainment. I call these manifestations of ethos "a cause beyond oneself" (Glickman, 1985). Teachers of effective schools see themselves as part of the total action, with an agreed-upon purpose and belief that as a group they can attain their goals. Similarly, research on ineffective schools has noted lack of a common purpose, finding that those teachers see themselves as isolated individuals, an "island unto themselves," concerned with their own students within their own four walls. To improve instruction, we must give constant attention to bringing teachers together to work on common instructional concerns.

Obstacles to School Improvement

There are five factors in the work environment that prevent this from happening: (1) one-room schoolhouse mentality, (2) inverse beginner responsibilities, (3) invisibility and isolation, (4) lack of professional dialogue, and (5) restricted choice (see Chapter Nine, p. 106).

At last, we have the real challenge to supervisors: to improve instruction, we must reshape the work environment of the teacher into one that is conducive to reflective and collective dialogue among staff members who are given power to act upon their decisions.

All supervisors must assess their own school situation, staff members, and community to determine how to approach the problem. Here, I offer suggestions for moving teachers away from individualistic and fragmented action toward a cause beyond oneself.

Increase Responsibility

First, we must gradually increase the responsibilities of the beginning teacher. With experienced teachers, we must plan a way to make the first year of teaching a situation of lessened responsibility, involving peer support and help in easing the beginner into the profession.

We must plan a buddy system matching experienced teachers with beginners so that the latter has someone to turn to for information and help.

Increase Visibility

We must encourage teachers to visit each other and as a result find out what others are doing. The visited teacher can ask the visiting teacher to observe and give feedback on particular classroom concerns.

We must hold after-school meetings in different rooms, where teachers are asked to defend the what and how of their instruction. Barth (1980) wrote of how teachers in his school presented their instructional plans to each other. They continued the intellectual task of asking, "In which ways does my teaching support yours, and in which ways does my teaching contradict what you are trying to do?" Teachers can see more easily where curriculum inconsistency exists from teacher to teacher and grade level to grade level.

Increase Professional Dialogue

We must make time for professional talk among teachers during faculty meetings. Give teachers time to propose plans for what *they can do* to change current problems. Keep talk focused on actions the staff can control.

We must invite teachers to help interview teacher candidates. This involvement not only gives recognition to their experience but also enables them to examine and explain the workings of their school to an outsider. The need to articulate school purpose becomes apparent when a candidate asks, "What is it like to teach here?"

Increase Professional Choice

We must encourage teachers to work in groups where they can control part of their own teaching schedule, materials, and curriculum. Teachers across grades or subjects can be grouped together and given complete responsibility for planning some activities for the year. Whether the work involves a special extracurricular project, a study group in discipline, or curriculum change, the power to implement as a group can help build collective action.

We must continuously ask staff members to think about an active philosophy, not a theoretical one. What is the purpose of the school? Is it academic achievement on a test, or is it other ways of knowing? Do we value memorization and recitation, or experimentation and inquisitiveness? Do we want students to become aware of self-values? Do we want conformity, or autonomy? Or do we want to do everything? These are not pie-in-the-sky questions; the research on effective schools has shown that faculty members in an effective school clearly know their priorities, no matter how narrow or broad they may be, and that using their human and fiscal energy clearly reflects those priorities. Clarity does not occur by itself. It occurs when we ask teachers, "What do you want your students to become? What do you do in your class? What do you do in the school that either supports or negates those goals?"

Conclusion: The Challenge

The challenge is clear: supervisors have to move forcefully to eliminate factors in the school environment that impede improvement and replace them with collective action—a cause beyond oneself.

References

Barth, R. *Run School Run*. Cambridge, Mass.: Harvard University Press, 1980.

Brookover, W., and others. "School Social Systems and Students' Achievement." In *Schools Can Make a Difference*. New York: Praeger, 1979.

Edmonds, R. "Effective Schools for the Urban Poor." *Educational Leadership*, Oct. 1979, pp. 15–24.

Glickman, C. D. *Supervision of Instruction: A Developmental Approach*. Boston: Allyn and Bacon, 1985.

Goodlad, J. I. "A Study of Schooling: Some Findings and Hypotheses." *Phi Delta Kappan*, Mar. 1983, pp. 465–470.

Little, J. W. "Norms of Collegiality and Experimentation: Workplace Conditions of School Success." *American Educational Research Journal*, Fall 1982, pp. 325–340.

Rutter, M., and others. *Fifteen Thousand Hours: Secondary Schools and Their Effects on Children*. Cambridge, Mass.: Harvard University Press, 1979.

Part Four

Teaching, Learning, and Service

Chapter Twelve

Democratic Education

Judy and the Dance

Goddard College sits off a rural Vermont highway, up on a hill, near the small town of Plainfield. In 1994–95, I accepted a visiting faculty appointment at the college to teach in the master's degree residency program, which would involve working with twelve students for one year (two ten-day institutes, one in early summer and the other in January, and ongoing communication with all twelve while they completed individual contracts leading to a master's degree in teaching or a professional certification). The final product of their work was a portfolio, a thesis, and a public exhibit of their learning. In accepting this position, I was one of a team of seven faculty members—five like me in a visiting, part-time position, and two full-time faculty who taught year round in the undergraduate and graduate programs.

After twenty years of teaching at a large university, I was eager for this small community experience. I had friends at Goddard, my spouse's family was from Vermont, and for the past thirty years I had spent every summer at family dwellings in the northern part of the state. Furthermore, I was raised in New England and began my education career in small towns in Maine and New Hampshire. So returning to a small town and a small college in New England had obvious attractions. However, the greatest reason for me to be at Goddard was the reputation of the college as Deweyan in origin and an embodiment of progressive education and community life.

The author wishes to thank colleagues—students and faculty—at Goddard College and the University of Georgia for their insights and suggestions in shaping this chapter.

That year, I took a partial leave from my own university (the University of Georgia), where I hold a special career appointment as University Professor of Education. Among my duties, I serve as chair of the university's Program for School Improvement, which operates a nationally recognized collaboration with more than one hundred schools involved in the renewal of democratic education, the League of Professional Schools (see Glickman, 1993).

I took this partial leave to study the historical, political, legal, philosophical, and sociocultural connections between democracy and education. I hoped that teaching at Goddard would help me make concrete connections, give me a way of thinking about my own teaching, and suggest how to improve teacher education programs at my own university.

My spouse, Sara, who is an extraordinary public school teacher, took a leave with me, and we planned the year to include visits to other universities, public schools, and educational organizations throughout the United States, Canada, Turkey, and Greece. As part of my leave, I returned to Georgia every six weeks for a month at a time to continue collaborating with schools and state and college policy work, attend to the development of a new department, complete essays for a forthcoming new book,[1] and generally stay in touch with colleagues about other college and university matters.

The University of Georgia (UGA) is the oldest state university in the United States, chartered in 1785. Like Goddard, it is nestled up on a hill. But the similarities stop there. UGA is in the city of Athens, with a student population of about thirty thousand students within a city of about one hundred thousand total. The College of Education is the second largest in the nation, consisting of 220 faculty members and several thousand undergraduate and graduate students. The town and the university are a thriving mix of academics, sports, art, music, and vibrant night life.

There are great differences between Goddard and UGA. Goddard is tiny in size (550 students), private, and high-tuition. Its academic programs offer an array of choices for students; the structure of its programs, core requirements, and grading systems are vastly different from most other colleges and universities. Goddard attracts mainly out-of-state students; the student and faculty bodies tend politically to the moderate or the radical left, with a sprinkling of a few independent conservatives.

By contrast, the University of Georgia is large and public, with very low or free tuition (state funds pay full scholarships for almost all entering students); more than 90 percent of undergraduates and approximately 50 percent of graduates are from the state. The student body tends to be moderately conservative to moderately liberal, and the faculty is moderately liberal. Athens is often cited as the most progressive town in Georgia (in reference to music, art, politics, and lifestyles). It attracts a substantial group of people of counterculture ideologies. The majority of citizens voted for Jesse Jackson and the Rainbow Coalition in one of the past presidential elections, and it has a two-term female mayor who won as the candidate of a progressive coalition of preservationists, artists, and liberals.

Being in the southern bible belt, UGA and Athens draw a diverse student body from all areas of the state and have a substantial number of conservative and religious people with fundamentalist beliefs. The university is best characterized as a very good major public university with competitive admission requirements and a loyal following of alumni, friends, and legislators throughout the state. Its undergraduate academic preparation programs are mostly traditional with large introductory classes and a two-year requirement of core liberal arts for all students before they can major in a discipline or a professional field. Most undergraduate academic advising is done by staff members, not by faculty.

Although Goddard is a small, private college with faculty hired to teach and advise students, UGA is a comprehensive, land-grant, sea-grant, research university where all education faculty are budgeted one-third time for research. The College of Education at UGA consistently ranks as one of the top national research institutions, measured by publications, research conducted, and grants received ($10–12 million a year in external grants). Promotion and continuing employment of faculty at Goddard are weighted toward developing excellent courses with students, carrying on personal advisement, and providing service and research to one's local community. Promotion and tenure at the University of Georgia also must include evidence of strong teaching, but it is weighted toward research, grants, and publications in national and international journals. This is not to say that Goddard faculty and students could not succeed at the University of Georgia or that UGA faculty and students could not succeed at Goddard; rather, student and faculty expectations are quite different. Goddard students expect and demand that faculty respond to their individual needs. UGA students expect to attend large classes, take required courses, and generally not receive much individual faculty attention.

My Beginnings

Two days before the first residency at Goddard, visiting faculty arrived from many parts of the United States and Canada. We all met with the two regular faculty for dinner at a local restaurant. Preparatory discussions continued the next day on the campus of Goddard. Since I was the only new visiting faculty member, the rest of the group reviewed for me procedures, requirements, advisement schedules, and short courses. We then finalized details for the upcoming ten days.

I immediately felt comfortable in the discussions. They were free of the personal tension that I often experience in an academic department meeting. (I later learned that this absence of tension was due in part to the ad hoc and temporary nature of this faculty group rather than the normal Goddard faculty interactions. The full-time academic faculty at Goddard were in the midst of intense personal and professional conflict as a result of a controversial and divisive administration.) I was impressed with my Goddard colleagues—their experience, their care in reviewing student work, and their thoughtful dialogue. Any previous snobbery that I might have held about faculty at small, private, and nonhighly selective colleges not being of the same intellectual caliber as faculty at selective research institutions was discarded immediately. I quickly came to the conclusion that my Goddard colleagues could clearly persevere, academically and intellectually, in other institutions and were at Goddard by their own choice.

My own thinking about students, teaching, learning, and programs seemed to fit nicely with theirs. However, I did hold on to private fears that I might not be up to the task of the "Goddard mission" in my own teaching practice. At the University of Georgia, I have received honors for my teaching, yet I did not know how well I could work with Goddard students, who were not coming to learn from me but were instead expecting me to adapt to what they wanted. At Georgia, I was known for using participatory methods and had learned such practices from some of the most acclaimed masters of progressive education.[2] I knew how to involve students in activities and assessments. But Goddard students would be different; they would expect such involvement as their right, not as part of a special situation.

Frankly, I wasn't sure how to handle this. I anticipated uncomfortable times with Goddard students because I know, as a teacher, that I want the ultimate authority over student work. At UGA, I remind my students from time to time that what they want to do may not be the same as what they need to do. When UGA students are not taking their assignments, activities, and learning seriously, I have the traditional authority of the academy to back me up. I wasn't sure, in this new situation, if push came to shove with students, whether such a student-centered institution as Goddard would foster a climate supportive enough for me to exert faculty authority. Goddard had few attendance policies, gave no letter grades, and had no required courses. Virtually all aspects of the program were negotiated between students and faculty. Readings, activities, and fulfillment of requirements were open to discussion and negotiation. I was concerned that either I might simply let students have more freedom than I thought desirable or I would restrict their choices more severely than other faculty members and be perceived as a tyrant.

The residency commenced. It went nonstop, all days and most nights. Students would have a daily schedule consisting of a group meeting or individual conferences with me; two short courses with me and other faculty; and a selection of collegewide seminars, presentations, or special events given by faculty, students, or special guests. The previous year's graduating students were in attendance at the beginning of the residency to present their theses, and everyone attends the graduation ceremony, where every graduating student has a chance to speak. Besides the activities that I have mentioned, a number of other academic, social, or recreational activities were added daily.

I was given an office (the graduate residency program occurs on campus when the regular undergraduate program is on break) and a dormitory room. I brought four cardboard file boxes full of books and reference materials from my office at UGA in anticipation of what students might find helpful. (Given that I have a bad back and there are no elevators in Goddard's teaching facilities, once the materials were in place, they stayed!) We (faculty and students) had breakfast, lunch, and dinner together each day in the common dining hall. The last night of each residency was devoted to a talent show conducted by willing students and faculty.

After nearly twenty years of an academic routine of preestablished times for office hours, set time for class, and strict separation of my professional and personal lives, I found myself on a very different schedule. For the next ten days, students would become an integral aspect of almost every waking moment. Even when I might find time to be alone, I would be aware of students outside my door or on the same walking paths or waving to me from the garden. The only physically separate time from students would be when sleeping, a one-hour faculty meeting each afternoon (devoted to talking about them), and finding time before breakfast to prepare for them.

Other faculty warned me that by midresidency, feelings of exhaustion would set in and I would need to steal away and find more personal time for quiet.

Judy Couldn't Dance

Let me dwell on a few events that symbolized what I learned at Goddard. My group of twelve students was a mix of people from all over the country, all U.S. citizens; one from Vermont, others from Korea, Minnesota, France, Washington, New York, and California. Nine were working on a master's degree and three were working on a postgraduate teaching certification. Eight were women, four were men, age twenty-two to forty-four, and years of formal teaching experience ranged from none to twenty. We sat in a circle in heavily used chairs in a very warm room.

I began the first meeting with our residency group by looking at this casually attired collection of students and explaining how this group would belong to all of us. If it worked well, it would be because we all took responsibility for the group. Since I was new, I asked students with previous experience at Goddard to help explain the expectations, rules, and forms that I had. I then asked them to develop a list of what they each wished to accomplish in our scheduled time of group meetings over the next ten days. I concluded by asking them to each explain why they had chosen Goddard.

The first responses to my question were predictable and pragmatic. Students cited reasons of career advancement, wanting to learn about something in particular, and needing a flexible program. Until we came to Judy. Young, tall, and pleasant looking, with a strong physical presence, Judy was from a community farm in the Midwest. She spoke softly of why she was here. She explained that she had come to Goddard because of what happened to her in grade school. As a very young child, she had loved to dance—out in the fields, at home, and with playmates. In her first year of school—kindergarten—she was asked by her teacher to dance for the entire school in the auditorium. She readily agreed and enjoyed every moment of her performance. After the conclusion, the principal then went to the lectern and announced that another child had won the contest. Judy remembers feeling confused and humiliated. She did not know until that moment that she had been in a contest, and now everyone in the school knew that she couldn't dance.

Since that moment, she has not danced in public. The idea of public performance puts a knot in her stomach and she wants to run and hide. But now, as a mother and an adult, she is at Goddard to become a teacher. Yet being a teacher is a public performance, and thinking about being in front of students continues to trigger deep anxiety. She wishes to learn to be comfortable as a teacher so she can help students develop their own talent without public fear or shame. But she must overcome her own fear first.

Her statement, said at first quietly, slowly, and haltingly, increased in volume, anger, and emotion, and the rest of us were moved to tears. In that moment, our group was born. Individuals thanked Judy for speaking from her heart, and then each of them spoke to their own private issues of education: religion, race, faith, gender, abuse, cultural identity, and finding one's way in the world. I spoke of my own private fear of trying to do a job worthy of them and me.

We became a major part of each other's lives from this residency to the next, and beyond. For a year, we were a group. Together we organized learning topics, students counseled each other, they socialized together, and they offered each other endless support. Students helped plan one another's learning contracts; they selected, facilitated, and discussed readings; and they built a library for each other. I had been prepared for Goddard students to bring personal issues to the residency, but I was totally unprepared for the sheer, unadorned candor. The last time that I had heard such private expressions made public to new acquaintances was in 1968, when I participated in sensitivity training as part of the Teacher Corps program (one of the national programs to address poverty in schools). In 1968, I remembered being hesitant about the openness and lack of restraint. Now, in 1994, I was excited by the candor but concerned that our group be more than a support group, become a learning group over ideas, practices, issues, and methods that built upon but moved beyond personal experiences. bell hooks (1994) refers to this as moving personal experiences to "theory in action." Experience is essential to, but not synonymous with, learning. I realized that my job would be to facilitate personal expression only as it built toward new intellectual knowledge, application, and reflection.

How Did It Work?

I was most conscience of being a colearner with students, but not their social peer. Memories that I hold of a few professors and their relations with students during my own undergraduate days at a small liberal arts college remain distasteful. Those faculty members took advantage of their position by imposing themselves on students in both social and personal situations. Students, no matter what setting or age, are vulnerable to faculty members who use them for personal attention and social belonging. Students often allow faculty to intrude in their social settings, allow them to dominate social conversation, and pretend to laugh at a professor's storytelling or humor to placate them. Many students, because of their unequal status with faculty, often feel obligated not to offend. This faculty intrusion and student compliance occurs everywhere in education settings, but it is potentially more apt to occur in a small, intimate community setting.[3]

I observed that faculty members at Goddard had worked out the delicate line of maintaining a professional distance while being personally attentive and supportive. For me, this separation was more difficult because of my unfamiliarity with the gripping emotional disclosures on the part of students and my wishing to be open to them. So I had to work hard and consciously establish my role. I did this by not inviting myself to student social activities and declining many well-intentioned social invitations from them. Through such acts, I let it be known that our mutual work together was to emphasize professional engagement over personal friendship. By doing so, I gained the reputation of perhaps being nice but hard with students, expecting them to do more than they initially wanted. This does not mean that I didn't become friends with them; some of us still correspond and visit years later, but it did mean that we were fellow travelers, not peers.

According to solicited, anonymous feedback, the two ten-day institutes went extremely well. Students were very busy and so was I, with endless last-minute preparations for advising individual students, organizing group meetings, conducting short courses, and participating in seminars. During the six-month interim between residencies, I was in constant communication with every student, receiving and reading their progress reports and papers and sending them feedback every three weeks.

Depending on my travel schedule, I occasionally met with students in their home locations. They created a partially successful electronic mail network that connected them with each other, and every six weeks I would write and disseminate a common newsletter to them on what I was studying, what I was hearing from each of them; I would notify them of the various deadlines approaching.

In one case, a most able student stopped sending in her assignments. I called her one Sunday morning to find out what was happening. She told me that teaching and family responsibilities were overwhelming and she couldn't keep up with graduate work. She had been feeling depressed and decided to quit the program. Knowing her as an exceptional student with great insight into issues of postmodernism and education, I told her that I understood, but if she decided to reconsider I would work with her to get back into sequence. I told her what I thought of her abilities and how much I had learned from her. She called me back a week later to tell me that she had reconsidered and wanted to continue, and we worked out a new schedule. She graduated a semester later than normal, with an outstanding thesis. The last occasion I had at Goddard, she came over to me, gave me a hug, and thanked me. She told me that it was that one quiet Sunday call that had given her the encouragement to continue.

When I think about the overall experience with these twelve students and what resulted, I am quite satisfied and proud of their work. There were four high-quality master's theses, as good as some doctoral dissertations that I have guided. All the students, except one, secured or advanced in their professional jobs; three took new leadership positions, and two went on to doctoral studies at Union College and Teachers College of Columbia University. The Goddard experience seemed to work for me.

Comparisons

The experience gave me specific applications to try out upon my full-time return to the University of Georgia, as well as thoughts about what Goddard could learn from UGA. I found that both institutions—in their operations and academic programs—could learn from each other. What I found most significant in comparison were (1) faculty discussion about students, (2) personal relations as part of—not separate from—academic learning, (3) diversity of field experience, and (4) diversity of intellectual perspective. Finally, my greatest overall learning as a teacher was reconceptualizing the old content-process dichotomy through balancing three dimensions of teaching to guide student learning for democratic education.

Discussion

I found at Goddard that faculty talk about students constantly. They talk about how individual students are progressing, ask each other to review student work, advise one another on how to work with a particular student or group of students, and review with each other their own teaching and student assessments. Goddard faculty, in their interaction with each other, are like faculty at excellent public or private primary and secondary schools. With the exception of a small, regional university that I taught at early in my higher education career, I have never experienced such depth and comprehensiveness of discussion about learning and students.

Faculty in most academic departments at the large universities that I am acquainted with rarely talk with each other about progress or their concern with an individual student, unless it is to complain about someone; nor do they talk about their own teaching and the assessment of student learning. There are notable exceptions in a particular department or program, but most department meetings are about procedural matters, academic program components, internal politics, the enrollment, and the budget. The nature and quality of the learning experience for students is rarely discussed. Most other professional discussions among faculty are usually about their research, their papers and publications, or their presentation to a professional organization.

At Goddard it is nearly impossible for a student to become lost. Each faculty member knows his or her own students extremely well; furthermore, faculty know by name and interest most of the students other than their own. Knowing students well is a high priority for almost everything Goddard faculty do. These ongoing discussions about students and how to improve teaching and learning for them is, as I said previously, characteristic of successful K–12 schools that colleagues and I have studied (Glickman, Gordon, and Ross-Gordon, 1998). For example, at home I constantly hear my spouse, Sara, talking at night with her middle school colleagues about students, teaching activities, and curriculum plans for the next day. Goddard reminded me of Sara's ongoing and endless conversation with her team members. To have such discussion at a large research institution, it must generally be galvanized in a special forum, connected to a research agenda, or tie in with a special invitation to like-minded people to work together. Such conversation simply doesn't come with the territory of everyday normal responsibilities at a large university.[4]

At Goddard, a focus on students and teaching is the culture of the institution. New faculty are assimilated into it. If you don't participate in these conversations, you are regarded as atypical. At a large university, the culture is more of independence, allegiance to one's discipline, and individual academic freedom. If a faculty member does participate in discussion about students and teaching, it is usually due to special initiatives that attempt to modify the institutional culture.

Personalization

Another striking difference is personalization of learning as integral to education. At Goddard, students know faculty as people living the same everyday lives as themselves. At UGA, students know faculty as professionals who teach classes and hold set office hours. With the exception of advanced graduate students and undergraduates fortunate enough to be in an experimental teacher education program, Georgia faculty typically do not know or remember by name most of the students they teach. This is due to the greater number of students, of course, but also to expectations of faculty work as well as the distinct separation of faculty from personal life.

Diversity of Field Experience

A major state research university like UGA has a much richer environment of diversity than an institution like Goddard. At Goddard (in the residency program), student field work, internships, and student teaching is done off campus, most often in the area where the student lives. The selection of site, supervisor, and cooperating teacher is left mainly to the student to secure and then is approved by Goddard faculty. With limited faculty and with students spread across the country and around the world, such a process of selection by students is understandable, but quality control over the diversity of settings is lost. UGA has developed ongoing relationships with a number of public schools as Professional Development Schools, where the university and the school work together in planning an optimal experience with student teachers.

In addition, there are a large number of individual teachers, K–12, across hundreds of schools, who have been screened as good teacher models and mentors for practicum and student teaching. If a UGA student does not have a good working site, the university intercedes and makes corrections. Over their time at Georgia, most students have experiences with many teachers; several schools; diverse classrooms; and different populations of students who vary by socioeconomic class, race, and ethnicity. At Goddard, because the student in the residency program is relied on to seek his or her placement, there is no such assurance of quality and diversity of placement. For example, while I was at Goddard a few students did their student teaching in affluent, private school settings but later took teaching assignments in public schools. They were simply not prepared to handle such a different setting. This matter of placement is not a major issue for mature graduate students who are already teaching and working toward a master's degree, but it is for those working on initial licensure.[5]

Intellectual Diversity

Another area of contrast and application is for students to be informed by a variety of perspectives, experiences, and ways of thinking. Students at the University of Georgia have a major research library to draw from; they receive instruction from highly specialized researchers who have mastered a specific field and hold definite points of view, often contrasting with each other. Students thus learn of differing ideologies about education from faculty and other students who can confidently explain their position. A state university like Georgia (with its affordable, and most often free, tuition and its more inclusive reach to attract students from all regions of the state) also contains a greater plurality of thinking among faculty and students than a college such as Goddard. Students and faculty tend to think more alike at Goddard than students and faculty at a place like the University of Georgia.

It is hard for those who argue for a conservative or fundamentalist position to be of significant numbers and to have influence at

Goddard; not so at Georgia. At UGA, you often see students sitting side by side, one with a clean, pressed suit and tie and the other with clinging garments and pierced body adornments. In these settings, in my opinion, students can more readily understand diverse expressions of truth and make public judgments about what decision or course of action should be taken. To do so at Goddard, faculty need to be extremely deliberate about bringing oppositional ideas, different from their own, to students. This is not meant to imply that Goddard faculty are closed to the range of ideas, but it is more difficult for Goddard students to hear from the oppositional believers themselves. To bring a greater range of academic ideas into a respectful, thoughtful discourse for students, Goddard faculty, with students, might need to do more selection of oppositional books, readings, speakers, and settings.

Discussion and Applications

Since my Goddard experience, I have found that it is not simply the scale of an institution that creates a participatory learning environment; rather, it is the mission and purpose of faculty within an institution. For example, there are larger research institutions that have small teams of cohorts of students, faculty, and public school educators that capture some of the features of the Goddard experience. Of course, there are small colleges across America, the size of Goddard, that can be more highly structured, impersonal, and nonengaging of students than a large institution. Large numbers of students and faculty usually create more bureaucratic rules, regulations, centralization, and program standardization, but it doesn't have to be an absolute limitation.

Some departments of teacher education at UGA have developed undergraduate and graduate degree programs based on small-scale interaction and negotiated curriculum—not to the extent of Goddard's student-centered approach, in that grades and some required courses still exist. But students and teachers are part of a learning community and work together intensely in field settings and ongoing problem solving and reflective seminars (Graham and

Hudson-Ross, 1999). Our new Ph.D. program in social foundations was developed with aspects of the Goddard experience in mind: cohort groups, a shared curriculum among students and faculty, community learning and action research teams, and individual contracts. Goddard, in turn, might further improve its small residency programs with the borrowed features of a large university by purposefully supplementing the program with varied speakers, settings, readings, and ideas.

But before leaving this section on application, let me describe how Goddard personally affected me as a teacher upon my return to Georgia.

In my department at UGA, we gave ourselves the freedom to reconceptualize the large introductory course that we teach to all education majors. Some of my experiences at Goddard helped me rethink how I would do it. I accepted that I could not possibly know most of the 240 Georgia students who would take the course, as well as I knew every one of my 12 Goddard students. However, I realized that I could know Georgia students better by making simple changes. For example, now I arrive at my UGA classes at least a half hour before starting time and mill outside with waiting students. They know that I will be there, they can ask me quick questions, and I can talk to them informally as to the latest news on campus. I also remain after class so the same type of interaction can take place and they can ask me questions about the day's class or the upcoming assignment.

I followed up on the Goddard experience of calling students at home, and even in my largest classes now I call five or six of my Georgia students on Sundays to find out how they are doing, how the course is going, and if they need help with any questions. After my first Sunday of such calls at Georgia, word spread throughout my entire large class that I call students, not because they are in trouble but just to check on them. Most students were both amazed and appreciative. Such calls have resulted in decisions with students that would not have occurred if I had waited for the students to initiate them. On the basis of these Sunday calls, one student changed her major; another learned about a particular graduate program that she was later accepted into; and another decided that education, as a career, was simply not what she wanted to pursue.

The reality at Georgia is that I could not have students as involved and making as many choices as Goddard students, but again I saw that I could have Georgia students more involved and making more choices than ever before. By seeking help from experienced UGA colleagues who had the reputation for working well with large classes, I was able to make a traditionally passive lecture course into a highly interactive one, including community learning; provocative discussion; fast-paced technology with videos and music; team projects; student-led forums; and student-initiated introductions, questions, and critiques of guest speakers.

After my experience at Goddard, I wanted to see if participation-oriented teaching (although most easily done in small groups and community settings) could still be used in a large-group setting. The final anonymous and confidential evaluations of my first attempt to do a required (and large) undergraduate UGA course confirmed that more than 90 percent of students found the course to be intellectually challenging, provocative, open, and demanding. The success was due to reorienting my thinking as a teacher about the capacity of students, regardless of the size of the class. Of course, I had to spend a full five weeks of my summer in planning the learning environment and activities; colleagues and I had carefully chosen teaching assistants who could manage small-group discussion and student contracts, and I had the benefit of a number of faculty colleagues to call upon for help. When the first class of this large course began with an amplified version of Pink Floyd singing "We don't need no education," students knew they were in for a different kind of large-class experience.

Balance and Tension in Democratic Education

I think public universities such as UGA and specific private institutions such as Goddard have a public purpose as to why they educate. What I mean is that these institutions—in standards, expectations, and educational programs for students—have a responsibility to prepare teachers who teach their students as equals—deserving dignity and respect—and provide an education that affords each and every student life, liberty, and the pursuit of happiness (Glickman, 1998). The goal is to educate students to think independently as they learn to contribute to a more just and democratic society. Public purpose education must work to create a generation of citizens more intelligent, caring, and committed than the generation before. To achieve such purpose, schools and programs need to employ a pedagogy of learning that demonstrates to students in day-to-day interaction the power of democracy as the most powerful way to learn and live together.

Schools and colleges with democratic aims use the process of governance to implement learning that results in wiser and more participatory students. John Dewey knew this point well (his colleague William Kilpatrick much less so). Democratic education in the classroom does not translate into moment-by-moment egalitarianism, where students and teachers have the same authority. Dewey held that the teacher has the moral duty—thanks to experience, knowledge, and commitment—to establish educational conditions that guide such student learning. Dewey found no dichotomy in teachers asserting control to ensure that learning occurred from the interaction between current knowledge and the natural interest of students. He differed forcefully with Kilpatrick and others who advocated that a teacher's role was facilitating the interest of students through projects (see Dewey, 1938).

Democratic education is achieved when faculty use authority to help students gain authority. This is done through a set of intentional activities. Eventually, such a democratic education enables students to question, synthesize knowledge, and make new applications. It results in citizens who can make private and public judgment (Massaro, 1993).

So what I learned in contrasting, applying, and synthesizing my experiences at Goddard and the University of Georgia is that democratic education can be done in multiple settings—small and large, public and private. It is conditioned on attending to three realms and keeping them in constant balance and tension. The dimensions most helpful to me are knowledge, relations, and participation.

By knowledge, I am referring to content, understanding, and skills within and across disciplines. I mean knowledge that equips students to gain mastery of "cultural capital," knowledge that allows one to access and critique one's life in relation to society and then choose how to live. (I believe that writers as divergent as E. D. Hirsch and Lisa Delpit are correct in saying that there is a cultural literacy of those in power in America, and students not privy to learning it are limited in their ability to gain, resist, or change existing conditions.)

By relations, I am referring to the dignity and respect accorded to and among students and teachers to listen and learn from each other, and the high confidence, care, and expectations that teachers and students have for each other.

By participation, I am referring to the interaction between knowledge and the learner that defines a learning experience. This involves student choice, activity, application, demonstration, and contribution of what is learned from, to, and with others. Through participation, students move from knowledge to wisdom and find new paths of interest and talent to pursue.

If teaching focuses on one or two realms to the exclusion of the others, potential learning is obstructed. For example, if I as a teacher focus on participatory methods and personal relations and neglect knowledge, then students may be more interested and involved, but they acquire little outside information. If I focus on knowledge and relations, and disregard participation, then the student is not able to make applications beyond what has been immediately learned. If I emphasize participation and knowledge and fail to attend to personal relations, then students are not open, emotionally, spiritually, or personally, to learn with and from others. Knowing these three dimensions in tension and integration allows democratic education; students gain the authority to determine what is correct, from understanding a range of perspectives, considering various actions, and examining reasons for their decision.[6]

Conclusion

My last memory of Goddard was our group's final time together. We walked through half a foot of fresh snow to the community hall for the culminating and celebratory talent show. We sat together, took numerous pictures of each other, and reminisced about past events. As the show began, a few members excused themselves. The lights went down and the master of ceremonies announced that we were about to hear a recently formed band. When we looked up, there were four members of our group on stage, instruments in hand, ready to play. As they launched into their opening number, a dancer entered from the side stage with tambourine in hand. She was exuberant, graceful, and radiant. It was Judy, and she was dancing!

Judy's journey was a metaphor for the learning journey we took together. We learned about what is possible when education and democracy are treated inseparably from each other. Democratic education is a dance with both structure and improvisation, performed on many stages and in many halls, where performers, observers, and directors are all part of the performance. It is quite exhilarating to dance!

Notes

1. *Revolutionizing America's Schools* was published in 1998.
2. I participated with Jon Bremer of the Parkway Program, was a principal of an open education school in New Hampshire that Jean Piaget and Barbara Inhelder visited, was an assistant professor at Ohio State University, and greatly influenced by the faculty of the laboratory school; more recently, I worked as a colleague at Georgia with Eliot Wigginton of Foxfire acclaim.

3. Faculty at all institutions, traditional or progressive, have influence over students in both obvious and subtle ways. Faculty have the power to negotiate away certain requirements for students, give official approval of student work, or make a student's progress more difficult.

4. At UGA, I have been heartened by focused attempts to galvanize such discussion recently in (1) collaboration between the faculty of the College of Education and the College of Arts and Sciences in extended retreats, (2) new teacher education programs by invitation to faculty to form cohorts with students and selected public schools, and (3) priority funding of college grants to faculty wishing to study their own teaching.

5. Remember that I am referring to criteria for placing students in the part-time residency program. I am not referring to the full-time undergraduate program at Goddard, which I am not familiar with.

6. Reasons can be communicated from multiple ways of knowing and not only from the use of scientific positivist logic (Barber, 1992, Chapter Four).

References

Barber, B. R. *An Aristocracy of Everyone*. New York: Ballantine, 1992.

Dewey, J. *Experience and Education*. New York, Collier, 1938.

Glickman, C. D. *Renewing America's Schools*. San Francisco: Jossey-Bass, 1993.

Glickman, C. D. *Revolutionizing America's Schools*. San Francisco: Jossey-Bass, 1998.

Glickman, C. D., Gordon, S. P., and Ross-Gordon, J. M. *Supervision of Instruction: A Developmental Approach*. (4th ed.) Needham Heights, Mass.: Allyn and Bacon, 1998.

Graham, P., and Hudson-Ross, S. (eds.). *Teacher/Mentor: A Dialogue for Collaborative Learning*. New York: Teachers College Press, 1999.

hooks, b. *Teaching to Transgress: Education as the Price of Freedom*. New York: Routledge, 1994.

Massaro, T. *Constitutional Literacy: A Core Curriculum for a Multicultural Nation*. Durham, N.C.: Duke University Press, 1993.

Chapter Thirteen

Listening to Students

"You have to know the kids. They teach me how to teach them. They may be from all kinds of backgrounds and cultures, but if you really listen to them, they'll tell you how to teach them" (Delpit, 1994, p. 120). When we hold large conferences for educators that include concurrent sessions, the sessions that are usually packed and most highly favored are the ones that feature students (elementary, middle, or secondary) describing their significant learning experience in the classroom and school. The students conclude the presentation with suggestions to teachers and administrators as to what they could do to change their own practices to help their own students learn better.

Overhearing the conversation of attendees as they leave a presentation like this is both encouraging and perplexing. One hears teachers and principals rave about the insights and reality of what these students say. They often note on their conference assessment forms that they learned more from the students than from a national expert flown in from afar to give a keynote address. Yet what is puzzling to me is that these students who capture such attention are just like students that the attendees have every day in their own classroom and school. They really don't have to go to a conference to listen to them. It simply doesn't occur to many of us to ask the same questions and gather the same suggestions from our own students.

Young children, adolescents, teenagers, or adults—students in all classrooms and schools across all subject areas have definite ideas about their education. Why do so many educators not ask or listen to their own students discussing issues and practices of education? The only answer I can surmise is that, outside of ignorance (which I don't think is the case), if we ask our own students for input they will tell us what we might prefer not to know. To not know means not having to act. If asked, students tell us what is wonderful and engaging, as well as what is boring, shoddy, and disrespectful. They clearly explain what teachers do to inspire their best work, but they also explain what teachers do to bring out the worst in them.

Wasley, Hampel, and Clark shadowed students in reform-oriented schools for three years and uncovered a dichotomy. School faculty complained that their students were apathetic and irresponsible, made little effort, and were always expecting to be entertained. The same students in these classrooms confided to the researcher that their teachers were inept. According to one female student, "It's just the same old thing. I go to class, and we do what we do almost every day. . . . It's just so boring." A student referred to by his teacher as apathetic said, "I don't do all the work because a lot of it seems like busy work. . . . Sometimes, it feels like he gives us the work to keep us busy rather than because it is important for us to know" (1997, p. 25). These students, who were constantly labeled as making no effort (some received good grades, some did not), expressed that their behavior was totally different in the classroom of a teacher who came to class prepared, interested, and ready to push, who respected students and took their intellectual exchange seriously, and who truly enjoyed their company.

It would appear to be just common sense for educators to listen to their own students, but the risk of doing so is often perceived as high. In our own private conversation with students, they tell us about what is helping them learn. They cite particular projects, lessons, and ways of presenting materials. They talk about good teachers and teaching, but they also tell us just as clearly about the other side. Students have openly told us about growing hostility and discrimination with their teachers around gender, race, and socioeconomic class, within an individual classroom and throughout an entire school. Students have told us of long-standing sexual harassment by a teacher and about how, when they raised the issue, it was ignored by the teacher, other faculty, and administrators. Students have reported to us on drug usage and physical intimidation. In several instances, what students said about their experience has contradicted what the adults in the school say ("We have few or none of these problems here"). Of course, it is possible that students might be distorting and exaggerating, and every incident is considered an allegation until verified. Public knowledge of unverified claims could lead to a manufactured crisis and harm among colleagues, parents, and the school board.

I don't wish to make light of the matter of asking students what they think. Virtually everyone who devotes a life to a career believes that what they are doing they are doing well. Without critique or data, the comfort of a continuing perception of one's own success is kept intact. But refusing to let students (and others) examine one's work comes at great cost. Many students do not learn as well as they could; furthermore, they learn from the refusal of teachers to gather and listen to student feedback that they (the teachers) do not really value the democratic ideals of freedom, inquiry, and free dissemination of information. Students learn that what is real for adults is protection of their ego and self-image.

The fact that most of us as adults do not typically seek information about our performance is not due to any inherent character flaw but is instead attributable to how we learned as students, and later as adults, to survive in a world of power (in school and at work). Most teachers were fairly good students, which is defined as being obedient; knowing when to smile; learning the game concerning when to initiate or defer, depending on the teacher's clues; and knowing how to keep the teacher's authority, self-importance, and ego intact. By figuring out what the teacher wanted, we learned to gain his or her approval and the desired grade, reward, or recognition. Thus, to lower our guard, to lose control over information, and to self-correct are actions that go against what we have learned about how to successfully gain comfort and security in a world dominated by authority. However, Sarason (1996) has noted that healthy individuals and healthy organizations are not in a mode of self-preservation but instead in one of self-correction—always gathering data, assessing, validating, critiquing, and adjusting according to progress made toward goals.

My experience as a university instructor might be revealing as to why our current conditions exist—why student feedback is not openly solicited, and what an individual can expect when trying to rectify the balance of power between teachers and students in creating an intellectual community where all members are held to standards of important learning. In giving my personal experience as a teacher, I might exaggerate success on my part and downplay failure. I'll try to be honest, and I hope that my past and current students and colleagues will continue to provide me with an honest rendering of what occurs in the name of good learning and poor learning.

Furthermore, I do not equate my experience of teaching in a public university setting with teaching in a public school setting of young children, adolescents, and young adults. Teaching older students who have all experienced traditional academic success and have chosen and been admitted to a college or university is substantially different from teaching younger students who have a greater range of behaviors, attitudes, and academic experiences and no choice but to attend. Teaching in a public school (preschool through twelfth grade) is much more challenging than university teaching in the range of management and learning-related decisions required. (For explanation and description of teachers successfully using student feedback at various public school levels and settings, see Fried, 1995; Ladson-Billings, 1994; Wood, 1992; Wolk and Rodman, 1994).

For most courses that I teach,[1] whether through team teaching or alone, I bring to the class an incomplete syllabus that includes:

- A course description
- Description of course content—skills, knowledge, and understandings—to be learned

- Central questions of the course
- List of readings and some assignments, including a community service or field experience requirement and a team project
- Expectations for assessment, evaluation, and grades

On the first day, I tell students why we are there—that we've agreed to come together for so many hours and weeks to learn about a topic we might not normally learn if we were left to our own devices. I then use a teaching method learned and adopted from my years of involvement with the Foxfire Network in Georgia, a method used in public and private classrooms in all content fields and at all grade levels (see Wigginton, 1985). I ask students to write individually about the most positive, memorable learning experiences they have had in school, at whatever level. I ask them to read their written descriptions to each other in pairs, and then I move them into larger groups for discussion.

I ask each group to identify, from their collection of individual experiences with positive learning, what the characteristics of a good classroom, a good teacher, and good students are. After doing so and soliciting their findings, I ask them to define for me what good students are able to achieve, demonstrate, or show at the end of a course when they have "learned exceptionally well the content of the course." Exhibit 13.1 is a summary of the common characteristics generated by my most recent undergraduate class of students.

Students tend to enjoy this activity, and after they have finished I tell them that I will rework their list to include my expectations and we will complete our course syllabus with mutual standards of practice and assessment. We then spend another three hours over the next few class days to complete the syllabus. In the interim, I tell them to do the readings and activities assigned, and I organize each class period during the first half of the course. At the conclusion of the very first class, I ask if students have questions. Most students stare at me or shrug their shoulders, but a few are brave enough to bring up the inevitable question, "What do we

Exhibit 13.1. Students' Suggested Characteristics of a Good Classroom, a Good Teacher, and a Good Student

Course: Spring 1996

Characteristics of a good classroom

- Discussion
- Respect for individual students
- Positive reinforcement
- Out-of-class experiences, variety
- Flexibility concerning needs and wants of students
- Sharing of experiences among students
- Ability of teacher to learn from students
- Good attitude from class
- Involvement of students
- Variety of teaching methods
- No negative reinforcement or motivation
- Disciplined, orderly, respectful
- Changes in environment, varied format
- Structure, to create a comfort zone

Characteristics of a good teacher

- Earns respect
- Sets rules; time to learn and time for fun
- Makes students feel special
- Finds creative ways to learn
- Doesn't stereotype students
- Listens to what students have to say

need to do to get an A?" I answer that my expectations for an A can be found in the syllabus and are based on a student's doing excellent work as defined by our joint expectations and standards of quality. Furthermore, I tell them that as a class we will, together, differentiate student work that is judged excellent, good, average, or poor.

For the next six weeks, I give some lectures, organize panel forums, help them individually develop their community learning

Exhibit 13.1. (*continued*)

Characteristics of an effective student

- Alert, attentive
- Open-minded
- Responsible
- Willing to learn
- Conscientious
- Considerate and respectful of teacher and others
- Confident of own ability
- Motivated
- Involved in learning
- Willing to interact with others

What students should be able to demonstrate

- Evidence of having synthesized and analyzed the readings, class activities, community service, and field experiences according to the central questions of the course, through communicating (orally, graphically, or in writing) what the theoretical or abstract problems presented in the course have been and how they can be solved with clarity, logic, and reasoning
- Application of a solution to these problems in an actual situation at the local, state, national, or international level

contracts with me, and hold much discussion around their assigned reading, in small and large groups. I scan these discussions to see that everyone has the opportunity to be involved, and I alter the discussion format depending on the degree of participation from students. In discussion, I try to accept all of their contributions and ideas, and I keep pushing them to explain their perspective by asking them to make reference to the readings as well as their own experiences. I also insist that they give me more than their opinions—that they give me the reasons behind the opinion, so that their classmates and I can understand them. After the first few weeks, during discussion, I move out of their line of sight and have them direct their talk to one another rather than to me. From time to time, I ask them to write thought pieces, and I give them a few short quizzes (as outlined in the initial syllabus). Occasionally, I review at the beginning or end of class what we agreed were the criteria of a good teacher, a good student, and a good classroom. I remind them that we need to hold ourselves personally and collectively accountable for meeting these criteria.

At the midpoint of our course schedule and after detecting confusion and grumbling about the class and the grades that they are receiving on their quizzes and assignments, I have us stop as a class and look again at our mutual criteria. I ask them individually and privately to write down "how you, I, and we are doing in regard to our criteria of a good student, good teacher, and good classroom." I assure them of anonymity (they are told not to write their names on their paper, and I pledge not to do any detective work). After they write down their individual reactions, I ask them to share within a small group and ask a group reporter of their choosing to let me and the entire class know what individuals (again anonymously) have said.

Although from the very first class I make a point to talk informally with students before, during, and after class; in passing in the halls; and at office hours, where I encourage drop-in visits, I never really find out what they think about the class until I stop and take classroom time to formally do so. When I formally ask, and they tell me, no matter how often I have done this in the past, I'm never prepared for their critical appraisal. I know intellectually that students can learn well without thinking that I'm a nice person, but still, I often get my feelings hurt. Here are examples of their unedited comments:

> I feel like this class has been a waste of my time. I don't feel like I have learned anything and I have attended every class. I feel we just talk back and forth and never learn what you want us to. I would not advise anyone to take this class!! . . . . Your teaching is not very good.

One of the characteristics of a good teacher is to "prepare students for examinations." This has not been done at all. I wish the class was more structured.

This is not how I expected this class to be. I wish this class was more straightforward.

Instructor is very opinionated and fails to present both sides of an issue.

I wish there was more facts, more lectures. The instructor is too theoretical, vague, and boring.

Other students responded that I was "too liberal," and still others stated that they never knew where I stood on an issue. Finally, one student remarked that as an instructor I had an "eccentric style."

There were a number of positive comments to help balance the negatives, such as "I do feel you are intelligent and have much to offer, but your teaching needs more structure." What I was trying to glean from these responses was information that (1) could make me a more effective teacher; (2) could make students take more responsibility for their own learning; and (3) would make us all problem solvers concerning how to make the course better, so that we could document that substantial and valuable learning would transpire.

Up to this point in the course, the activities I have done with them in the first class and over the first few weeks to develop standards of practice and complete the syllabus are seen by most of them as simply a simulation exercise. They truly don't believe that what they are doing is something that we will actually adhere to. So, when this midterm assessment of the class and of me is finished, I remind them that this is "our" class, we all have responsibilities in it, and I am asking them (and myself) to reflect on the information presented (including my comments, both positive and negative, about individual student performance and the class as a whole).

I direct them to come back for the next class with a plan of action, and I tell them I will do the same. Mine is about becoming a better teacher, theirs should be about becoming better students, and both of ours are about how to become a better community of learners. Many leave that day skeptical about doing such an assignment, thinking that I as a teacher still just don't get it. (However, one male student who was very quiet through the first half of the course pulled me aside after class and said that when I told the class that we are all adults and we couldn't make learning better unless we really talked to one another honestly, those words really hit him. He candidly confessed to me that after the first few quizzes, he figured that he couldn't get an A and thus lost incentive and was just sliding by to pass the course. He realized now that he was acting irresponsibly, treating the course as a game to get a grade, not as an education, and now he wanted to talk about being more responsible.)

This one day of formal assessment generally turns the course around for me and for most of the students. We come to the next class with our improvement plans. We agree that I will lecture more and give clearer directions. They assume responsibility for some group presentations on agreed-upon topics and conduct activities that vary from my previous teaching formats. Finally, we agree to construct together a final examination that is fair and rigorous and uses weights and rubrics for scoring.

The second half of the course is quite different from the first. One group of students spends several nights producing a video to illustrate universal concerns about pedagogy. Another group finds an interactive distance laboratory and uses visual artists to show the advantages and disadvantages of technology in education. Another group creates a television format to debate the controversial issues of education. Prior to final papers and exams, they develop a system of coaching each other on their drafts of written response to the core questions of the course. At the end, they generate a comprehensive set of closed- and open-book questions about what every student should be able to answer, and then I select from the questions for the final exam.

I ask my university colleagues who teach the same course to review the exam questions developed by the students. My colleagues conclude that the degree of difficulty is far beyond what they normally expect in their own classes, and one even asks me if it is fair to expect so much from my students. My answer is that we as a class have decided that it is fair to hold ourselves to such standards.

So, did I succeed, or not? At the end of one course conducted in this fashion, not many students received A's, but I did see greater involvement, enthusiasm, and deeper thinking on the part of students than I see in most university classes where the course belongs solely to the instructor. Other faculty would drop in from time to time to observe this "unusual" class, and one student invited her mother to attend. After the last class session, we conducted a final assessment of the course to help me organize for the next time I would teach it. Here is a selection of their anonymous and unedited responses:

> I was more permanently and universally affected by the class discussion we had on the first Monday of the second half of the quarter. That day you sat us down and asked us what we thought about the class and we told you. I have never before had a teacher open himself up to such criticism and I have never had a teacher accept such criticism from students.

> The second half of this course was quite different from the first. I am used to abiding by unchanging rules that the teacher makes because he or she knows best. Now, all that talk about democracy, education, Jefferson, and Liberty-equality-fraternity finally make sense.

> I could tell something was different and special about this class. . . . We had some problems and difficulties between teachers and students. I found it to be particularly sensitive and noble that a teacher

would give so much effort and place so much importance in considering student ideas rather than imposing one's beliefs on a class. This experience changed my life and the importance I place on teaching, learning, and education.

I have had many memorable experiences in my school career, both good and bad, which have led me to want to be a teacher. However, it was not until midpoint of this quarter that I found the true definition of being a good teacher. I finally figured out what it was about those great teachers in high school or elementary school. . . . They led democratic classrooms, ones which catered to everyone, are open to new ideas, and make the student feel welcome.

This course has changed my way of thinking about education. I thought those first few days were kind of silly but now I know we were a part of this class. I look around the room and see familiar faces that I have shared my thoughts and ideas with. We were forced to become involved in learning not just for ourselves but for the good of everyone. It seems so strange (after fourteen years of being a student) that almost all my teachers have overlooked such a beneficial way of learning.

I keep copies of many of the students' final products. I show them to other colleagues and give them as examples for future students. But to be honest, there continue to be students who do not like the class and/or me to the extreme. And despite the high praise of some students for my teaching, I know that I'm not a great teacher. I'm not a well-organized lecturer with a dynamic delivery. In discussions that I lead, I have a tendency to ramble. I'm forever having to remind myself to focus on content and not spend undue time on process, and the directions I give students are often unclear. I'm aware that I need to be more diligent about responding quickly to students' written assignments. And I have to become more current in some of the fields in which I teach. Last of all, my humor is often funny only to me, and narrating my own personal experiences is often not of much interest to undergraduate students. So even though I've been recognized by students and faculty for my teaching, no one should ever equate me with any of the great teachers in universities, public schools, and other education settings.

Teachers, that is, such as Corla Hawkins, who works in a destitute urban middle school, or the thousands like her who teach in our public schools in all types of setting and listen to and act with their students in acutely more insightful ways than I do (Kozol, 1991). They have patience, organizational skills, clarity of speech, and mastery of content beyond mine. So what I find striking about my teaching and why it appears to be life-changing for many students is simply that what they experience with me is novel. They rarely have prior experience of a teacher treating them with the recognition, attention, and consideration that any respectful adult would confer upon another. After all, what I simply do is check with them, call them at home when pleased or displeased with their work, and listen to them in the same way I would want people to listen to me. I try to use my authority as a teacher to see that they learn well. I don't do everything they want. I get annoyed at them, and they get annoyed at me. But above all else, I'm responsible, as bell hooks (1994) says, for creating a learning context that we are all committed to.

In many ways, it is sad that these students have such praise for my methods of asking them for their ideas and acting upon them; it shows how rare this approach is in education. Students who have not experienced such a setting in their entire school career and then become teachers don't have any lived experience of democracy as education. As hooks points out, even those who have made a stellar career out of the study and espousal of inclusiveness, deconstruction, constructivism, feminism, postmodernism, liberation, and empowerment and have continually embraced new ways of thinking are still too often "attached to old ways of *practicing teaching*" (hooks, 1994, p. 142, emphasis in original).

Student Responsibility

There is a reciprocal obligation between student and teacher. The power is clearly not equal, but the student has a responsibility to press the issue of influence with the teacher in an effort to improve learning. The typical strategy in the classroom and school for involving students is to ask them to handle peripheral matters such as deciding what the school colors should be, organizing the prom, holding fundraisers, and voting in class on whether they want to have free time now or later. What I have discussed in this essay is not influence on the periphery but instead on the core issues of education: teaching and learning, curriculum development, and assessment. If students are bold enough—and aren't immediately removed from a classroom or school for doing so—they need to ask and suggest how they can become involved with their teachers and administrators in determining how to improve learning. At the school level, sympathetic peers, teachers, and administrators can help by putting such issues on the agenda of the school council and student government. Assuredly, power in the classroom and school should not be shared equally between teachers and students in all matters, but how to learn is a matter best informed by all those involved. Even a classroom teacher's (or school's) rejection of such an issue creates public awareness that there is an issue and opens the possibility of further pursuing it.

Last, it is important that educators, parents, and community members understand that I'm not advocating a student-run class-room or school. I'm not advocating parity between students and adults on all matters. Teachers should have more authority and responsibility, because of their experience and wisdom, to determine students' educational experiences. Not all student ideas are good; some students might make a dishonest, vindictive, naïve, or unworkable plan, and some might see a teacher's asking for their feedback as a way of avoiding hard work. But the same can be said of educators' ideas: some are purposeful, others are not. It is the responsibility of an educational institution fulfilling democratic purpose to see that as much information and as many ideas for improvement as possible be solicited, entertained, and studied, in the widest possible forum, before any further decision is made to improve education. A critical source of such valuable information and ideas passes by us every day, in our own hallways and classrooms.

Note

1. I'm referring here to classes of fewer than forty-five students. I do teach an occasional course with several hundred students, wherein I have to use a much different organizational plan to increase participation, involvement, and facilitation with such a large number. I omit that discussion because most educators do not teach such large groups, and the details of what I do (with varying degrees of success) would be quite lengthy.

References

Delpit, L. *Other People's Children: Cultural Conflict in the Classroom*. New York: New Press, 1994.

Fried, R. L. *The Passionate Teacher*. Boston: Beacon Press, 1995.

hooks, b. *Teaching to Transgress: Education as the Practice of Freedom*. New York: Routledge, 1994.

Kozol, J. *Savage Inequalities: Children in America's Schools*. New York: Harper-Collins, 1991.

Ladson-Billings, G. "Toward a Theory of Culturally Relevant Pedagogy." *American Educational Research Journal*, 1994, *32*(3), 1994.

Sarason, S. B. *Revisiting "The Culture of the School and the Problem of Change."* New York: Teachers College Press, 1996.

Wasley, P. *Teachers Who Lead: The Rhetoric of Reform and the Realities of Practice*. New York: Teachers College Press, 1997.

Wasley, P., Hampel, R., and Clark, R. *Essential Connections: Kids and School Reform*. San Francisco: Jossey-Bass, 1997.

Wigginton, E. *Sometimes a Shining Moment*. New York: Anchor Press/Doubleday, 1985.

Wolk, R. A., and Rodman, B. H. (eds.). *Classroom Crusaders: Twelve Teachers Who Are Trying to Change the System*. San Francisco: Jossey-Bass, 1994.

Wood, G. "Restructuring Time, Size, and Governance: Steps Toward Democratic Schooling." *Democracy in Education*, 1992, 6(3), 3–13.

Chapter Fourteen

Co-Reform as an Approach to Change in Education

The Origin of Revolution

Carl D. Glickman, Barbara F. Lunsford,
Kathleen A. Szuminski

Debate about educational change has failed to recognize the original mission of pubic education: preparation of educated citizens to participate in a democratic society. Education for a democratic society suggests the need for public school educators and teacher educators to work in unison to create and achieve a common agenda for long-standing educational change. Co-reform, an approach to educational change that brings together educators for the mutual benefit of both public schools and teacher education programs, holds promise for achieving and sustaining educational change for all students.

In this chapter, we outline a moral framework for making decisions about symbiotic programs and discuss the issues that emerge as the co-reform process begins. Constraints common to public school educators and teacher educators during the co-reform effort, and suggestions for increased understanding, are discussed.

The word *revolution* was originally an astronomical term for revolving back to some preestablished point. The English civil wars and the French and American revolutions were not about creating new ideas, but about revolving back to or returning to fundamental, old ideas (about "the rights of man"). These struggles were about restoring the liberties and freedom that should have been the conditions of a natural state. Thomas Jefferson wrote about creating a society that would foster a revolution by the people every twenty years. He was referring to decisions by the people to break the accumulation of cumbersome, undemocratic structures and replace them with structures that moved back to the original intent of the Declaration of Independence and Bill of Rights. Thus, the revolution was to be an ongoing, cleansing process to keep government rooted in its earliest aspirations.

Unfortunately, in discussion about the reform of public education and teacher education, this original intent has been lost. The clamor for change is couched in terms of student academic achievement, international competition, and economic or workforce preparation (see *America 2000*, 1991) and has resulted in pedagogical and school innovation of teaching methods, learning assessment, scheduling and placement of students, decentralization, and site-based management. Although these innovative changes are well intentioned toward improving student academic achievement, they are changes on the basis of political or personal agenda and are made without the original intent of public education as a priority. Because these changes are not focused on the original mission of public education, they are haphazard, unrelated activities that do little to improve education (Goodlad, 1992). In this chapter, we discuss democracy and public education, including the central goal of public education in a democracy and one means of achieving that goal. It is our belief that uniting the teacher educator with the public school teacher in a co-reform process may be the means to achieve the goal of public education in a democratic society.

The changes many of us in public education have experienced are sometimes seen as a political and ideological agenda supporting innovation as a response to a crisis. The poor success rate of innovation in public and teacher education is depressing. Innovation is often viewed by many experienced educators with skepticism, and justifiably so. Over their careers, too many public school teachers have seen too many innovations implemented with little background preparation, minimal staff development, and a weak rationale for making the change. The innovation is generally brought to the classroom from an external source (a university professor, an outside consultant, the district office, the state education department, the legislature). Examples of innovations that have come and gone and returned again are open education, competency-based education, performance contracting, core curriculum, individualized instruction, direct instruction, mastery learning, cooperative learning, and higher-order thinking. The lack of success or any long-term change in the schools is not the fault of any of these changes; it is because the change was not clearly driven by a commonly acknowledged mission of education.

Change in public education is devoid of the revolutionary process driven by the original intent for democratic public education. If educators don't center their work on the intent of education in our democracy, then pedagogical and structural reforms will continue in the pattern of passing on after a few years, replaced by the next generation of hot ideas that have the political backing and media attention of the time. We will continue to educate on shifting sand and amid pendulum swings, with no firmness of direction (see Barber, 1993).

The inadequacies and failures of prior public educational reform result from lack of attention to both the goal of public education and the process that should be followed for successful implementation of the goal. The common goal of teacher education and the public schools has been fuzzy to many outside the field of education, and unclear to many within the educational arena. The problems that exist for either teacher education or public schools have often been dealt with by blaming the other for lacking understanding. This constant debate about fault has done little to push the dialogue toward a common agenda for teacher education and public schools. Further, constant debating has kept both teacher educators and public schools from seeing why they have to work together to accomplish the same goal.

Perhaps the only way that teacher education and public school educators can get past throwing criticism and begin collaborating is to engage in a common revolution that weeds out those practices inconsistent with education and democracy. This bonding of teacher educators and pubic school teachers for the mutual benefit of public schools and teacher education programs is defined as co-reform.

Common Goal of Education

Education in a democracy is established as an instrument of the society to promote the healthy participation of its future citizens. This is why public school educators and teacher educators are contracted employees of the state. They share the obligation to prepare students to contribute to the public good.

The U.S. Supreme Court, in *Board of Education v. Pico* (1982), concluded that "the constitution presupposes the existence of an informed citizenry prepared to participate in governmental affairs, and these democratic principles obviously are constitutionally incorporated into the structure of our government. It, therefore, seems entirely appropriate that the State use "public schools to . . . inculcate fundamental values necessary to the maintenance of a democratic political system" (p. 876).

According to Thomas Jefferson, public education has two corollary purposes: to produce an educated citizenry to participate in decisions about promoting the future good of our democratic society, and to allow leadership in a democratic society to develop from the merits, abilities, and talents of the individual. Leadership in a democratic society should not be based on family privilege, economic wealth, religion, race, or group privilege (see Lee, 1961). Following this line of thought, we can quickly articulate the basis toward which all efforts in public education reform should be directed. With the insertion of a few words, we have the central goal: "All students are created equal; they are endowed by their Creator with certain inalienable rights; that among these are an education that will accord them life, liberty, and the pursuit of happiness; that whenever any public school becomes destructive of preparing students for these ends, it is the right of the people to alter or abolish it."

Teacher education programs are responsible for preparing future teachers to make appropriate decisions (with their colleagues and students) to realize this central goal. At the same time, public school educators have the responsibility of refining their current practice to help all students become true participatory citizens. In conceiving, designing, and implementing their educational programs, public school educators and teacher educators must be morally consistent with their common goal.

What Is Good Education?

Research on effective teaching will never answer the question of what a good education is. "Effective" connotes efficient accomplishment of intended learning results. "Good" connotes determination first of what worthy learning results are, and second which methods are appropriate to achieving those ends. Effective teaching can be good, and good education must be based on effective teaching, but the terms are not synonymous (see Glickman, 1993). Therefore, debate over the use of particular instructional strategies cannot be resolved by research data. Both sides can always find evidence to support their own preference and refute other points of view. This is why there is endless argument over what research says about phonics versus whole language, cooperative learning versus individualized instruction, or homogeneous versus heterogeneous grouping. The only way to decide upon these research issues is to deal with them in accordance with the higher question: What should students be taught, and how should they be taught so that the methods of teaching are consistent with an education for a democratic life?

Good education would ensure that all students:

- Enjoy and exercise freedom of speech and accept the obligation to show respect for the rights of others

- Understand the key importance of separation of church and state in governmental affairs
- Know and are committed to the steps of due process prior to being deprived of life, liberty, property, or the pursuit of happiness
- Are knowledgeable and conversant about the issues of our society
- Know how to reason well, consider various perspectives, test ideas, and shape informed opinions
- Practice and communicate the acceptance of the equality of all humans

Once it is clear what is meant by a good education, appropriate teaching practices become more apparent. The research line that runs from the developmental research of Piaget, Bruner, Inhelder, Kammi, Vygotsky, and Kohlberg to the constructivist reach of Gardner, Slavin, Joyce, Resnick, and others yields the strategies and techniques that engage, challenge, and involve students in active, participatory learning, consistent with democratic principles. In the same manner, structural school reform debates about grade level versus multiage grouping, authentic assessment versus standardized testing, and tracking versus nontracking of students can also be screened according to the concept of democratic education (see Gutmann, 1987).

Grouping students to label and limit their aspirations is wrong. Allocating more money to privileged students at the expense of underprivileged students is wrong. Keeping intellectually advanced students from moving beyond their peers is wrong. Restructuring teaching to a daily routine of compliance and passivity is wrong. Not allowing students to develop their ability to think, reason, and solve problems is wrong. Teaching teachers to apply these strategies to public school children is equally inconsistent with the common goal of educating for a democracy. Therefore, the problem with current educational solutions and reforms is a problem with public educators and teacher educators alike.

Of course, there will be thoughtful disagreement about the degree of activity, participation, and involvement of students, but the direction is set. Our schools must reflect the democratic principles of our society if students' experience in school is to have relevance and meaning to their lives outside of school. We must purge our schools of practice that is in direct contradiction to the democratic principles that guide our society. Changing our schools means changing our university teacher education programs as well. In doing so, we will create the Jeffersonian concept of revolution as a continuous recentering to permit long-term substantive change in education.

So far, we have made no mention of subject matter or academic content achievement as part of a democratic education. One might incorrectly interpret good education as being process. Students need to master reading, writing, mathematics, history, art, music, science, economics, and technology. Without substantive knowledge, understanding, and skills, a student has little chance of becoming an independent, proactive, and valued citizen. The focus on education for a democracy, however, assists students in learning academics in the context of choice, activity, application, relevance, and extension to one's life in immediate and future communities. To teach content without visible connection to how it is applied to individual power and influence in a large democratic society is to relegate at least half of our students to not learning content; performing poorly on achievement measures; and continuing the generational cycle of disengagement, cynicism, illiteracy, and hopelessness. To put it succinctly, students who do well in school know how school learning will help them (even if this is conveyed more by their parents than the school). Those who do not perform well in school will never perform better until learning is connected to a viable and real democratic future (Glickman, 1993).

A Common Agenda for Co-Reform

Teacher education and public education have the same ultimate purpose. Faculty in both are contracted agents, commissioned to serve the higher purpose of education for democratic citizenship. If public schools are to reflect democratic principles and give the student the opportunity to experience firsthand acquisition of knowledge and understanding of democracy, the opportunity to be actively engaged in one's own learning, and application of that learning experience to the society at large, then teachers in public schools must possess certain qualities. They must have a clear understanding of the mission of the school, have firsthand experience in being engaged in their own learning, have a broad base of knowledge and content, possess appropriate pedagogical strategies, and be able to assess their own work and the needs of their students.

This type of teacher will not exist unless teacher educators understand the goal of public education and create a learning environment for future educators that enables them to graduate from a teacher education program with the attributes we have just listed. Historically, rather than working together toward this common goal, public school and teacher educators have attacked and kept each other at a distance. Restructuring too often has become what one party sees as the need of the other to correct, instead of a joint responsibility for both to assess and change. For example, many public school educators deplore the practices of college and university teacher education programs. They criticize them for being too easy, too boring, and too detached from the real world of the school. Tit for tat, teacher educators launch criticism at public education as being too convention bound, too focused on control, and too theoretical. Both groups see the hope for educational improvement in rectifying the decaying operations of the other. Ignoring the obvious relationship (public educators were prepared by teacher educators, and most teacher educators were public educators), they each take comfort in the other's lack of responsiveness.

On the other hand, collaborative and simultaneous reform of public schools and teacher education programs on the basis of understanding reinvigorates the natural symbiotic relationship. As a public school improves, it fosters a better preparation site for teacher education students and yields insight into future changes in teacher education programs. As a teacher education program improves, it gives future teachers the skills for further change in public education. For a teacher education program to change in isolation and without compatible educational changes in the public school means inadequate preparation for the future teacher and therefore an inadequate educator of future citizens.

For a substantive co-reform revolution to occur, both institutions have to develop a moral framework for decisions about symbiotic programs. Co-reformers need to develop:

- A covenant of learning based on the democratic goal of education (mission, vision, and principles of learning) that serves as the core values of education at both the public school and the teacher education institution
- A democratic charter for decision making that ensures equal representation of both parties in developing the covenant and subsequent implementation decisions
- A critical study process that includes a data collection process (action research) to assess the effects of programmatic change on public school students, future teachers, and current teachers

In other words, to prepare students for the goal of democratic citizenship, the co-reform collaboration among teacher educators and their students, and teachers currently teaching, must include the same belief in democratic principles and the same procedure for decision making about structure, activities, and resources of the joint effort.

Co-Reform Dimension

Programmatic linkage can now be illustrated using these program elements as an illustration:

- Interdisciplinary curriculum
- Team teaching

- Portfolio and performance assessments
- Peer coaching
- Extended communities of learners
- Technology integration
- Project-centered learning
- Student choice and involvement
- Cooperative learning

If both institutions are to assist each other toward a common, moral goal, then it becomes apparent that what is good for the goose is good for the gander. For example, if one party (teacher education or pubic school) is moving toward greater implementation of integrated and interdisciplinary teaching, so should the other. If one party (teacher education or public school) is moving toward peer coaching, so should the other. When a joint decision is made for one institution to move toward greater implementation of a specific strategy on the basis of action research and close examination of the goal and the current results, the other institution should support this strategy as well.

A common vision for education founded on democratic principles should result in similar program components and educational practices. It is a contradiction for a teacher education program to exhort authentic assessment, teach teaching, and encourage heterogeneous learning for public schools if its own program is based on standardized examination, individually led teacher classrooms, and homogeneous grouping. In the same way, it is a contradiction for a teacher education program to use constructivist, student-oriented, and technologically infused learning methods if the public school uses regimented, teacher-centered, textbook-driven learning methods.

If professionals across settings have a common goal or direction, they can then check for compatible activities that allow both institutions to gain greater insight and power for educating their students. With some notable exceptions, the array of teacher education programs and public schools are unlinked; both groups tolerate the other, taking up space in each other's facility and classrooms and going about education in their own separate ways and with no clear common purpose. A clear understanding about the original intent of public education and the priority of democratic principles is not articulated. Without this common understanding, the two groups proceed each with its own agenda and without a common link.

To begin the co-reform process, awareness and understanding of each other are necessary. For many classroom teachers in public schools, knowledge of what is happening in teacher education is limited to what was taught or current when they were in college. There is little opportunity for teachers within a public school to meet teachers recently out of college and find out what is being taught or how field experiences are being implemented. Likewise, many teacher educators have little or no experience with practitioners and what is currently happening in public schools. To understand and prepare teachers, teacher educators have to be current about issues facing public schools. This can be achieved by visiting schools and talking with teachers, students, administrators, and parents.

This initial awareness is not enough to put the two groups on a common course. Opportunity for working with each other, exploring the issues, problem solving, and accepting joint responsibility for programmatic and symbiotic changes is essential. Such collaboration requires drastic changes in how the two faculties think of each other and respond to the idiosyncratic content of their respective work.

Different Constraints, Same Issues

We three authors of this chapter work at a large teacher education institution and have been involved for many years with university and public school reform. We coordinate two networks of public schools, involving more than eighty schools in thirty-seven districts. The focus of that work has been assisting the schools to make internal educational improvement consistent with democratic principles and procedures. At the same time, we are involved as participants or researchers in the internal reform of our own university preparation program, including new undergraduate programs in elementary, middle, and secondary teacher education and new graduate programs in educational leadership. Some of our university faculty collaborate with a few of our network public schools (as professional development sites) for simultaneous, co-reform programs.

In our dual roles with both public school reform and higher education reform, we have been struck by the similar difficulties experienced by both. For example, university faculties have the same problems as school faculties in developing a clearly articulated program; in creating a covenant of mission, goals, purpose, core values, and guiding learning principles when establishing a charter for democratic decision making; and in developing a critical study process.

Among ourselves, we have found the same problems of miscommunication, conflicting ideology, apathy, lack of sufficient time and money, and discomfort with change. In both settings, faculty tend to see their work as individuals with allegiance more to their department or grade level than to their school or college. In both settings, faculty are more concerned about their immediate, day-to-day work and less concerned about interdepartmental or interdisciplinary planning. Organizational structures make it difficult for even the most eager to achieve broad-based, long-term change. In both institutions, one finds faculty eager and change-oriented, willing to challenge existing structures. Yet they tend to become isolated from the rest of the faculty who are content with existing practices. In both, the vast majority of faculty are caring, well intentioned, and committed to their students. They simply have learned how to work within the existing framework of autonomy and isolation and see no reason to change (see Cuban, 1992; McNeil, 1998).

There are intra-institutional differences that can impede change in some insignificant ways. Many university faculty members have difficulty accepting public school educators as their peers. Higher education means to many that public schools are "lower" education and of lower status, esteem, and expertise. Democracy is based on equal rights and power, but the norms of the two institutions have not been equal. Even if higher education faculty members are open to the idea of equality, the institution can impede equality in many ways:

- Lack of recognition for such planning (it doesn't count for tenure or promotion)
- Lack of released time for such planning (other research, writing, teaching, and service obligations in one's department receive higher priority)
- Lack of a previous history of peers within the same institution knowing of each other's work (meetings are begun with wheel spinning and finding out the who, what, and how of each faculty member and department)
- Lack of a mutual time for planning with public school colleagues who have less flexibility as to when meetings can be arranged

These factors can create inertia among university faculty in moving beyond the planning-to-plan stage and on to program purpose, features, and implementation. The institution of the public school exerts its own difficulty for co-reform activities, as when public school teachers and administrators:

- Do not have the academic freedom to make changes in their own schools (control from the district or state)
- Are unable to respond quickly to school planning and implementation owing to the day-to-day incessant demands of students, parents, unpredictable crises, and community resistance

- Harbor traditional skepticism toward university people about whether they will roll up their sleeves and work and understand a public school setting

University faculty members do have greater flexibility in use of their time, but they feel much constraint on how to use it. Public school faculty have less flexibility in scheduling time for planning but endure institutional pressure to be involved in schoolwide efforts (site-based management, strategic plans). The ultimate result is that members of neither group can truly understand the life of the other until they work in each other's setting.

How can these understandings be developed?

- Teacher education programs can hire clinical practitioners from schools to be part of the university setting.
- Public schools can invite university faculty to teach in their settings for an extended period.
- Educators in different settings can trade places with one another for a short period of time.
- Teacher education classes can take place in the public schools.
- Both parties can shadow each other during part of one another's normal work.
- Both parties can jointly sponsor extra-educational activities (summer school programs, after-school programs, tutorial programs).

Ultimately, the best way for people to understand one another is through active participation in mutually important work. Unfortunately, because of different institutional constraints, it is hard to identify the mutually important work (co-reform) until other cross-collaboration has occurred.

Messy Work for a Clear and Common Goal

There is no algorithm for the specifics of how a co-reform program should be developed or what it should look like. Clarity about common goals and purpose is the beginning. Programs that mutually reinforce educational activity across teacher education and public education are the means. The end is a perpetual quest: the ongoing revolution to educate future generations of democratic citizens. This is no small task by any means, but it is the task that gives meaning to our professional lives.

References

America 2000. Washington, DC: U.S. Department of Education, Sept. 1, 1991.

Barber, B. R. "America Skips School." *Harper's*, Nov. 1993, pp. 39–46.

Board of Education v. Pico. 457 U.S. 853, 1982.

Cuban, L. "What Happens to Reforms That Last? The Case of the Junior High School." *American Educational Research Journal*, 1992, 29(2), 227–251.

Glickman, C. D. *Renewing America's Schools*. San Francisco: Jossey-Bass, 1993.

Goodlad, J. I. "On Taking School Reform Seriously." *Phi Delta Kappan*, 1992, 74(2), 232–238.

Gutmann, A. *Democratic Education*. Princeton, N.J.: Princeton University Press, 1987.

Lee, G. C. "The Precious Blessings of Liberty." In G. Lee (ed.), *Crusade Against Ignorance: Thomas Jefferson on Education*. New York: Columbia University Press, 1961.

McNeil, L. M*. "Contradictions of Control. Part 2: Teachers, Students, and Curriculum." *Phi Delta Kappan*, 1998, 69(6), 432–438.

Part Five

Standards, Policies, and Authority

Chapter Fifteen

Open Accountability for the 1990s

Between the Pillars

Those of us who've been involved with public education for more than two decades have seen significant shifts in the agenda of school reform. We now stand in the midst of two apparently contradictory movements, one entitled "legislative reform" and the other "empowering reform" (Wise, 1988). What appear to be polar opposites, however, under closer scrutiny become complementary frames to guide a new center of change.

A Bounded Center

In an earlier period, school reform legislation was mainly enabling rather than controlling. States gave schools the autonomy to develop their own instructional programs, curricula, teaching methods, and evaluation systems. Which student data would be reported by schools was largely a local matter. Local control was a sacred cow, not to be tampered with by politicians. In the mid 1960s and early 1970s, the banner of reform used the operant word *open* to refer to project- and student-centered education. *Diversity*, *uniqueness*, and *innovation* were words embedded in school reform.

The more recent school reform movement has been categorized as the era of legislated learning. The banner of academic excellence has been translated into blue-ribbon commissions, supported by "education" governors who establish laws and regulations

---

The author wishes to acknowledge the contribution of Ray Bruce in his reactions to previous drafts of this chapter.

about school standards, uniform curricula, teacher evaluation, promotion and retention policies, and standardized data on student achievement. *Accountability* has been the operant word for justifying increased funds for schools and staff. State legislators and state department officials have increasingly controlled both the ends (what data will be used to evaluate schools, teachers, and students) and the means (the curricula and programs of instruction) of school improvement (Wise, 1988).

These two contrasting eras represent educational reforms reflecting either the political left or the political right. As in most generalizations, these characterizations are more nearly true than false; still, there are exceptions to the rule. What is more significant, however, is to acknowledge the successes and failures of both reform movements and to suggest that combining the success of each period into two fixed frames will create a new balanced movement for the future.

By establishing the two pillars, policy makers might trade the proverbial pendulum swing from one extreme to the other for a new, improved—and wiser—center. Without such a bounded center, reform will continue to swing first toward and then away from excessive freedom and excessive control. The prior excesses of the open education movement propelled the later emphasis on accountability, and the recent excesses of the accountability movement have propelled a new emphasis on restructuring the schools. It's no accident that the current language of school reform (with terms such as *empowerment, site-based management, career ladders,* and *integrated curriculum*) is a hauntingly familiar refrain for those who taught in schools during the open education movement. At that time, the phrases were *shared governance, the school as the center of inquiry, differentiated staffing,* and *spiral curriculum*. Further, it's no accident that the language of future reform efforts can be predicted to include such terms as *outcome-based instruction, mastery teaching,* and *performance appraisal systems,* which reecho the recent accountability movement that began with *management by objectives, behavioral objectives,* and *performance contracting*.

The Signs

Open education arrived in the United States, freely (and a bit enviously) borrowed from the British primary schools, at a time when our federal government was appealing to the social involvement of the baby boom generation of young adults. Teachers with a social activist bent were actively recruited into education (the Teacher Corps, VISTA, the Peace Corps). Schools addressed issues of freedom, relevance, elimination of racial discrimination, and winning the war on poverty. Experimentation with school practice that differed from the conventions of thirty seats, six rows, and the self-contained classroom was encouraged. A wave of the politically left youth generation (those who rode the freedom buses, marched against the Vietnam War, and openly questioned the values of the previous generation) made inroads in the schools. The result was a young teaching force that was reshaping schools. In fact, some schools no longer looked like schools: students roamed from room to room and sprawled on the floors, discussing controversial topics with their teachers. Teachers often taught in teams, and many classrooms were without walls. Grades were eliminated. To the previous generations of adults who remembered school from their childhood, these new schools had the appearance of chaos.

Whenever a school made available the resources and support to hard-working, committed, and knowledgeable teachers, open education was an operation of awesome beauty. Behind the noise and activity was a purposeful commitment to educating students in the fullest manner of thinking and acting knowledgeably and ethically. The results of student success in some schools were quite remarkable (see Jennings and Nathan, 1977). Yet when schools gave teachers autonomy to improvise without support and planning, or when teachers were told to innovate with neither the commitment nor the knowledge to study and apply the principles of open education, such operations were disastrous. They resulted in the miseducation of students in its fullest sense—activity without rhyme or reason other than being new or fun. (Lawrence Cremin noted in 1964 that the demise of progressive education schools in the 1930s happened in a similar manner.)

When the decline of student performance on nationally standardized tests (particularly SAT scores) began to appear in the media, critics of open education had a field day casting the blame on this new type of experimental schooling. The argument went like this: open education had neglected the basics, was too permissive, and had sacrificed the essential values of Western civilization to meaningless relativism. Simultaneously, in the 1970s, the agenda of the nation was shifting from a predominantly liberal and social agenda to a predominantly conservative and economic one. Once more, the economic downturn in the United States was traced to the schools. Because of open education, the argument went, students lacked the basic skills and knowledge to work, and the United States lost its economic competitiveness in the world (National Commission on Excellence in Education, 1983).

Accountability thus became the central tenet for a return to a traditional conception of the school. Now schools were to show improvement in basic skills; stop fooling around with course electives and projects; and get back to drill, practice, homework, direct instruction, and serious time-on-task schooling. Leaving schools to educators, the reasoning went, had resulted in loss of rigor; the task now was to shape the curriculum and schools through legislated policy. A common core of knowledge was to be taught to all students, and uniform programs and teacher evaluations were to be enforced by state officials. As states mandated by means of legislation, the department of education became the enforcer. At first, teachers and principals screamed about the straitjacket of standardization and top-down control. Later, these screams became whimpers, as it was clear that state legislators, powerful business leaders, and citizens were not sympathetic. Legislation piled upon prior legislation, swamping schools in a pool of regulation. Teachers and principals became passive workers following someone else's orders. Morale among educators plummeted; the loss of flexibility and respect for the profession were seen as part and parcel of the same problem (Boyer, 1988).

In the mid-1980s, reformers had begun to talk seriously and visibly about making teaching a better recognized and remunerated profession to attract and keep the best and brightest teachers. (At the same time, these reformers were squeezing out any discretionary decision making about curriculum and instruction by those they wished to attract and keep.) Finally, in the late 1980s, a turnaround began to occur. The National Governors Association, composed of the majority of "education" governors, said that legislation had gone too far, that it was time to return more decision making to the local school. The National Association of State Boards of Education (1988) issued a report that urged loosening of state policies, procedures, and curricula for schools. One of the most heavily legislated states, Florida, released a report about the emerging consensus of state legislators, business leaders, and educators that "state and district policies should reflect greater freedom and accountability at the local and school level for decision making" (Office on Policy Research and Improvement, 1988).

The Two Pillars

We've witnessed two decades of school reform, each characterized by a major pillar undergirding the change efforts within it. We could probably agree that both pillars are essential to guiding the future of public education. In the next decade, choice and responsibility should rest between these pillars.

The decade of social activism and civil rights advocated that education should be built on a foundation of equal access to knowledge. Open education was in large part a delivery system of flexible instruction for adapting to the individual and group needs of students. In its best form, open education afforded continuous progress, active interest, and steady achievement for an eclectic, heterogeneous body of students. In its worst form, it became a rationale for depriving some students (those classified as "slow," "poor," or "disadvantaged") of equal access and therefore teaching them differently, translated as "less." Now, we can all agree that the concept of *equal access* should be a fundamental pillar; all students will acquire a core body of knowledge basic to citizens of the United States. This goal does not translate into a set curriculum of detailed objectives, competencies, materials, and activities but rather into a core group of understandings that an education citizen should acquire, encompassing language, communication, literacy mathematics, science, technology, history, and values.

The second pillar is the legacy of the accountability movement of the 1980s. We may disagree on the importance, validity, or priority of particular data, but who would argue that the schools and the public shouldn't know how their students are doing? To refuse to collect, disseminate, and use data about students' attitudes, achievements, and performance would be irresponsible. So the second pillar to bind reform in the 1990s is *public demonstration and display of student performance* (see Figure 15.1).

The Open-Accountable School

The two pillars—equal access to knowledge and public demonstration of results—will define the boundaries for the decentralization of decision making about curriculum, delivery of instruction, staff development, and evaluation. Schools operating within these poles have already sprung up across the country: the NEA project (Mastery in Learning), the AFT Project (Research into Practice Network), the National Network for Education Renewal, the Coalition of Essential Schools, the Massachusetts Carnegie Commission of Schools, the Georgia Program for School Improvement, Dade County (Florida) schools, and Jefferson County (Kentucky) schools. These schools have implemented such ideas as team teaching, teaching less content in a deeper manner, integrating curriculum across discipline areas, portfolio evaluation of students, and nongraded continuous progress. In these settings, the view of pro-

Figure 15.1. School Reform Between the Pillars

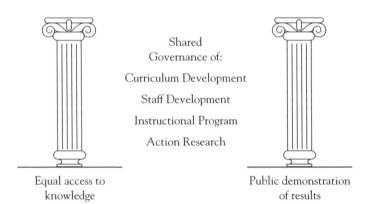

Shared
Governance of:

Curriculum Development

Staff Development

Instructional Program

Action Research

Equal access to
knowledge

Public demonstration
of results

fessionalism as involving the teacher in decisions about collective work has been embraced through establishing shared governance operations and school councils. State departments not only tolerate these schools but encourage them because they operate between the two frames of access and documentation. The states are willing to lessen control over the means *and* the ends of education for schools that can document their operations between the pillars.

Where We Sit Now

The foundations of the next phase of school reform are set. The state has a vested interest in a common curriculum and in student results. However, as long as a school or district can demonstrate (1) provision of equal (nondiscriminatory) access to a common body of knowledge and (2) the results of such efforts in regard to student learning (through, for instance, narrowing disparate achievement gains among various student groups, improved student attitudes, better attendance, fewer disciplinary actions, reduction in the dropout rate, and so on), the state's role moves toward greater freedom and local discretion. Without such demonstrated efforts and results, the state's role shifts toward greater control and centralization.

Of course, there are competing notions of what constitutes a common body of knowledge (Brandt, 1988) and of what appropriate results are. This defining continues to fuel the reform debate as it is negotiated between local districts and state departments. For example, in Vermont, accountability is being defined, in part, as each school holding a public meeting in the spring to answer questions townspeople have about their schools. In other states, accountability is defined uniformly and narrowly as student performance on state, criterion-referenced, and nationally normed tests. Similarly, definitions of a common body of knowledge vary, from detailed K–12 core curricula (including the textbooks and materials to use) in some states to broad goals and objectives in others. E. D. Hirsch, Jr., the author of *Cultural Literacy* (1987), recently suggested that a common curriculum should be taught for 50 percent of a school's instructional day (Hitt, 1989). Two examples from our northern neighbors are illuminating. In British Columbia, the provincial government requires that at least 25 percent of a school's curriculum be locally developed by teachers. In Nova Scotia, the ministry of education requires that language and literacy programs *not* be founded on basal readers but on real books and magazines and other teacher-chosen materials.

Definitions of common knowledge and important student results are profoundly influential, and each school or district has to negotiate an agreement with the higher authorities. But, the point is that discretionary activity between the negotiated definitions is allowing creation of a new reform movement. "Restructuring" connotes a movement toward open *and* accountable education. Decision making in schools is being released from top-down control and from conventional structures of grouping and teaching students. The curriculum is being expanded from textbook-centered to project-centered. Instructional activities of drill, practice, and competition are being opened to exploration and cooperative learning. Learning within the traditional four walls of the classroom is being enlarged to learning outside the school walls, in community and field sites. The typical arrangement of one teacher with twenty-five students is being opened to concepts of team teaching, flexible grouping, and lead teachers. If we are to take the best from the most recent reform efforts, then we could have the best of accountability without the excess of prescriptive legislation and the best of open education without the excess of laissez-faire attitudes toward student performance.

To Policy Makers: Learning from Reform

The improvement of schools must come through the motivation of professionals, which is premised on two dimensions: (1) having the choice to make knowledgeable decisions about one's collective work (teaching), and (2) taking the responsibility for implementing and accepting the consequences of one's choices (Deci, 1975). The open education movement gave educators choice with little responsibility. The accountability movement gave educators responsibility without choice. Earlier, we had freedom without control; recently, we have had control without freedom. The effect of both eras has been to shortchange students.

The message to policy makers (at the district, state, and federal levels) is to hold schools accountable for achieving negotiated goals but not to legislate how they are to achieve those results. The first assumption should be that people in schools know and care about their students and programs, and figure possibilities for improvement. Policy makers should ease uniform standards, statewide teacher evaluation systems, and prescriptive curriculum but should not erase equal access to knowledge and documented achievement of goals. Those schools that can't document success should reap the consequences of higher authorities' using external systems to ensure high-quality education for students. Those schools that *can* achieve success between the two pillars should be allowed to fly! Only then, in the nineties, will we learn about the capabilities of the public school to be a truly educative institution.

References

Boyer, E. *Report on School Reform: The Teachers Speak*. New York: Carnegie Foundation for the Advancement of Teaching, 1988.

Brandt, R. S. (ed.). *Content of the Curriculum*. (1988 Yearbook of the Association for Supervision and Curriculum Development.) Alexandria, Va.: Association for Supervision and Curriculum Development, 1988.

Cremin, L. A. *The Transformation of the Schools*. New York: Vintage, 1964.

Deci, E. L. *Intrinsic Motivation*. New York: Plenum, 1975.

Hirsch, E. D., Jr. *Cultural Literacy: What Every American Needs to Know*. Boston: Houghton Mifflin, 1987.

Hitt, J. "Who Needs the Great Works?" (Forum.) *Harper's*, 1989, *278*, no. 1671 (Sept.), 43–52.

Jennings, W., and Nathan, J. "Startling, Disturbing Research on School Program Effectiveness." *Kappan*, 1977, *58*(7), 568–572.

National Association of State Boards of Education. *Right from the Start: The Report of the NASBE Task Force on Early Childhood Education*. Alexandria, Va.: NASBE, 1988.

National Commission on Excellence in Education. *A Nation at Risk: The Imperative for Education Reform*. Washington, D.C.: U.S. Government Printing Office, 1983.

Office on Policy Research and Improvement. *Restructuring Education: The Florida Experience*. (Conference proceedings.) Tallahassee: Florida State Department of Education, 1988.

Wise, A. "The Two Conflicting Trends in School Reform: Legislated Learning Revisited." *Kappan*, 1988, *69*(5), 328–333.

Chapter Sixteen

Holding Sacred Ground

The Impact of Standardization

When you look at students in their magnificent diversity—of language, culture, ideas, economic background, religion, expression, and manners—what do you hope that schooling will do for them? What is schooling for, anyway? What constitutes an educated person? W.E.B. Du Bois (1970) described learning for African American children as the most fundamental human right because it allows students to challenge the world and determine how they can work toward a different and better future.

In the 1840s, Horace Mann proposed the need for common schools that would function as the great equalizer of human conditions, the balance wheel of social machinery. Public school would be free, for poor and rich alike, and nonsectarian. The common school would not be a school for common people but rather a school common to all people, developing educated persons who exercised free and deliberate choices (Cremin, 1964).

Thomas Jefferson viewed the educated person as a farmer, a person who lived apart from others; pursued interests in science, philosophy, and art after a long day of self-sustaining chores; and then determined when to participate in neighborhood and community affairs. The educated person combined self-reliance, individuality, and self-learning with minimal but significant civic responsibility.

In the late 1980s and until the late 1990s, the "restructuring" period of education, we saw perhaps the largest and most sustained rethinking of schools along the lines of the larger purpose of democracy, with inclusion of all students as active, curious, and wise citizens.

My contention is that the work of K–12 schools—to sustain an education for all students built on active, participatory, integrated, and contributory learning—is messy, difficult, and up close. Powerful intellectual education is respectful, challenging, and democratic, preparing students to use their skills, knowledge, and understanding to exercise choice about how to self-govern and to govern with others—to have choices of life, liberty, and the pursuit of happiness (Glickman, 1998).

Many collaborative networks throughout the United States work toward such educational goals. The Coalition of Essential Schools, the Accelerated Schools, the Child Development Study Schools, the ATLAS Project, the Four Seasons Project, and the Annenberg Urban and Rural Challenge are just a few of the collaborations that have brought together the enthusiasm of the school and local community to develop intellectual expectations among faculty, students, parents, neighborhoods, community resources, and businesses; these expectations move far beyond the traditional view of teaching as isolated, controlling, and passive (McDonald, 1996; McDonald and others, 1999).

Thousands of individuals are committed to this work, including such noted educators as Deborah Meier (1995), George Wood (1998), James Comer (Comer, Ben-Avie, Haynes, and Joyner, 1999), Henry Levin (1991), Lisa Delpit (1995), Linda Darling-Hammond (1997), and Theodore Sizer (1984). With their efforts have come astounding realization of what students are capable of doing. The work of these educators represents the very best in the tradition of progressive education (Ravitch, 2000).

How do we sustain such work when recent history indicates that it will be curtailed? We are already seeing that by way of the standards, assessment, and accountability movement, which has, in many states, increasingly locked teachers and schools into focusing their teaching on high-stakes tests that reward or punish the school and determine whether students graduate or progress to the next level of school. The state standards and accountability movement has been an unstoppable train, with only one state (Iowa) left in the United States without such a scheme.

Standards, Accountability, and Tests

The movement for state standards and accountability is a complex phenomenon.

First, the states are not all alike; the scope of standards, the nature of assessment, and the usage of both vary. Accountability plans in such states as Texas, Connecticut, New York, Massachusetts, Alabama, and Michigan are highly prescriptive and maintain tight control over the curriculum; the consequences of test results are high for students, teachers, and principals. Other states—Maryland, Maine, and Vermont—use assessment that is broader, incorporates more constructed response, and allows more options and discretion on the part of the school and district.

Second, variance or waiver differs by state. Some states—through charter school laws or other state deregulation programs—allow the school and district that is disgruntled with the existing state plan to opt out if it develops its own accountability and assessment plans. The trend, however, is toward reducing local control and forcing schools to comply with state assessments.

The governors, as part of the National Governors Association, advocate tight state controls over standards, and the federal government's Goals 2000 legislation has added further momentum for more testing with greater consequences. The issues of standards and accountability pervade educational conferences and literature on reform.

Standards policies are a significant issue in education because they affect nearly every student, faculty member, and school in the country and have a direct bearing on how we define the well-educated student, the curriculum to be taught, and the ultimate purpose of our schools.

To the consternation of many of my friends, I have seen much good come out of the standards movement:

- The standards movement expects every student—regardless of socioeconomic class, gender, race, or ethnicity—to achieve at a higher level than ever before, and it holds teachers and schools responsible for proving that all students can achieve standards.
- The standards movement provides greater funds and targeted assistance to classrooms and schools where groups of students are not achieving at an equitable level.
- Some schools that have shown no improvement over many years have been closed or reconstituted.
- In some states, stronger equalization and redistribution of state funding of schools has accompanied implementation of schemes for state accountability. Poor schools are receiving more, and wealthier districts are receiving fewer, state funds.
- State legislatures—or, more often, state courts—are saying that a quality education for all students is a constitutional responsibility and must be funded accordingly.
- Some states have built inclusive and participatory consensus on key learning standards and assessments not tied to one way of knowing or to one format of testing. Some states also have sophisticated accountability schemes that weigh differences among students and communities and give useful information, assistance, and overall purpose to a school's work. Such state plans are rare, but they do exist.

Now that I have mentioned some of the good, let me explain what is bad about state standards:

- States exercise major, unilateral control over all operational aspects of a school: standards, assessment, curriculum, consequences of a test, budget, resources, staffing, and governance.
- States establish narrow standards for many academic areas, require frequent and extensive testing of students using a test with

a single format; and they often follow one group's idea of what every student must master by a certain time.

- States use bad science to make decisions: comparing non-comparable schools in reward and punishment systems, not accounting for improvement within schools, and relying only on test scores to assess achievement and accountability and to grant student promotions (Schrag, 2000).
- There is no allowance for prototype schools or districts to develop their own standards and assessments to challenge the state model.
- Consequently, there are few challenges to the state's idea of what a well-educated American is.

This last point is the critical flaw of any universal state or national system of standards and accountability.

Who Defines the Well-Educated Person?

If we define education for democratic life as George Wood (1998) does—as making wise citizens and good neighbors who can think deeply and intelligently about issues of self and society, care for and respect others, take care of their family's needs, and contribute to the welfare of others—then what knowledge and which type of schooling are essential to this definition? Presumably such an education includes developing an intellectual understanding of other humans and of local, national, and international living conditions; ways of communicating with diverse others; skills of analysis and problem solving; and the competence to choose what one will do with one's own life in economic, social, leisure, and aesthetic pursuits.

Does one need three years of college preparatory mathematics for this? Does one need to learn French or Chinese? What level of mastery does one need in the various disciplines? What is the priority of learning discipline-based subject knowledge versus integrative knowledge, with applications and contributions in the world outside of school? What are the intellectual skills, understanding, and core knowledge needed of a good neighbor and proactive citizen?

I am neither devaluing the worth of specific subjects nor suggesting that we water down expectations for all students. Instead, my battle is about who should determine, and for whom, the essential standards and the degree of public accountability for students.

In a high school curriculum controlled by college admission criteria, certain core courses and scores on the SAT or ACT are essential (even though the most selective colleges consider a much wider range of knowledge and skills). College bound or not, most students will not use most of what they are required to learn in high school, whether they study mathematics, history, language, or science. Is this knowledge still essential? Again, says who? Dare I ask whether one can be a wise and productive citizen without going to college?

Is the purpose of public education to train a highly skilled workforce to support the economic engine of our high-technology information and service corporations? If so—and, of course, there are good reasons to have a healthy economy—then the push for standards, assessments, tests, and skills reflects the idea of what successful corporate employees need to know; thus, we have the college core courses supplemented by a huge concentration on technology.

Again, I am not arguing whether there is the need for expertise in technology; rather, my question is about who should determine, and for whom, what a well-educated person is.

For example, the Waldorf schools in the United States (Oppenheimer, 1999) have children work with natural materials for the first three to five years of schooling; children use only wood, clay, paint, and water to work on long, painstaking projects for several years before the manufactured world becomes a source of their learning. TVs, phones, and computers do not belong in this early and primary childhood education. The primary emphasis is on imagining and working in a completely natural environment. Are these students less well educated than their peers? According to what criteria?

The standards movement defines the well-educated citizen as a college graduate who is technologically prepared to lead a successful economic life. The idea of an educated citizen as someone who may not want to make a great deal of money or work in a corporation, who instead might seek success in quiet detachment from or even resistance to college or corporate life, has eroded in America. Even mentioning the idea that education is not mostly about jobs or money but about how to choose to live is seen as a romantic, utopian throwback to another time.

My point is not to convince others of my definition of a well-educated person, but to share the open doubts about one single definition and to explore the need for more varied concepts of education—concepts that also thrive on student accomplishments and successes and promise a toehold in the future of American education and democracy. How might we do this?

Furthering Democracy

A democracy flourishes only when it protects the marketplace of ideas and a diversity of perspectives. One learns only through disagreement that is civil, respectful, and thoroughly understood (Yankelovich, 1991). What we need are special protections for classrooms and schools that have articulated different perspectives of students—their capabilities, their outcomes—and how to organize for them. We must protect these places in the same way we protect religious communities, native and ethnic cultures, historic places, and national parks. We need alternative concepts of education—not as historic artifacts, but as thriving places of practice that are built into systemic state and district policies. We need schools without grade levels, without mental or physical walls from their communities, with different forms of student expectations, work, assessments, and performances.

Without these alternatives, we have a single concept and a simple system that focuses on raising certain test scores and that silences other possibilities for public education. If this single system does not work as legislators expect, then more private schools will proliferate—with or without public purpose—able to operate in ways that have not been available to public schools. The transition will be complete: state control will be turned over to private hands and the grand democratic idea of education for public purposes— wise citizens and good neighbors—will be gone.

Within Public Purpose

Alternative concepts of an American education and the role, indeed the obligation, of public schools to test our forms of teaching and learning must be mindful of criteria different from those for private or religious schools. Public schools must be open to all, nondiscriminatory, and reflective of the range and diversity of student needs and abilities; such schools must be public in all that they do. Students, parents or caretakers, and faculty should have a degree of choice over the curriculum and method. Further, all such schools must make known what they intend to accomplish and must publicly share their progress, or lack of it, with their community, district, and state. Finally, all meetings about schoolwide decisions and the use of funds must be open to everyone. In being public, and no matter how different from one another, schools have a responsibility to make known their definition of a well-educated American, their practice of attainment, and the results. Further, they must abide by the U.S. Constitution and not promote private or sectarian purposes.

Unfortunately, protecting a loyal-opposition school movement in the next decade will be extremely difficult. Between the powerful groups that want a single system at the state and district levels and the extremists who want to abolish state support and allow all families to educate their own children however they see fit, we need to find a middle ground: state support with divergent concepts of education for public purpose.

What Can We Do?

How might nonstandard classrooms, schools, and districts continue their work at a time of great state standardization? Let me suggest some viable options.

Rebel Openly

Knock the current accountability and testing system out by force. Parents and educators in Wisconsin halted what is widely regarded as a bad, arbitrary set of exit tests. Some Massachusetts schools refused to administer their state tests. Even some test developers and proponents agreed that the tests were unrealistic and time-consuming, often measured trivial knowledge, and were not used appropriately (Schrag, 2000). Rebellion is the clearest stance, but it has obvious disadvantages. Power against power means one group wins and the other loses; if one is on the losing side, even greater rigidity is the likely result. The other problem is that opposition to a single public accountability scheme for a state must have in its place a locally developed public account-ability plan to set higher expectations for all groups of students in a legal way. This accountability entails major commitment on the part of teachers, school leaders, students, and parents (Gal-lagher, 2000).

Propose Variances in the Current Accountability System

Don't fight the entire state system, but argue instead for more pub-lic charter schools and more state deregulation programs that give waivers to state assessments. Argue that—just as all successful corporations work on a future design to help improve the larger system—education needs prototype schools and districts to pilot and test new forms of standards and assessments for guiding further state improvements.

Accept the State Testing, But Develop a Community-Based Standard and Assessment

A community-based standard and assessment as a culminating demonstration, portfolio, or exhibit can integrate what students need to know on the state assessments with a larger, more applicable contribution. The school realizes a higher purpose without reducing the chance for students to do well on the state assessment. Schools work with parents and others to find out what the local community expects of students and their schools. In the last month of each school year, there might be an open house for the community to view this culminating work; Maine, Vermont, and Minnesota have pioneered this work.

Accept the State Standards and Tests, and Make Them Work

Make the state standards and tests work by involving students in activities that allow other types of learning. Some schools and communities—many in low-income areas—have created an environment of joy, love, and pride, where mastery of the state test is one important part of showing the rest of the world that, as students and a community, they are as good as anyone else (Scheurich, 1998).

Ignore the Test

Mainly ignore the test, and then do a crash preparation close to the date of the test. Or allow only a fraction of time weekly for test preparation.

Resign

Resign, and find another school within or outside public education. Then practice what you believe.

Conclusion

In my experience with schools that have grounded their work on such alternative visions of education, I have uncovered incredible stories of savviness and courage: principals who have been fired and some reinstated; teachers taking on their union to meet more often, control their own hiring, and teach larger classes as a way to redistribute money for more specialized services for students; schools ridding themselves of colleagues who had great community power but were incompetent or uncaring about what was possible for all students; and educators engaging the public in discussion about school change.

Many unsung heroes—school boards, superintendents, and community members—have fought to keep alternative concepts of the school alive. But many other teachers and principals have quit, unable to sustain the commitment, energy, and time to educate students in a way that continued to challenge them. I have seen vicious attacks on such caring people by those frightened about allowing students to judge the world for themselves.

Others, over the years, in quiet voices and loud ones, have carried an idea about education and democracy as being inseparable from each other, an idea of the public purpose of education, taking place in all types of location and in view of others—within the school and the larger community of parents, neighbors, and citizens (Glickman, 1998).

When we no longer see the inseparability of education and democracy, we lose our way. We are at a time when we must hold to a sacred concept of public education, a concept of the pursuit of truth in the marketplace of ideas. When one concept of education wins over all others and we are left with a single definition determined by others for all of us, then we all lose. We are at a time when we must hold this sacred ground, reaching out to our students, reaching out to one another, and helping to define our future.

References

Comer, J. P., Ben-Avie, N., Haynes, N. M., and Joyner, E. T. *Child by Child: The Comer Process for Change in Education.* New York: Teachers College Press, 1999.

Cremin, L. A. *Transformation of the School: Progressivism in American Education, 1876–1957.* New York: Vintage, 1964.

Darling-Hammond, L. *The Right to Learn: A Blueprint for Creating Schools That Work.* San Francisco: Jossey-Bass, 1997.

Delpit, L. *Other People's Children: Cultural Conflict in the Classroom.* New York: New Press, 1995.

Du Bois, W.E.B. "The Freedom to Learn." In P. S. Foner (ed.), *W.E.B. Du Bois Speaks.* New York: Pathfinder, 1970. (Original work published 1949)

Gallagher, C. "A Seat at the Table: Teachers Reclaiming Assessment Through Rethinking Accountability." *Phi Delta Kappan,* 2000, *81*(7), 502–507.

Glickman, C. D. *Revolutionizing America's Schools.* San Francisco: Jossey-Bass, 1998.

Levin, H. M. *Building School Capacity for Effective Teacher Empowerment.* Brunswick, N.J.: Consortium for Policy Research, 1991.

McDonald, J. P. *Redesigning School: Lessons for the 21st Century.* San Francisco: Jossey-Bass, 1996.

McDonald, J. P., and others. *School Reform Behind the Scenes.* New York: Teachers College Press, 1999.

Meier, D. *The Power of Their Ideas: Lessons for America from a Small School in Harlem.* Boston: Beacon Press, 1995.

Oppenheimer, T. "Schooling the Imagination." *Atlantic Monthly,* Sept. 1999, pp. 71–83.

Ravitch, D. *Left Back: A Century of Failed School Reforms.* New York: Simon & Schuster, 2000.

Scheurich, J. J. "Highly Successful and Loving Public, Pre-K–5 Schools Populated Mainly by Low SES Children of Color: Core Beliefs and Cultural Characteristics." *Urban Education,* 1998, *33*(4), 451–491.

Schrag, P. "'High Stakes Are for Tomatoes': Statewide Testing of Students, with Penalties for Failure, Has Run into Opposition from Parents Across the Political Spectrum." *Atlantic Monthly,* Aug. 2000, pp. 19–21.

Sizer, T. R. *Horace's Compromise: The Dilemma of the American High School.*
    Boston: Houghton Mifflin, 1984.
Wood, G. H. *A Time to Learn.* New York: Dutton, 1998.
Yankelovich, D. *Coming to Public Judgment: Making Democracy Work in a Complex World.* Syracuse, N.Y.: Syracuse University Press, 1991.

Chapter Seventeen

Dichotomizing Education

Why No One Wins and America Loses

I did not lightly take pen in hand in writing this article (yes, I still use a pen). I have devoted my entire professional life to working with colleagues in creating, establishing, and sustaining public schools that are driven by collaboration, personalization, and active and participatory student learning (Glickman, 1998). I will continue to do so, because I personally believe this is the best way to prepare all students for the intellectual, social, and aesthetic life of a democracy.

Yet even in the fervor of my beliefs, I still see other concepts of education that raise a degree of uncertainty in me. My memories of my own best teachers are revealing. Most were highly interactive teachers, but one grand elder taught behind a lectern in a huge auditorium with little interaction with students. Nevertheless, he was perhaps my greatest teacher. The discrepancy doesn't change the strength of my own beliefs; it simply reinforces to me that the viable and powerful possibilities of educating students well are beyond what I can imagine.

Ultimately, an American education must stand on a higher foundation than the beliefs of any one individual or any one group. It should encourage, respect, and support those conceptions—no matter how diametrically opposed to one's own—willing to be

Particular thanks to colleagues Donna Alvermann, Gene Hall, Alice Sampson, Bobby Starnes, Margaret Wilder, and many others—too numerous to mention—who graciously provided feedback, reaction, and thoughts to this chapter.

tested openly and freely. Furthermore, it should involve the willing and nondiscriminatory participation of *all* students, parents or caretakers, and educators. That is what should be at the core of an American education. But with the winner-take-all wars being fought today, I am seriously concerned for the future of our students, our public schools, and the vitality of a better democracy.

Ideological Absolutes

The either-or debates about standards versus no standards, intrinsic versus extrinsic motivation, core versus multicultural knowledge, direct instruction versus constructivist learning, and phonics versus whole language are symptomatic of ideologies that attempt to crush each other, with only one solution left standing. Whether the ideology is education anchored in traditional, behaviorist authority or progressive, inquiry-based learning, the stance toward the final outcome is the same. One group possesses the truth and the other side is a pack of extremists—scary, evil people. Articles and books present educators and the public with a forced choice that unfortunately undermines the reality of the world and endangers the very concept of an American education.[1]

Let me illustrate the incompleteness of ideological absolutes with one of the most emotive societal issues of today: assessment of race and socioeconomic achievement. One side of this debate argues that America is the land of opportunity, where freedom rings, where anyone—regardless of race, religion, gender, or class—can work hard and rise to a position of authority, success, and accomplishment. The other side of this debate argues that America is a hegemonic system, protecting the ruling class and existing privilege, and keeping the poor, the dispossessed, and people of color stifled, oppressed, and marginalized. Well, which side of this debate is correct? After all, determining which perspective is right has great implications for what needs to be changed in societal practice and programs, and in directing resources. The truth is that two contradictory realities have compelling evidence and must be used together to figure out what has to be done next.

Consider the economic component of this debate. Lipset (1996) compares the United States with other western industrialized nations. Since the civil war, America has been an extremely wealthy country, with a steady rise in living standards and unparalleled increase in social and economic advances for the poor and working class. Yet the poorest fifth of this nation continue to *decline* in their relative income position.

The African American scholar Henry Louis Gates, Jr., takes on this same dichotomy in reference to race. He observed that since 1967 middle-class African American families have quadrupled, the top one hundred African American businesses since 1973 have moved from sales of $473 million to $11.7 billion, and in 1970 "only one in ten blacks had attended college; today one in three has" (Gates and West, 1996, p. 19). He goes on to discuss the continuous wrenching poverty of a third of African Americans today and concludes: "We need something we don't have: a way of speaking about black poverty that doesn't falsify the reality of black advancement, a way of speaking about black advancement that doesn't distort the enduring realities of black poverty. I'd venture that a lot depends on whether we get it" (p. 38).

In truth, America has been one of the leading countries of opportunity for disenfranchised persons, and at the same time it has been a country of great economic stratification between the luxury of the wealthiest and the wretched conditions of the poorest (Myers, 2000). In essence, the beliefs of Ayn Rand and Pete Seeger are both correct. To speak only of one side and ignore the other is to create disbelief in most ordinary citizens, who know firsthand of examples that counter any single view being exhorted. This is what I believe to be the danger of ideological truth in education. Many educators feel they have become pawns to the reformers' and policy makers' propaganda of a single truth; hence the conclusion that there is a single best way to change the system of American schools.

Education Ideology

The current attacks by E. D. Hirsch, Jr., against progressive education and the equally strident attacks by others such as Alfie Kohn against traditional education are wonderful examples of this either-or ideological stance.[2] Hirsch argues that a core, common knowledge is essential for all students to succeed in mainstream society. Without a common framework of fluent and written English, historical and cultural reference, and direct instruction, marginalized and poor children are deprived of the education that wealthier children automatically pick up from their parents and caretakers, and peers. Thus there is the need to rid our schools of the overwhelming "permissive" practices of activity-based education and use common-knowledge tests to ensure that all children are acquiring the "cultural capital" needed for success in later life. Kohn in turn speaks against standards, core knowledge, and tests and says that children, regardless of their circumstances, are innately curious and teachers should move with this curiosity to open up new freedoms and possibilities. Each proponent has their version of truth, and it is on their side.[3] Both see little validity in any research as to success in the methods that oppose their ideology. Again, the reality is that education is composed of many complexities that defeat any singular truth of how the world can and should work.

For example, might it be that both Hirsch and Kohn have a valid perspective? Striving for core knowledge that students themselves might not choose but that gives them access to a society in which they might possibly change the current world of power, wealth, and control seems quite reasonable. Endeavoring to facilitate students' curiosity to learn multiple histories, cultures, and intelligences in an intensely involving way also seems quite reasonable. It is important that school be a joyful and engaging place. Yet, is all learning intrinsic or extrinsic? Most would say it's both; we learn for the joy of it. But some of the most useful learning has been done because others, not we, demanded that we do it and do it well until we got it right.

The polemic around standards versus no standards does not account for complex realities. Are external standards bad or good? Might they be both? Might we have public system state standards as well as no state standards in the same state system? Some states have standards and assessments that have been well received by educators and the public, and not seen as heavy handed, intrusive, or unfair. Many states have standards and assessments that are volatile in makeup, format, pressure, and consequences.

The standards polarization (again, only one side can and shall win) has come about by using the term to ascribe the same properties to all. However, the properties are not the same; Maine's standards are quite different from Virginia's. Elements of standards can be quite good, such as to focus on the progress of all students through disaggregated data, equalization of funding for poor students and communities, and additional or targeted resources. Some states allow for variances for schools and districts to develop their own assessment. And yes, there are cases where it is good that standards can be used to close and reorganize a school that has done a disservice to students and parents. Standards can be demeaning and harmful in equating education with single, narrowly derived tests and standards, and they can be terribly positive in challenging schools and communities to leave no student behind (Gallagher, 2000).[4] We need to acknowledge simultaneous realities as pieces of the real world if we are to educate all students better than before.

Pedagogical Moves and Hurt

The "single-truth" wars have created much pain among teachers and school leaders who are swept onto the battleground: whole language versus phonics, activity-centered versus direct instruction, competition versus cooperative learning. When whole language gained currency as the way to teach reading, teachers using phonics were lambasted, swept over, and made to feel they were evil, archaic, fascist practitioners of an indefensible method. Recently, the opposing force has won in states led by California and Texas. They have blamed language immersion and inventive spelling as the cause of literacy doom in America. Now teachers of whole language feel abandoned and rejected as feel-good, self-esteem contributors to the demise of basic skills. These periodic surges and countersurges occur because one set of believers ignores any possible merit on the other side. Isn't it possible that many highly literate and culturally diverse people you and I both know were taught how to read mainly by decoding, phonics, and grammatical rules? Isn't it equally obvious that many highly literate and culturally diverse people have learned to read through literacy immersion, writing workshops, and experiential learning? Why is it so difficult to accept that having an open mind about education possibilities should be a virtue rather than a liability?

Cooperative versus competitive learning is another such brawl. Cooperation is a key aspect of how one learns with and from others; it undergirds much of community, civic, and business life. Research exists that demonstrates the power of structured team activity in academic and social behavior. Yet humans, as part of the animal kingdom, also have other learning traits of dominance, power, and testing self against others that have allowed them to survive. Cooperation and competition are not different versions of humanity; they are different dimensions of the same humanity. Thus there is evidence that both cooperation and competition bring out high performance in an individual.

The overarching debate about progressive, learner-centered schools versus teacher-centered direct-instruction schools will be my last venture into the foolishness of single truth. This debate simplifies and silences cultural and family values, as Lisa Delpit so eloquently writes in *Other People's Children* (1995). To expect students to conform to certain manners, to expect them to learn what adults determine is important for them, to be didactic in instruction, and to use call-and-response measures has been the source of great success for teachers and leaders such as Marva Collins, Jaime Escalante, and Lorraine Monroe, and a number of school programs.[5]

Regardless of what one personally believes about the atmosphere of such classrooms and schools, students and parents in these settings see didactic methods as an expression of teachers' love, care, and cultural solidarity (Carter, 1999; Irvine, 2000). To demand that students learn and to go to almost any length to see that their students can compete with other students in the country are sources of great pride, not despair. Even so, progressive classrooms and schools that are activity- or project-centered cultivate imagination, problem solving, and self responsibility, and a variety of intellectual pursuits have, in the hands of the most dedicated teachers, also attained incredible success for students. Thus such educators as Elliott Wigginton, Deborah Meier, David Smith, George Wood, Gloria Ladson-Billings, Sonya Nieto, and J. Mahiri have shown the power of inquiry-centered, progressive learning. Why is it that progressive educators almost never cite the success of nonprogressive schools, and likewise, traditional educators never cite the success of progressive schools? It can only be that each group has divinity, intelligence, and all-encompassing wisdom on their side.[6]

My point is *not* that all methods, techniques, curricula, and structures are of equal worth and that "anything goes" is acceptable. My point is that when a group of students and parents or caretakers choose to be with a group of educators dedicated to a particular philosophy and way of learning, the results for students can be awesome. No one group should have the presumption or power to tell another group that only their way is the right way. Instead, within public purpose and criteria, we should be seeking, testing, and developing research-based alternative conceptions and practices of successful education. Kenneth Wilson, a Nobel laureate in physics, remarked about the need to test a multitude of educational approaches through longitudinal research and self-correction to find out what works well and how to use, discard, or adapt to other settings (Wilson and Daviss, 1994), not so we can eventually prove that one way is the only way but instead to allow differing conceptions of education to flourish in the marketplace of public education.

Religion in America and an Educated American

America is the country with the highest percentage of citizens actively involved in religious and spiritual practice of all Western nations (Lipset, 1996; Nord, 1995). Why? Because it is historically the only country that has no official state religion and no divine story behind its creation. Those countries that do have a history of official state religion—a one way to believe for all—have the lowest percentage of citizen involvement in religious practice. This example offers detail as to why we must avoid a single-government (local, state, or national) conception of education. The analogy with religion ends at a certain point, as government needs to be neutral and not use public funds to promote any particular set of religious beliefs. But government must use public funds to support a public education consistent with democratic ideals (Dayton and Glickman, 1994; Barber, 1992; and Gutmann, 1987). The best way to do so is to create a system of state schools that promote various conceptions of an educated American within public criteria.

Public education can be defined in several overlapping ways. Public education is funded via taxpayers, it is an education for the public, it is open and without cost to students and caretakers, it is compulsory, it is governed by public authority, it is nonprofit, and it always *should be* nondiscriminatory and nonrepressive of students and parents or caretakers (Gutmann, 1987). It is public because of a common good to achieve, to educate students to have a choice of life, liberty, and the pursuit of happiness for themselves and for others.

Within these definitions of public, American democracy, and thus American education, is always an experiment—most hopefully, a thoughtful one—that must constantly test how to further realize the hopes and aspirations of all its people. Whenever one truth stamps out all others, whether it be through one system of tests, one approach to curriculum, one conception of knowledge, a single method of instruction, or uniform structure of all public schools, democracy itself and education for a democracy are subverted.

Conclusion: What Do We Do?

My point, as a reformer who advocates and assists schools in the progressive tradition, is not to find an eclectic, "all things of equal merit" ground,[7] but instead to move beyond finding common ground toward a higher ground of public education that incorporates complexity and competing conceptions, a higher ground where contradictory truths must be part and parcel of American democracy. What we need is a view of our education system that supports multiple conceptions of an educated American. We need a view that holds all such conceptions to the scrutiny of research and public accountability, cementing all actions in the classroom and school within the criteria of equitable access and results for all students. American students and schools lose each time one truth gains currency and suppresses competing notions of public education.

Let me end by stating that, in my experience with schools, educational reformers, policy makers, legislators, corporate personnel, community activists, and citizens and residents at large, when it comes to education I find people of astonishingly goodwill and passionate intent who labor in the light of controversy about what our schools need or deserve. They are accused by their opponents as being self-indulgent conspirators with sinister motives, but most of them (or at least those that I know) are not so. However, many of those who are most influential or powerful are singularly convinced that theirs is the true way to improve education, and all other ways are false, bad, and corrupt.

We need to come to a realization that most of the time life does not hold single truths but instead is about predicament, competing views, and apparent opposition that must be part of a principled system of American democracy and the marketplace of ideas. All public schools must be devoted to public purpose and accessible to all, and the system must value and allow multiple conceptions of education that students, parents, and faculty can choose from—some purebreds, some hybrids, and some yet to be known, but all devoted to study and examination of what happens to students and their pursuit of the American Dream.

We do this by building multiple concepts of education into every school district and state in the union. We must fight against any single model, structure, method, or system of education. We expand freedom of schools and choices for parents, faculty, and students to test new concepts of standards, assessments, and accountability under public authority. Ultimately, we hold every school and district responsible for whether they have provided an education for all children that can be documented to increase choices of life, liberty, and the pursuit of happiness. This is an American education.

Notes

1. See Hirsch (1996), Kohn (1999), Ohanian (1999), and De Pommereau (1996).
2. Both Kohn and Hirsch are against state and national standards. Hirsch believes that there must be common core standards developed at the local level; Kohn is suspicious of any standards developed outside of local educators, parents, and students within their own schools.
3. Raspberry (1999) likens this argument to jazz versus classical music. Those who advocate education as jazz see spontaneity and improvisation within great freedom as the elements of key teaching. Those who advocate education as classical music see the need for an accomplished rendition through close adherence to a single conductor. Raspberry says jazz is wonderful with greatly skilled and creative musicians, and a disaster with those who are not. Classical composition is exquisite when played by the best, but still pretty good when played by those less talented who know how to follow. So, he claims, progressive schools are jazz, great with the best; traditional schools are classical, great to pretty good with a broader range of teacher expertise and talent.
4. Again, this is a complex issue. I know of cases where a disenfranchised population of people of color and poverty have been

great supporters of traditional schools and state tests, core knowledge, and accountability schemes, and other cases where such groups have led a legal assault against traditional schools and uniform state tests and accountability plans.

5. See, for example, such schools as P.S. 161 in New York City, KIPP Academics in Texas and New York, and the Frederick Douglas Middle School in New York City.

6. I do think it's time to dismantle patron saints in education. No matter how brilliant John Dewey was—and his work has tremendously influenced me—he never wished to be an embodiment of all that it is important to know about education or the world. The same can be said about Carl Rogers, B. F. Skinner, E. Thorndike, or M. Foucault, as well as other more contemporary figures. Not coincidentally, these pedestal figures are almost all white European males, but that is a matter for another time and another discussion.

7. Actually, I prefer the term *renewal* rather than reform. As defined by Goodlad and associates, renewal is the professional practice of continuous study and improvement of schools for democratic purpose (see Glickman, 1993).

References

Barber, B. R. *An Aristocracy of Everyone: The Politics of Education and the Future of America*. New York: Ballantine, 1992.

Carter, S. C. *No Excuses: Seven Principals of Low-Income Schools Who Set the Standards for High Achievement*. Washington, D.C.: Heritage Foundation, 1999.

Dayton, J., and Glickman, C. D. "Curriculum Change and Implementation: Democratic Imperatives." *Peabody Journal of Education*, 1994, 9(4), 62–86.

Delpit, L. *Other People's Children: Cultural Conflict in the Classroom*. New York: New Press, 1995.

De Pommereau, I. "Tougher High School Standards Signal Greater Demands on Students." *Christian Science Monitor*, 1996, 88(141), 12, 1C.

Gallagher, C. "A Seat at the Table: Teachers Reclaiming Assessment Through Rethinking Accountability." *Kappan*, 2000, 81(7), 502–507.

Gates, H. L., Jr., and West, C. *The Future of the Race*. New York: Vintage, 1996.

Glickman, C. D. *Renewing America's Schools: A Guide for School-Based Action*. San Francisco: Jossey-Bass, 1993.

Glickman, C.D. *Revolutionizing America's Schools*. San Francisco: Jossey-Bass, 1998.

Gutmann, A. *Democratic Education*. Princeton, N.J.: Princeton University Press, 1987.

Hirsch, E. D., Jr. *The Schools We Need and Why We Don't Have Them*. New York: Doubleday, 1996.

Irvine, J. I. "Seeing with the Cultural Eye: Different Perspectives of African American Teachers and Researchers." DeWitt-Wallace Reader's Digest Distinguished Lecture at the annual meeting of the American Educational Research Association, New Orleans, Apr. 24, 2000.

Kohn, A. *The Schools Our Children Deserve*. Boston: Houghton Mifflin, 1999.

Lipset, S. M. *American Exceptionalism: A Double-Edged Sword*. New York: Norton, 1996.

Myers, J. "Notes on the Murder of Thirty of My Neighbors." *Atlantic Monthly*, Mar. 2000, pp. 72–86.

Nord, W. A. *Religion and American Education: Rethinking a National Dilemma*. Chapel Hill: University of North Carolina Press, 1995.

Ohanian, S. *One Size Fits Few: The Folly of Educational Standards*. Portsmouth, N.H.: Heinemann, 1999.

Raspberry, W. "Editorial Opinion: Educational Jazz Often Just Won't Work." *Houston Chronicle*, Star ed., June 25, 1999, p. A34.

Reyes, P., and others (eds.). *Lessons from High-Performing Hispanic Schools: Creating Learning Communities*. New York: Teachers College Press, 1999.

Wilson, K., and Daviss, B. *Redesigning Education*. New York: Teachers College Press, 1994.

Chapter Eighteen

Standards, Freedom, and Authority

Systemic Sense About Schools— A Commissioned Proposal to the Georgia Governor's Commission on Educational Reform

After more than a decade of contentious debate about standards, accountability, and freedom, there appear to be a number of lessons about which policies work (or would work) best for improving the educational lives of children and the capacity of schools.

As classroom teacher Philip Manna wrote:

> What makes a good school has very little to do with how rich or poor the students are or the type of curriculum that's taught. It has very little to do with special programs, expensive playing fields, huge endowments, snappy uniforms, celebrity alumni, or whether the school is wired to the Internet. What makes a good school, whether it's public or private, *is* . . . a feeling shared by the entire staff that . . . their school belongs to them. . . . When an individual school community feels it's really in control of its destiny, teachers, parents, and administrators are more inclined to do hundreds of little things it takes to make their school work. . . . This feeling only forms when a particular school community is given the freedom and authority to try what they believe is best for their students [1997, p. M7].

Recently, I was invited by the governor of Georgia and his Commission on Education Reform to write a research-based paper containing a proposal for future legislation and policies about standards and accountability for the next decade. I found the task refreshingly challenging, one in which I needed to check my own previous advocacy and carefully study what other states have done with what learning results for students, and to ask various educators and community members from a variety of economic and regional settings to react and revise my ongoing drafts. Upon final consultation with legislative and academic policy makers, I submitted a research-based plan that would be "bold, yet conservative." It was bold in the idea that all students should be educated to a high level of achievement; it was conservative in the idea that democracy and accountability flourishes at the individual school and community level closest to students.

The Systemic Tension

Newman and Wehlage (1995) found, in one of the most comprehensive national studies ever done correlating student achievement and school characteristics, that "collective responsibility" was critical to school success. It was defined as "the autonomy of the school from external constraints," "teachers' influence over their work," and often "significant authority over curriculum, school policies, and hiring" as well as "substantial authority over budget." Such collective responsibility of the school accounted for a higher level (from 54 to 137 percent) of achievement of students in mathematics and science (grades eight to ten, and grades ten to twelve). The researchers noted that "school autonomy from external constraints was a necessary condition but not sufficient" (Newmann and Wehlage, 1995). A school must *willingly* want the autonomy to serve the instructional needs of students. Simply having authority without the desire or ideas for what to do to improve teaching and learning across the school had little effect on achievement. This research is consistent with a number of other studies about decentralized authority for schools with high student achievement (Glickman, 1993; O'Neil, 1995). A school must use its authority for determining and realizing a common vision of learning—what virtually all students should be able to know and do before leaving their elementary, middle, or secondary school. Furthermore, successful schools are more than accountable for achieving learning goals determined by the district and state but hold themselves responsible for developing—with students, parents, and community members—standards and assessments of learning that require students to demonstrate and apply their accumulated learning publicly.

Simply put, there are, and always have been, extraordinarily successful schools at all K–12 levels, in all socioeconomic, geographic, and racial or ethnic categories in America that have had the leadership, talent, and human resources within their own school and surrounding community to develop outstanding educational programs and achieve higher student performance than what others in the local school district or state could determine for them. Rules and procedures from the local board or state board cannot improve a school whose employees are knowledgeable, caring, and intelligent. In fact, such rules and procedures often make student education worse by driving talented educators away. Smart people don't work well in a place where their own thinking is systematically discouraged. The best people often move out of a highly controlled place, and many leave the profession altogether.

Internal motivation is an important factor for school success. Many schools change for the better and attain a high level of achievement for all students when people within the schools have:

- Studied student progress, or the lack thereof, and targeted areas of improvement
- Kept their focus on improving teaching and learning for all students within and across classrooms
- Used authority, flexibility, and control over internal resources, operations, and budgets to carry out their plans for school improvement and high standards for all students
- Shared in the decision making and held themselves publicly accountable for the results.

The danger of research findings is that these results can lead to a simplistic perception of the school and the teaching profession.

Not all schools have the leadership, willingness, or knowledge to change for the better. There are classrooms and schools stuck in routine that does not challenge all students. Their educators either do not know what to do or blame others for the conditions of student nonlearning. They are content with a secure, low-threat environment of mediocrity. Nevertheless, there are other schools where people are willing to take on greater autonomy and responsibility but need more knowledge, study skills, and professional development to change teaching and learning for the better. Thus a comprehensive state policy (or local district policy) for school improvement is not a single recipe, as in thinking that total local control for all individual schools is best or that centralized and mandated reform is best. Education policies, rules, and procedures must account for the complex reality of differences between schools and the need for a combination of top-down and bottom-up initiatives.

Comprehensive policies should account for giving all schools the total school-based authority *that they request* for a pilot period of time, to find where the actual capability, talent, and commitment exist in the school. At the same time, policies should provide more assistance and targeting of schools that need or request external structure and models of instruction. As noted researcher Robert Slavin points out (1998), there are three types of schools: "sand," "brick," and "seed." Sand schools always are shifting and have no foundation for improvement. They are not stable enough to study, change, and follow through on their plans. Brick schools have basic stability, cohesion, and interest in improvement; they need examples, guidance, and technical assistance. Seed schools are places that, when given support and autonomy, take their own ideas, plant them in fertile ground, and nurture them to fruition. Seed schools lead in developing new ways of education that result in ongoing improvement for all individuals and groups of children. They demonstrate superior ways of grouping students, developing and using new curriculum and learning methods, extending student learning into the local community and vice versa, embracing technology as a tool for a higher level of student utilization of knowledge, and reinvigorating the public part of public education.

All schools, in time, must be viewed as having the potential to become seed schools.

The Right Standards and Assessments for Accountability

Any specific recommendation about school authority in regard to a comprehensive policy of state and local accountability must take into consideration the specific nature of standards, assessments, rewards, and sanctions made. Authority within an accountability system is only as good as the standards, assessments, and benchmarks of accountability.

Particular legislation in Texas, Maryland, North Carolina, Kentucky, Maine, Vermont, Wisconsin, Minnesota, Washington, and California was reviewed; the positions on standards, assessments, and accountability given here are from those states where student achievement gain and ranking have led the nation. New policy can take the best lessons and greatest successes from these states and add and revise according to successful large-scale school change efforts (Fullan, 1999; Elmore, Peterson, and McCarthey, 1996; Darling-Hammond, 1996), and create powerful variation accounting for the unique features of a district or state (its population, demography, economy, and educational history). A comprehensive policy supports autonomy for the purpose of pushing schools to reach a higher level of educational achievement for *all* students and pushes the district and the state to sustain constantly improving standards, achievements, and educational design as an example for further changes in policy.

State standards and corresponding assessments should be guided by six core principles.

State Standards and Assessments Must Be Done Right!

Assessments and student tests must be referenced against state standards, and assessment must incorporate knowledge, understanding, skills, problem solving, and applications—not merely recall of information. The assessments must be developed and implemented in multiple forms. A student performance mastery level must be kept at an absolute measure that does not change for five to ten years. In this way, the percentage of students passing the mastery level can be constantly adjusted upward, and the school and district can measure themselves against a fixed, absolute point. Improvement, or the lack thereof, with increased expectations for all students, parents, and schools is then clear and easy to gauge.

Do Assessments at Specific Grade Levels

State assessments of student achievement for high-stakes evaluation of schools and districts and for advancement or graduation of students must be done at no more than three or four ages or grade levels (such as fourth year, seventh year, and eleventh year). The reason for requiring state assessments at three or four age levels is to give the district and schools the opportunity to determine their own needs, additional standards, and assessments in intervening years. This has been the decisive strength in achievement gains made in Kentucky, Vermont, and Maine that allow schools and districts to supplement or support the state assessments with their own way of improving teaching, learning, configuring of classrooms, and instruction time. An optional battery of state-developed tests on key assessment standards (reading and mathematics, for example) should be available for the individual school to use for yearly diagnostic purposes to help focus improvement efforts.

Vary the Assessments

Assessments have to be provided to students at multiple times and in multiple ways for demonstrating mastery of state standards. For example, high school exit assessment related to science standards should be available for students to take a number of times, if needed, during the tenth, eleventh, and twelfth grades. There must be at least two methods for a student to demonstrate mastery of the standard (perhaps a paper-and-pencil test and a controlled science experiment with external evaluation criteria). Differing versions of assessments of the same standards can be found in Maryland, Milwaukee (Wisconsin), and Maine. This type of assessment ensures that students can demonstrate the knowledge, skills, and understanding required of the subject and not be penalized by use of one particular form of testing or overreliance on written language.

Assessments Must Be Independent of Coursework

High school students must be able to take assessments regardless of having taken the courses aligned with the particular standards. If passed, students automatically receive credit and an appropriate grade for the course. This option for students to earn credit through examination at any time in their schooling allows schools and districts to offer a variety of instructional models, including tutorials, independent study, apprenticeship or internship, and learning via technology, in addition to or in lieu of a traditional course. Credit through examination already exists as a normal procedure in high school advanced placement exams for college credit and for students from a home school environment to receive course credit upon entering a public school. This shift to student performance, rather than seat hours in a class, challenges students to move through school at a rigorous pace, and it challenges each school to develop alternative instructional models of time and delivery. Many schools will continue with traditional courses as the primary means of learning, but such a system of examination for course credit gives advanced students, as well as those who have struggled in a typical course, an incentive to move more quickly.

Make Assessment Guidelines Explicit and Public

Every high school, middle school, and elementary school must have, as part of high-stakes state standards, at least one school- and community-based academic learning standard with explicit guidelines and assessment criteria for what every student must demonstrate to fulfill graduation or school promotion requirements. Assessment of such a locally derived standard must be done in a public setting where the larger community of parents, local school board members, and others can view how students have used the accumulation of their learning (that is, science, mathematics, technology, English) with direct application to one's community (a library project, a character education initiative, a study and analysis of economic opportunities, a history of one's town or local environment, a community service project). This school- or community-based academic standard should be developed *with* parents and other community members, as an expectation of what the local community expects of students and their schools. In the last month of each school year, there should be an open house for the community to view this culminating work. Emphasis on standards developed locally with parents and community members reinforces the traditional, democratic aim of the public school to educate students who can use their knowledge, as active and wise citizens, to help strengthen their community. Maine, Vermont, and Minnesota have been pioneers in this work.

Use Appropriate Data

All assessments of state standards used for public accountability of schools—in earning awards, designations, rewards, assistance, sanctions, and penalties—must use disaggregated data from students according to race or ethnicity and socioeconomic level. Public schools must be held accountable for the learning of *all* students. In the past, aggregated and averaged student achievement scores of schools often masked the uneven quality of expectations and education for groups of students of various races or ethnicities and socioeconomic classes. The strength of the Texas accountability system, according to a recent Heritage Foundation report (Palmaffy, 1998), has been holding each Texas school accountable for its entire school population. No rewards or recognition can be earned without a satisfactory success rate for all groups of students. For example, all groups, including the three major subgroups—African American, Hispanic, and low socioeconomic class—must show an 80 percent pass rate on all assessments to receive a positive, recognized rating.

If any one subgroup falls below the minimum passing rate, the school receives an unacceptable, low-performing designation. The result of holding schools accountable for all groups of students has resulted over the past five years in achievement gain for all, including white, upper-class, and middle-class students, and the most dramatic achievement rise in the nation of low-income and minority students. The gains on the Texas criterion assessments have also paralleled a rise on other indicators, such as college and admission rates, SAT and ACT scores, national education assessments, AP examinations, improved attendance, and reduction of the dropout rate.

This deliberate attention to socioeconomic class and race or ethnic groups has sent a powerful message that education can and will work for all students, with a no-excuses mentality embraced across the ideological and political spectrum of citizens and legislators in Texas.

A Policy for Local School Authority, Assistance, and Designations

Here is a four-component policy proposed for school-based authority as part of the overall new criteria for standards, assessments, and public accountability. The states with the highest gain in student achievement have sent a message to each individual school that "You are responsible for improved student learning. . . . Here is the standard of progress you must achieve, and here is the flexibility you need to get there" (Cornett and Gaines, 1997). The message is based on four related ideas:

1. Most local educators (principals, faculty, and staff) can be trusted with school-based authority to improve education for all students.

2. Decentralized authority to the school becomes an ongoing and normal way of work when a school demonstrates that previous trust and flexibility accorded to it *does* lead to a higher level of achievement for all students.

3. If school-based authority *does not* lead to a higher achievement level for all students, trust is broken and local district school boards and the state have the responsibility to intervene and centralize control. They must give assistance until reasonable trust can be reestablished.

4. To ensure that the entire education system is always preparing for the future, there must be a limited number of state-approved prototype schools and districts developing and piloting standards, assessments, and accountability systems beyond current usage.

These four components, with necessary resources for planning time, professional development, equitable funding for schools, and collaboration with parents and community, are essential to achieving immediate standards and revitalizing the profession of education as well as ensuring that future improvement in the education system is ongoing.

What authority should the individual school have? It is time for a dramatic and reasoned challenge to normal school operations. It is recommended that over a three-year trial period all schools be granted by their local district, local school board, and state agencies all of the authority that each school believes necessary to achieve improved student results! In exchange for this flexibility, each school can be bound by letters of understanding with their district and the state for meeting academic achievement standards, including their own culminating academic standard developed with parents and the community. In effect, every public school will, for this three-year initial period, have the same authority, responsibility, flexibility, and process as outlined in the charter school guidelines that are currently used by many states for a limited number of schools. This flexibility and authority is to be accorded to every school that wishes to assume such responsibility, as determined by ratification by the internal governance process of the individual school and its parents.

Each school not wishing to have total school-based authority will propose a more limited letter of understanding with the school board and district, detailing the particular domains and variances over which it wishes to have responsibility. School boards and districts will continue to exercise their constitutional authority over the district as a whole, particularly regarding district vision, district standards, goals, assessment, student assignment, transportation, buildings and maintenance, public relations, and distribution and oversight of total district budget and district personnel. The district delegates internal control and authority as proposed and ratified by the school in its letter of understanding. It is imperative that school boards, districts, and schools honor an agreement of this kind for the three-year initial period and not intervene in the internal management and decisions of the school. Table 18.1 illustrates domains of authority that a school may acquire.

Of all these areas, the most crucial to school success are (1) having school-based authority over the entire operational budget for curriculum, instruction, teaching materials, and professional development; (2) allocation of instructional time, instructional placement of students, and instructional staffing patterns; (3) hiring of faculty, staff, and administrative leadership; (4) supervision and evaluation of staff and faculty; and (5) developing unique partnerships with parents, businesses, and community agencies. Over the three-year initial period, progress at meeting achievement standards and parent endorsement of the school's progress for improving learning for all students would be necessary if there is to be a four-year renewal of school-based authority. Endorsement of parents is determined by significant representation on a school-based

Table 18.1. Domains of Educational Authority for Schools

Minimal-Impact Decisions	Core-Impact Decisions	Critical-Impact Decisions
Parent programs	Textbook adoption	School budget
In-service days	Curriculum	Hiring of personnel
Small budgets	Staff development	Utilization of personnel
Duty-free lunch	Coaching and supervision	Personnel evaluation
	Instructional programs	Partnerships and parent participation
	Student assessment	Instructional time
	Instructional budget	
	Discipline policy	

decision-making council (33 percent or more representation), or by a formal vote of parents endorsing or not endorsing the value of education provided to their students. It is suggested that the vote for renewal be set at a minimum of 80 percent approval by at least half of all parents.

School-Based Budgeting

Responsibility for expenditures and resources is vital to school authority and accountability. Site-based management and shared decision making is often espoused in district and state policies but rarely practiced. The reason is that many local districts and states have not allocated total resources and budgets to the individual school. The result is often a wasteful and frustrating experience for a school that spends much time in a group making decisions but lacks the resources for implementation. Most often, any new expenditure or allocation decided by a school for staffing, hiring, programs, schedule, purchasing, or materials must be approved by the district. Thus the request for funds to the district keeps actual control of important decisions at the district level. In effect, without control of resources, the school really has little overall authority.

Odden and Busch (1998) found that high-performance schools actually had control over their budgets to create smaller size classrooms and provide more intensive tutorials and services to students and staff in a way different from normal, district regulations. In such places, the district created the formula of a base amount for all children, adjusted the formula for special student needs and size of the school, and then gave the budget to the school.

Odden and Busch recommend that:

- Seventy-five to 85 percent of the entire operating budget be given to the school in one yearly lump sum
- The individual school reserve 2.5–4.0 percent of its operating budget for planning and implementing ongoing professional development and study of ways to improve teaching and learning
- The school have the authority to determine its own resource allocation for ratios of aides, teachers, specialists, lead teachers, substitutes, and so on
- The school purchase its professional development activities

The Edmonton (Alberta) school district decentralized budgets to individual schools more than twenty-two years ago. The result has been significant achievement gain. Michael Strembitsky, the superintendent over that time period, remarked that it took several years for the schools and district to work out the new relationship of school control over the budget and how schools would purchase their own staff development services and assistance. At that time, many central office district personnel feared that their positions would become unnecessary. The reality was the opposite. The demand for district services went up as schools purchased—individually or in pools—certain types of district expertise and assistance. The Edmonton district also allows schools to carry money over from year to year. This has eliminated the fiscally questionable annual practice of spending out school accounts—whether expenditures were a priority or not—by the end of each fiscal year.

Once a district delegates control over the school budget to the schools in a lump sum, the schools can then do what they propose. As Strembitsky put it: "There are people who dismiss the importance of school budgeting, because they claim that they want their people interested in instruction, not money. The reality is . . . until you give schools control over how they use their financial resources . . . they are focused on resource acquisition [not instruction]" (O'Neil, 1995).

School Designations and Assistance

Each school determines with the district the type and degree of assistance needed for the initial three-year period. After the trial period has concluded, the school is classified by three or four performance levels, on the basis of a public accountability profile. Designations might be "excellent performance," "high performance," "acceptable performance," and "unacceptable performance." An excellent-performance school would receive recognition, a monetary reward used as additional resources to the school, and continue with unrestricted autonomy. A high-performing school would receive lesser recognition, a lesser monetary award, and continue with the same or more school-based authority over the next period of time. An acceptable school would receive no recognition or additional state monetary award and have to develop with its district a targeted plan for improvement and needed technical assistance. The district would determine the needed assistance. An unacceptable school would receive a warning and a one-year probationary notice either to show improvement or be in danger of closure or reconstitution. The state, with a team of assistants, would develop with the school and district an audit of needed changes and then provide targeted resources and assistance.

To make the needed assistance available to the school, the state develops a network of carefully screened exemplary school practitioners (teachers, administrators, and other distinguished educators) and expert personnel from the state department of education, universities and colleges, and other school improvement programs and networks with longitudinal evidence of successful work. A state team then offers the unacceptable schools:

- A follow-up audit that examines and analyzes the conditions, personnel, and reasons for low performance on the basis of effective school research
- Fifteen to twenty days of onsite assistance, and more if needed
- A bank of validated educational programs, curriculum models, instructional methods, and professional development that the low-performing school could choose, adapt, and commit itself to implement

These services also might be extended to schools in other categories, in rank order of need.

The Prototype Schools and Districts

Every time there is a major overhaul of state education policy, the tendency surfaces to think that the work is completed and the best system has been put in place. As policy theorists explain, if improvements are not readily forthcoming, then what usually follows is intensification by the state of the rules and regulations that simply are not working. Intensification of rules that do not work creates a larger monitoring state-bureaucracy, kills the spirit of reform, and deadens new ideas for improvement (Broder, 1999; Fullan, 1999; Tyack and Cuban, 1995). Successful businesses use future prototypes to fine-tune, adjust, or revise their current operations (Broder, 1999). Rather than wait another ten to fifteen years to rework the next education system, prototype schools and school districts should research and create policy modifications and future alternatives.

What is proposed—as part of new school-based policies, legislation regarding authority, public school accountability, and standards and assessment—is selection of ten to twelve individual schools and four to six school districts, in numerous regions and socioeconomic populations, to apply to become "prototype schools" and "prototype districts," with special authority to develop their own standards and assessments that have the potential to be more relevant and rigorous than the ones currently being developed and implemented by the state. These schools and districts would research and design their own assessments for public school accountability—including the expected criteria that *all* students and groups must achieve. The state may require these schools and districts to administer current state assessments solely for statewide data gathering, but not as high-risk student assessment or as a current public accountability measure.

Requirements for applying to be a prototype school or prototype district have to be carefully established. Application as a district should be initiated by the local superintendents and local school boards. Application as a prototype school can be initiated by a current public school with the support of its local school board and superintendent. In the case of a school to be newly created by a team of teachers and parents, it could be granted a prototype designation by applying directly to a state review commission. All such *public* prototype schools need to have a documented open admissions policy, reflecting the diversity of students in its surrounding community, and comply with other state and federal laws applying to public schools and public institutions. The prototype designation might be for a five-year period and require a commitment of the schools and districts to make public their standards, assessments, learning results, and accountability measures, and to participate with the state in ongoing improvement of the current state system. Becoming a prototype school or prototype district is not a way to circumvent state expectations and high standards that are expected of all students. Rather, prototype designation is for those schools and districts that want to develop and test higher and more comprehensive expectations, standards, assessments, and accountability.

Closing Thoughts

This comprehensive policy about standards and school-based authority represents a major change in the thinking and practices of most schools, communities, districts, and state agencies, which are torn by important and paralyzing ideological debate on the nature of standards, assessment, and decentralization. This policy incorporates the need to be respectful of freedom and authority balanced by comprehensive and public assessment.

Seymour Sarason reminds us, over and over again, that a major rethinking about education purpose, schools, and freedom has to include start-up and developmental time for implementation. The plan is realistic and research-based, and it reflects the reality of schools. If done as part of a whole system policy approach, it can lead to increasingly higher-level achievement for all students. The plan gives educators and local communities the authority and flexibility to be truly accountable for their actions. Those schools (with the assistance of their district) that plan and act upon the commitment to all their students will excel and be recognized or rewarded accordingly. Those schools and communities that cannot find a way to use their freedom wisely to educate all students well will be notified and greatly assisted (and if need be, foreclosed).

My final point is that we need to rethink three ideas about standards, freedom, and opposition. First, standards and assessment are essential to the idea of equity for, and the capacity of, virtually all students. Second, the freedom of a school to control its own resources and use the best of learning practices is essential to school success and the attractiveness of a profession. Third, oppositional work—in the form of individual school and district prototypes that challenge current standards and assessments—has to be integrated into a larger systemic policy. It may be time to think there can be a sane, research-based, and enthusiastic way to provide for a better future for all students and schools in America.

References

Broder, D. "Winning at Baldrige Has Special Meaning." *Burlington Free Press*, July 14, 1999, p. 8A.

Cornett, L. M., and Gaines, G. F. "Accountability in the 1990s: Holding Schools Responsible for Student Achievement." (Educational Benchmarks 1997, brochure). Atlanta: Southern Regional Education Board, 1997.

Darling-Hammond, L. *The Right to Learn: A Blueprint for Creating Schools That Work*. San Francisco: Jossey-Bass, 1996.

Elmore, R. F., Peterson, P. L., and McCarthey, S. J. *Restructuring in the Classroom: Teaching, Learning, and School Organization*. San Francisco: Jossey-Bass, 1996.

Fullan, M. *Change Forces: The Sequel*. London: Falmer Press, 1999.

Glickman, C. D. *Renewing America's Schools: A Guide for School-Based Actions*. San Francisco: Jossey-Bass, 1993.

Manna, P. "The Best Schools Are Hooked on a Feeling." *Boston Sunday Globe*, June 20, 1997, p. M7.

Newmann, F. M., and Wehlage, G. G. *Successful School Restructuring: A Report to the Public and Educators*. Madison: Wisconsin Center for Educational Research, 1995.

Odden, A., and Busch, C. *Financing Schools for High Performance: Strategies for Improving the Use of Educational Resources*. San Francisco: Jossey-Bass, 1998.

O'Neil, J. "On Tapping the Power of School-Based Management: A Conversation with Michael Strembitsky." *Educational Leadership*, 1995, 53(4), 66–70.

Palmaffy, T. "The Gold Star State: How Texas Jumped to the Head of the Class in Elementary School Achievement." *Policy Review*, Mar.-Apr. 1998, no. 88. Accessed June 30, 1999. [www.policyreview.com/mar98/gold-star.html].

Slavin, R. E. "Sand, Bricks, and Seeds: School Change Strategies and Readiness for Reform." In A. Hargreaves, A. Lieberman, M. Fullan, and D. Hopkins (eds.), *International Handbook of Educational Change: Part Two*. Dordrecht, Netherlands: Kluwer, 1998.

Tyack, D., and Cuban, L. *Tinkering Toward Utopia: A Century of Public School Reform*. Cambridge, Mass.: Harvard University Press, 1995.

Part Six

The Crux of Education, Democracy, and the Future of Our Place

Chapter Nineteen

Revolution, Education, and the Practice of Democracy

The greatest experiment in humankind began with the Declaration of Independence of the American colonies in 1776 (West, 1993). Though the experiment did not apply to women, the poor, or the enslaved, the democratic belief of each citizen being equal and having inalienable rights to life, liberty, and the pursuit of happiness made the future inclusion of previously denied individuals "at least possible" (West, 1993, p. 8).

What is often overlooked in today's exhortations and reports about changing, improving, reforming, and innovating schools is the primary reason U.S. schools exist, and thus what professional educators are hired to do. The means for enabling all persons to take their rightful place as valued and valuable citizens of a democracy was to be done through a certain type of education. The failure of U.S. education is not in the achievement of individual students (Mathews, 1996). Students from wealthy and highly educated families do as well academically today as they have done in the past (Berliner and Biddle, 1995). Rather, education has failed to complete the work of the revolution: to provide an education for virtually all students—across all economic classes and family cultures—to become successful citizens (Mathews, 1996).

Citizenship education is not simply narrow knowledge of how government works and how to exercise one's political vote; it addresses the more comprehensive understandings of freedom: active participation; deliberation; judgment; and choices of intellectual, economic, social, aesthetic, and recreational life. It is this comprehensive view of education for all citizens that we are missing. Though the United States is the wealthiest nation in the world, its most highly schooled citizens are withdrawing from the life of their community and neighborhood ("College Freshmen Less Interested . . .," 1998). After nearly twenty years of steady educational advancement by poor and minority groups, we are now seeing a pattern of retreat (Haycock, 1998).

I wish to begin with two simple points and then suggest specific applications for teachers and other school leaders. First, democracy is both formal government and a theory of how humans learn. Second, if a democratic theory of learning is practiced in our classrooms and schools, then we will educate all students much more powerfully than ever before. The next generation of all citizens is thus capable of individual and collective choices that revitalize the democratic revolution in a way that we currently cannot imagine.

For educators not to embrace democracy as the core practice of teaching and learning is to ignore our primary mission. Rather than being the stewards of the democratic dream, we would contribute to the apathy, cynicism, and stratification of citizens today who dwell in the same land but have no common journey.

The Educational Theory of Democracy

Democracy is best established and improved by a society that protects and ensures freedom of expression, general diffusion of knowledge, a free press, separation of church and state (so all religions and religious points of view may flourish), and unencumbered pursuit of truth. Thomas Jefferson said if he had to choose between government or a free press, he would choose a free press because free ideas interacting with the curiosity of citizens would always promote a far better democratic society than government control alone (Peterson, 1975; Randall, 1993).

A basic idea of secular democracy is that all humans are capable of educating themselves when given an environment that allows them to participate actively with knowledge. The result of such participation is that individuals grasp the accepted knowledge of the day; are able to challenge, critique, and deliberate upon it; and eventually are able to form their own judgments and conclusions (Dewey, 1916; hooks, 1994; Ladson-Billings, 1994; Piaget, 1973). Such an education in a free society results in citizens being able to govern their own individual and collective lives in a way superior to that of kings, aristocrats, and dictators. Jefferson, the chief writer of the Declaration of Independence, deserves criticism for inconsistency in his own beliefs and certain life practices; nonetheless, he underscored the primary educational theory of democracy: that citizens are capable of learning for themselves when endowed with a rich, interactive, and information-based environment (Glickman, 1998; Barber, 1992).

The simplest idea to understand rhetorically, but the most difficult idea to practice in the school and classroom, is of democracy as an educative process. The public school is the primary institution for providing an educated citizenry for democracy. Yet most schools show in everyday action a disbelief in such preparation. Most operate on the basis of hierarchy, control, and power. They do not embrace equality among faculty, staff, and administrators, and they bypass any substantial contribution from students, parents, and local citizens in making important decisions affecting the school community (McNeil, 1986; Sarason, 1990; Tyack and Cuban, 1995; Hill, Pierce, and Guthrie, 1997). Students every day see adults practicing a form of life diametrically opposed to what they hear espoused from the core questions of what we should be doing in schools, curricula, placement decisions, scheduling of students, allocation of resources, and teaching to give each child his or her inalienable right to life, liberty and the pursuit of happiness. What is just, fair, and democratic? Questions of that sort should be the heart and soul of school practice, yet they are rarely raised or used as criteria for classroom and school decisions. Issues of unequal allocation of resources, a rich learning environment for some students but not for others, and assumptions about students being capable or incapable of great learning are often avoided; thus, the status quo remains in effect (Delpit, 1995). There are no simple answers to core questions about race, class, ethnicity, gender, and culture. Yet without raising them and looking at what can be done to give access to a better future for virtually all students, we are as guilty today as those of the past who practiced great undemocratic contradiction and hypocrisy.

The Power of Democratic Learning

In previous work, I have cited the learning benefits for students in classrooms and schools that practice a pedagogy of democracy (Glickman, 1993). Studies involving thousands of subjects and hundreds of schools during the past fifty years show that students in prodemocratic elementary, middle, and high schools outperform other comparable students on virtually all achievement measures, including traditional standardized tests (Aiken, 1942; Joyce, Wolf, and Calhoun, 1993; Newmann, Marks, and Gamoran, 1995; Meier, 1995). This evidence cuts across ethnic, racial, and socioeconomic classifications. Students in such a pedagogy:

- Work actively with problems, ideas, materials, and other people as they learn skills and content
- Have an escalating degree of choice, both as individuals and as a group, within the parameters provided by the teacher
- Are responsible to their peers, teachers, parents, and school community, using educational time purposefully, intelligently, and productively
- Share their learning with one another, teachers, parents, and other community members
- Decide how to make their learning a contribution to their community
- Assume growing responsibility for securing resources (of people and materials outside the school) and finding a place where they can apply and further their learning

- Demonstrate what they know and can do in a public setting and receive public feedback
- Work together and learn from one another, individually and in groups, at a pace that challenges all

Prodemocratic pedagogy does *not* feature the absence of such skills as reading, writing, and arithmetic, or content studies in humanities, science, and the arts. Furthermore, students in a prodemocratic pedagogy do *not*:

- Decide for themselves if, what, or how they will learn
- Learn the same material at the same time
- Sit and listen passively
- Get categorized, labeled, and placed in fixed-ability groups

Democratic pedagogy in the school is a set of purposeful activities, always building toward increasing student activity, choice, participation, connection, and contribution. It aims for students, individually and collectively, to take on greater responsibility for their own learning. It is not a pedagogy in which teachers open the classroom doors and tell students to be free. The teacher has a unique responsibility of position, experience, age, and wisdom to guide students to the fundamental aim: learning to be free. As such, at any moment in time a student or classroom might not look active, busy, or egalitarian; but over time the teacher is responsible for seeking, supporting, and demanding greater participation, voice, choice, and contribution.

In forming a learning compact, an educator asks of self and students:

- What decisions should I as a teacher make to ensure that everyone learns well?
- What decisions should you as students make to ensure that everyone learns well?

- What decisions should we make jointly to ensure that everyone learns well?

Teachers as Democratic Agents

Educators, teachers, and other school leaders are the keepers of the dream; we entrust them, day by day, with the job of completing the American Revolution (Nord, 1995; Ladson-Billings, 1994). Furthermore, it is with those teachers and in those schools practicing the core elements of democracy in educational activities that virtually all students succeed. Sadly, teachers (and other educators) in most traditional schools must choose to rebel against attempts to condition, and do so openly, with "full awareness of the responsibility involved as well as of the risks" (Greene, 1973, p. 171).

Teachers first must seek out colleagues—other teachers, parents, and school leaders—as peer coaches and critical friends. They must find at least one other person in the school with whom to critique, observe, and solve problems about an activity or assessment of student performance. They should ask parents and community members to help students develop a demonstration of what they are learning and suggest how students might contribute new skills to their own home, business, or community agency. Feedback from parents and community members on classroom activity and student assessment can improve student learning and participation.

Change involves recursive human decisions among competing tension, and it rarely results in a utopian breakthrough in which students always accomplish excellent work. Democratic education is always purposeful but, moment by moment, not so predictable. As a result, inclusiveness and student participation in classroom activity can create spontaneous and awkward moments. A student may unexpectedly ask a teacher his or her own views on a politically charged, controversial issue in the school. If the teacher is momentarily at a loss as to how to reply, the student may feel encouraged to make his or her own learning arrangements. Should the student, in doing so, inadvertently offend a powerful community member, the teacher must reassert authority over the class-room, prompting challenge from students regarding classroom democracy. Or a parent may walk in unannounced and complain in front of the entire class that his or her child is not being taught anything. Or students may exercise what they believe to be their freedom of expression by being rude to a person who looks and acts differently from them. The constant leadership dilemma of a change-oriented teacher is when to assert authority, lessen it, or challenge a student. These decisions are not easily determined. An occurrence with a student, parent, or peer often does not have clear and immediate resolution. To acknowledge this unpredictability with others and ask for a progress check with students, parents, and colleagues both lessens their defensiveness and encourages further self-correction and student progress.

Educational Leaders as Democratic Agents

Ideally, changes in teaching and learning will occur in a school in which all members develop and share the same beliefs about the organization; education; decision-making rules; and planning and implementing changes in curriculum, instruction, staff develop-ment, and assessment. Perhaps most important is ongoing action research to study changes and assess the impact on student learn-ing as to the covenant of vision, the decision-making charter, and the critical study of action research (Glickman, 1993). School leaders (principals, department heads, and teacher leaders) should consider the suggestions given here in beginning or furthering any schoolwide change.

School leaders should challenge the school community to examine and explain what is meant by the word *democracy* and how it applies to schools and education. Many U.S. schools have a written mission statement or vision that uses the word. To ask fac-ulty, parents, staff, students, and others to "unpack" the word into educational and operational terms creates awareness that the school has a responsibility larger than each individual teacher's preference to exercise autonomy in his or her own classroom. The discussion helps all members move beyond a simplistic notion of democracy as majority rule, individual liberty, or a free market.

Asking for examples of curriculum, grouping, teaching and learning methods, and assessments that are congruent (or incongruent) with the definition of democracy encourages people to be specific, give practical examples, and develop a public rationale as to why the practice fits. Creating the opportunity for others to discuss whether they agree with the examples and rationale is another good idea. This is one reason networking with other schools is quite helpful. To critique teaching and learning practices of classrooms and schools different from one's own initially creates less defensiveness and more open discussion. The next phase is to discuss examples within their own classroom and program in a manner that encourages and models critical, serious, civil, and at times playful talk with each other.

School leaders should establish what actual demonstration of democratic learning would look like in student achievement—for all students across all levels of the school—and how they would be publicly assessed. What should students be able to do when they leave this school, and how will they demonstrate such learning? This process of establishing a schoolwide policy for demonstrating learning might take several years to plan, implement, and evaluate, but the school then has a pedagogical direction for everyone who works with students.

These questions might guide the work of a school:

• What does it mean to be a democratic school? Does it mean that democracy is only for professionals and not for others, or can democracy and professionalism complement each other? What should be the rules for parents, students, community members, and district representatives? With which decisions should educators mainly concern themselves, and which decisions—for a matter of expediency, expertise, and consequence—should be decided by others?

• What is democracy? Is it only governance and decision-making procedures, or is it a way of learning and living together among all those who attend and work in a school? Does a school show its belief in democracy by using curriculum and instruction in a way that demands more involvement, participation, choice, and contribution from students?

• What does a democratic school look like? Imagine what a classroom and a school would look like five years from now if they were truly democratic. What would an observer see? What would be the school's decision-making process? What would the day-to-day curriculum, schedules, and student activities look like across the school? How would action research be used to establish internal schoolwide demonstrations and standards of student learning?

• What do all students learn in a democratic and professional school, and how is it demonstrated, assessed, and measured? All student learning should involve comprehensive and ongoing participation, application, connection, contribution, and responsibility. What should the assessment standards be for such purposeful student learning? What should students be able to demonstrate? How and by whom should such demonstration be assessed?

There are also appropriate roles for parents, citizens, and students in activating the practice of democracy as both the means and ends of learning for all students (Glickman, 1998).

Establishing Enduring Beliefs

Contemporary values without a strong connection to a historic, fundamental vision of life are a faddish opinion with a short life span (Cox, 1995). Most values about public education fit that case. Each wave of supposedly new beliefs is replaced by the next wave, resulting in public schools either constantly turning with the wind or maintaining a secure routine and waiting for the new reforms to pass. What is lost to educators, parents, and citizens is the connection of education to an enduring belief about the purpose of the school. Mathews (1996), citing the Northwest Ordinances of 1787, stated that the purpose of education in the United States was to:

- Create and perpetuate a nation dedicated to particular principles
- Develop a citizenry capable of self-government
- Ensure social order
- Equalize educational opportunity for all
- Provide information and develop the skills essential to both individual economic enterprise and general prosperity

The paradox of democratic education is that there is nothing particularly new to learn about powerful education. Democracy must be both the means and the end; a means of decision making to achieve the ends of life, liberty, and the pursuit of happiness for all citizens. Using a democratic process to decide upon a pedagogy of democracy for achieving democratic purpose is the only way that all students can be educated well. The idea that all children—not some—within a classroom, school, or state should receive the most meaningful, challenging, and responsible education possible should not be startling. The response should be to ask what alternative could serve democracy.

Democracy is not merely a belief. It is the practice of common citizens living, working, learning, and ruling themselves in a way that is more just and equitable than what is derived by an oligarchy, monarchy, aristocracy, or dictatorship. A democracy protects free expression, general diffusion of knowledge, the marketplace of ideas, and open pursuit of truth so that citizens continuously educate themselves to participate, learn, and govern beyond the limited ideas of individuals. We must *revolutionize* our schools in the original sense of the word, "to revolve or return to the original point." Our fundamental purpose is to reclaim the natural rights of all men and women to be free. No society completely and truly practices the ideals of equality, justice, and liberty, and we do not have many public schools promoting such beliefs through pedagogy. The issue for educators is not whether the United States will survive; rather, it is whether democracy will ever become a pervasive way of life.

References

Aiken, W. *The Story of the Eight-Year Study with Conclusions and Recommendations*. New York: HarperCollins, 1942.

Barber, B. R. *An Aristocracy of Everyone: The Politics of Education and the Future of America*. New York: Ballantine, 1992.

Berliner, D. C., and Biddle, B. J. *The Manufactured Crisis: Myth, Fraud, and the Attack on America's Public Schools*. Reading, Mass.: Addison-Wesley, 1995.

"College Freshmen Less Interested . . . Higher Education and National Affairs." (UCLA annual survey.) *American Council on Education*, 1998, 47(1), 1, 3.

Cox, H. "The Warring Visions of the Religious Right." *Atlantic Monthly*, 1995, 276(5), 55–69.

Delpit, L. *Other People's Children: Cultural Conflict in the Classroom*. New York: New Press, 1995.

Dewey, J. *Democracy and Education: An Introduction to the Philosophy of Education*. New York: Macmillan, 1916.

Glickman, C. D.. *Renewing America's Schools: A Guide for School-Based Action*. San Francisco: Jossey-Bass, 1993.

Glickman, C. D. *Revolutionizing America's Schools*. San Francisco: Jossey-Bass, 1998.

Greene, M. *Teacher as Stranger: Educational Philosophy for the Modern Age*. Belmont, Calif.: Wadsworth, 1973.

Haycock, K. "Teacher Preparation." Presentation to the University System of Georgia, Achievement in America, Atlanta, Feb. 11, 1998.

Hill, P. T., Pierce, L. C., and Guthrie, J. W. *Reinventing Public Education: How Contracting Can Transform America's Schools*. Chicago: University of Chicago Press, 1997.

hooks, b. *Teaching to Transgress: Education as the Practice of Freedom*. New York: Routledge, 1994.

Joyce, B., Wolf, J., and Calhoun, E. *The Self-Renewing School*. Alexandria, Va.: Association for Supervision and Curriculum Development, 1993.

Ladson-Billings, G. *The Dreamkeepers: Successful Teachers of African American Children*. San Francisco: Jossey-Bass, 1994.

McNeil, L. M. *Contradictions of Control: School Structure and Knowledge*. New York: Routledge and Kegan Paul, 1986.

Mathews, D. *Is There a Public for Public Schools?* Dayton, Ohio: Kettering Foundation, 1996.

Meier, D. *The Power of Their Ideas: Lessons for America from a Small School in Harlem.* Boston: Beacon Press, 1995.

Newmann, F. M., Marks, H. M., and Gamoran, A. "Authentic Pedagogy: Standards That Boost Student Performance." *Issues in Restructuring Schools,* 1995, no. 8, 1–11.

Nord, W. A. *Religion and American Education: Rethinking a National Dilemma.* Chapel Hill: University of North Carolina Press, 1995.

Peterson, M D. (ed.). *The Portable Thomas Jefferson.* New York: Viking, 1975.

Piaget, J. *To Understand Is to Invent: The Future of Education* (trans. G.-A. Roberts). New York: Viking, 1973.

Randall, W. S. *Thomas Jefferson: A Life.* New York: Holt, 1993.

Sarason, S. B. *The Predictable Failure of Education Reform: Can We Change Course Before It's Too Late?* San Francisco: Jossey-Bass, 1990.

Tyack, D. B., and Cuban, L. *Tinkering Toward Utopia: A Century of Public School Reform.* Cambridge, Mass.: Harvard University Press, 1995.

West, C. *Beyond Eurocentrism and Multiculturalism.* Monroe, Maine: Common Courage, 1993.

Chapter Twenty

A Discourse on Education
and Democracy

This chapter contains three essays originally published in the *International Journal of Leadership in Education* in 1998 and 1999. I wrote the first, "Educational Leadership for Democratic Purpose: What Do We Mean?" The second is a commentary on that essay by James Joseph Scheurich, entitled "The Grave Dangers in the Discourse on Democracy." The third is another essay of mine, reflecting on Scheurich's commentary; it is entitled "A Response to the Discourse on Democracy: The Dangerous Retreat." All three essays have been edited for stylistic consistency with the other chapters in this volume.

ORIGINAL ESSAY

Educational Leadership for Democratic Purpose:
What Do We Mean?

Democracy is a word much used by educational leaders in the United States, yet in education it is rarely defined beyond general statements. The importance of defining democracy and determining compatible educational practice is critical to school success.

In this chapter, four definitions of democracy are examined. I then articulate my own definition and make a case for participatory, community-oriented democracy achieved through school and classroom structures and activities.

I conclude with the need for educational leaders to develop their own working definition with others in a school community to provide ongoing guidance to classroom and school renewal. The perennial question for the public educator is always how to focus change on what public schools should educate for.

Recently, I presented a commencement address at a college graduation ceremony on the topic of education and democracy. After concluding with the need to keep education rooted in the spirit of American democracy, I received a warm round of applause from the majority of the audience. A Native American woman in the audience, though, came over to me and privately (but adamantly) expressed discomfort with my use of the word *democracy*. She asserted that American democracy meant to her the systematic exploitation and eradication of her people. She made a most convincing point about the need for educators to carefully articulate what they mean by the word.

I find this issue of definition extremely interesting, complicated, and exciting. I have grappled with it in conversation with others of different racial, cultural, religious, and ethnic experience over the past two years. The writer John Oliver Killens explains why many African Americans do not see the word in the same way as European Americans: "the sooner we face up to this social and cultural reality, the sooner the twain shall meet. . . . Your joy is very often our anger and your despair is our fervent hope. Most of us came here in chains and most of you came here to escape your chains. Your freedom was our slavery, and therein lies the bitter difference in the way we look at life" (1996, p. 108).

I wish to make clear to the reader that as I examine the issue of definition, educational leadership, and appropriate practice, I am speaking of the word in the context of the United States of America. I welcome readers from other countries to determine if this examination is of similar value in defining their own purpose of education. I do not assume that it is, nor that it should be.

What do I mean by education with a public purpose? How do I define democracy? What should the central practice of schools and educational leadership be? In this chapter, I examine a number of conceptions of democracy and what, in my opinion, are understandings essential to the future work of educational leadership and school renewal in the United States.

Definitions of Democracy

There are a number of ways to define democracy. A former student of mine, political theorist Doug Dixon (1997), explains three conceptions of democracy: liberal, participatory, and community.

Liberal democracy is the belief in a republican government of elected representatives, government officials, legal structures, and expert consultants who make decisions for citizens. A bureaucracy and hierarchy of government agents are necessary to govern. Citizens at large are capable of determining their representatives from election to election, but they do not possess the time, interest, knowledge, and intelligence to deliberate and solve issues for themselves. Thus the rule of majority vote through election and referendum is the key to sustaining society and ensuring the rights and responsibilities of the individual.

Participatory democracy is the belief in active participation of citizens in the ongoing deliberation and decision making of representative, republican government. It is assumed that citizens are as intelligent as those they elect and those who are appointed as civil servants. The solicitation, initiative, and involvement of citizens in public forums, ad hoc committees, and task forces to help shape government decisions are critical to the success of society. Thus the focus of participatory democracy is not simply elections where voters determine preselected choices, but instead having citizens deliberate and shape the choice and consequences of a decision.

Community democracy is the belief that society is largely improved by how citizens live in everyday, personal interaction. The concern is not with a particular form of official government or legalistic structure, but instead how people listen, learn, and mobilize together to change their associative conditions for the better.

These three definitions are simplified here and in practice often overlap, but one might now glimpse how the word *democracy* resonates with people according to their own definition. Liberal democracy is embraced most often by those citizens who have benefited from the existing governmental and legal structures and who have the greatest influence on the republican political system. Participatory democracy appeals most to those who have been outside the liberal system but have found optimism in a strategy of protest and resistance, forcing deliberation and change in governmental decisions. Community democracy resonates mostly with those who view government as uncontrollable, or at best a noneffectual entity, and find value in the personal ways that people help each other.

To complicate matters a bit further, there are other conceptions of democracy, not academic or theoretical, that simply come from the lived experiences of individuals. In this light, democracy may be viewed as patriarchal by those who feel denied of their rights and as freedom by those who have experienced economic success in free market economics. In his careful analysis of educational reformers, Dixon (1997) has argued cogently that prominent educational leaders wrap their particular advocacy for change in the schools within the cloak of democracy but often do so without explaining what they mean.

What Is Meant by Democracy and Congruent Education?

Let me begin with five points. First, democracy in the sense of equality, freedom, and liberty for all its citizens has never been fully achieved in the United States. Second, the U.S. political system of state and federal governments is in practice more a designed liberal system of elected persons influenced most by powerful individuals, interests, and businesses than a participatory democracy of equal citizens (Arendt, 1963). Third, the essence of a community and participatory democracy (which is what the Declaration of Independence advocated—rather than what the Constitution legislated) is an educative belief about how citizens best learn. Fourth, when community and participatory democracy is used as a guide for educational leadership and school reform, there is significant personal, empirical, and cultural evidence of educating students extraordinarily well. Fifth, before public schools can improve the education of all students, leadership must practice the rhetoric of a community and participatory democracy in all aspects of school life, including whole school renewal and a curriculum with culturally responsive and participatory pedagogy and assessment (Wilder, 1995). Participatory governance alone won't improve schools. In sum, each school in its local community needs to continually answer this question: What should we be doing in our schools, our curriculum, our placement, our scheduling of students, our allocation of resources, and in our teaching that gives each child his or her inalienable right to life, liberty, and the pursuit of happiness? Democracy is therefore a means of decision making (shared governance) to achieve the ends of an education for students that helps them achieve life, liberty, and the pursuit of happiness.

In answering this question, faculty, administrators, staff, parents, students, and citizens bring a strong sense of mission, teaching and learning practices, standards of performance, and ongoing means for reflective schoolwide progress (Glickman, 1993). Powerful schools take democratic clarity and purpose seriously in everything they do. They create a pedagogy of learning, where participation, choices, connections, demonstration, and cultural respect and responsiveness foster high expectations for all. I define democracy as the belief that citizens can educate themselves well when a society ensures freedom of expression, a free press, the marketplace of ideas, the general diffusion of knowledge, and the pursuit of truth (truth with a lowercase *t*) so that each generation may uncover new and different truths. In effect, it is individual liberty and community freedom as a way of learning (Glickman, 1998b).

Democratic Pedagogy

How can an espoused democracy be revitalized to support and encourage individual liberty and community freedom as a pedagogy for learning? Cognitive research, personal learning experiences, and ideological faith offer evidence that democratic pedagogy is the most powerful form of student learning. Not only is the pedagogy consistent with the aims of democratic education, it is how students become knowledgeable, wise, and competent citizens.

What is a democratic pedagogy? It is one that aims for freedom of expression, pursuit of truth in the marketplace of ideas, individual and group choices, student activity, participation, associative learning, application, demonstration, and contribution of learning to immediate and larger communities. Such pedagogical effort is undertaken in the context of equality for all, consideration of individual liberty and group freedom, and respect for the authority and responsibility of the teacher to set conditions for developmental learning.

Let me clear up a potential distortion of democratic pedagogy with examples of what it is and what it isn't (Glickman, 1996, 1998b).

Democratic pedagogy is *not:*

- Students deciding for themselves if, what, or how they will learn
- Absence of such skills as reading, writing, and arithmetic
- Absence of content studies in areas such as humanities, science, and art

Nor is it:

- All students learning the same material at the same time
- Students sitting and listening, passively
- Students categorized, labeled, and placed in fixed ability groups and tracts

Democratic pedagogy *is:*

- Students actively working with problems, ideas, materials and other people as they learn skills and content
- Students having an escalating degree of choice, both as individuals and as a group, within the parameters provided by the teacher
- Students being responsible to their peers, teachers, parents, and school community in ensuring that educational time is being used purposefully and productively

- Students sharing their learning with each other, with teachers, and with parents and other community members
- Students deciding how to make their learning a contribution to their community
- Students assuming growing responsibility for securing resources (of people and materials outside the school) and finding a place where they can apply and further their learning
- Students demonstrating what they know and can do in public settings and receiving public feedback
- Students working and learning from each other, individually and in groups, at a pace that challenges all

There are a number of research studies on learning practices that increase student achievement, learning satisfaction, and success in later life. These results have been consistent across socioeconomic, "race," ethnic, and gender compositions of students. There is a strong case that such learning is culturally responsive in that it takes into account diversity of student history and background. For example, students who graduated from thirty high schools using education and democracy as the central concept of curriculum and instructional practices outperformed students who graduated from traditional high schools. It was found that in 1,475 matched pairs of students studied through four years of high school and followed four years afterward, graduates from democratic schools had higher grades, received more academic and nonacademic honors, had a higher degree of intellectual curiosity, and participated more in groups and international issues (Aiken, 1942). In a 1977 study of twenty-six urban and rural schools, the greater the democratic effort made in a school—in process and organization—the greater was the achievement of students (Joyce, Wolf, and Calhoun, 1993, pp. 76–78). In 1995, a study of 820 high schools and eleven thousand students, under the direction of Fred Newmann, found schools that reorganized their academic programs around active learning and in which this type of instruction was wide-spread throughout the school had significantly higher student gains on all achievement domains of mathematics, reading, social studies, and science, as measured by the National Assessment of Educational Progress (Newmann, Marks, and Gamoran, 1995). The same results held true for longitudinal studies of elementary and middle schools (Newmann and Wehlage, 1995).

There have been instructional studies around specific active and participatory methods such as cooperative learning, role playing, the jurisprudence model, inductive thinking, and concept attainment (see Joyce and Weil, 1996). For example, Shlomo Sharan's work shows that democratic process teaching generates twice the student learning as passive lecture and recitation teaching (Joyce and Weil, 1996).

The same type of effective pedagogy, when incorporating cultural differences of students, can be seen in the work of several recent scholars. For example, Norbert Hill (1993) wrote that successful Native American teachers provide "assistance and guidance, rather than domination and control" and that teachers "encourage students to engage their curiosity through co-generating and participating in a variety of activities." Sonia Nieto and Carmen Rólon (1995, p. 22) summarized studies of Latino (or Hispanic) students and found that successful teachers increased "students' active participation and leadership responsibilities inside and outside the classroom." Gloria Ladson-Billings described ideal learning in a school culturally responsive to African American students: "The student learning is organized around problems and issues. . . . The students have studied cities in ancient African Kingdoms, Europe and Asia. They are studying their own city. They have taken trips to City Hall. . . . Groups of students are working on solutions to problems specific to the city" (1994, pp. 140–141).

To summarize, those teachers and schools that define democracy as participatory and community oriented appear to have much greater success with all their students. It is a pedagogy that respects the student's own desire to know, discuss, solve problems, and explore individually and with others rather than learning that is dictated, determined, and answered by the teacher. It is the belief that all students can participate and excel. School leaders facilitate and develop such a school community through their love, care, and belief that each student is equal and educable, and that each can learn to become a valuable citizen of society (King, 1994; Scheurich, 1995).

Conclusion

Education is not public because it is publicly funded; rather it is public because of public purpose (Barber, 1993). That is why it is publicly funded. Therefore all schools in the United States with the public purpose of preparing the next generation of citizens for a democratic society need to carefully define what democracy means and what are appropriate practices in and across classrooms, within a school, and out in the larger community.

The Declaration of Independence stated that "all men are created equal, that they are endowed by their Creator with certain inalienable rights; that among those are life, liberty, and the pursuit of happiness." It stands to reason that educators need to ensure that students have an education that allows each and every student the attainment of those inalienable rights. Consequently, as schools study and determine their future changes and improvements, they must first define democracy and then make direct application in how they group, schedule, assess, and teach students.

I do not wish to leave the reader with the impression that, once educational leaders help to define what democracy means, solutions in practice are simple, obvious, and uncontested. But what I do believe is that with a working, shared definition, U.S. educators, with parents, students, and other citizens, will be answering the essential and perennial question of why schools exist.

So as I conclude, I welcome others to this conversation. What do we mean by democracy? What are our obligations to our students? Are we willing to practice a form of democracy in our everyday action in schools that makes possible a societal form of democracy that we have not yet reached?

COMMENTARY

The Grave Dangers in the Discourse on Democracy
James Joseph Scheurich

Numerous scholars and educators have given pride of place to democracy both for society at large and for schools and school reform (see, among others, Glickman, 1993; and Raywid, 1990). In emphatic contrast, I would like to suggest that this is a *dangerous* choice. However, in making my brief points, I do not want to speak "against" any particular individual who privileges democracy in this way. Instead I want to speak against the ways democracy, as a linguistic vessel of meaning, discursively circulates both in educator and scholarly discourses. I want to try to show those who participate in these circulations that they are involved in a complex discursive enactment that has deleterious effects. I would like for us to think together, to consider certain difficult problems in the discourse of democracy, to critically examine some serious dangers in this discourse. Specifically, I want to discuss how the promotion of democracy as the principal underlying value in society or in schools and school reform is not only particularly *harmful* to national minority groups, like African Americans or Mexican Americans, but also, in the long view, harmful to everyone. This discussion, though, should not be taken as a comprehensive critique, archaeology, or genealogy of the discourse on democracy (certainly something that is needed); what I provide here is but a bare beginning.

Before I can make my points, though, it is necessary to address and then move beyond the emancipatory claims for democracy. In this regard, democracy is appropriately taken to be a reallocation of power from a small elite to the citizenry at large; however, as everyone knows, in Athens, democracy, like the early U.S. democracy, was relegated to only certain citizens, like white, male property owners, so the application of democracy is not necessarily coterminous with the entire adult population. The most well known example of democratic emancipation in the United States is the revolution that overthrew British royal rule of the thirteen colonies. Other

subsequent U.S. examples are the expansion of democracy via voting rights to women and to people of color. In addition, interna-
tionally there are courageous movements whose principal goal is to
establish democracy in their societies. One clear example would be
the successful movement to end apartheid in South Africa.

It is exceedingly important, therefore, that it be understood
that, for the discussion that follows, I strongly support these efforts
to develop and expand democracy in whatever context—from
countries to corporations, from societies to schools. Democracy
rightly holds a critical significance in any context in which relatively small elites subjugate or have subjugated majorities. I do not
dispute that democracy, in this regard or context, is emancipatory;
I strongly agree that it is. However, it is precisely when democracy
has been obtained and implemented, precisely at this point, where
the dangers arise and thus where we must begin our critical inter-
rogation. More specifically, when a democracy has been established
in a societal context that encompasses minority subgroups along
with a dominant majority, we have a context that is literally dangerous for minority groups.

Said most directly, democracy is not equity, nor is it any guarantee of equity. This is the point that Glickman implies at the very
beginning of the preceding discussion, but I think we need to consider this issue in more depth and centrality than he does. This
point—that a society is democratic, no matter how democracy is
defined, does not guarantee that it is equitable—seems, on a kind
of superficially logical level, an obvious point. However, at the level
of human practices and their effects, at the level of how democracy
gets discursively enacted and thus "materialized" as practices, such
as in personal conversation, speeches, writings, school reforms,
classroom pedagogy, administrative actions, laws and policy, etc.,
this point is not widely discussed and thus is not socially obvious.

Indeed, the context that Glickman presents us with at the very
beginning of his piece is instructive: he gives a speech about keeping "education rooted in the spirit of American democracy." The
audience responds warmly, but a Native American woman
approaches him after the speech to suggest that democracy for her

and her people has literally been genocidal. Her suggestion to the speaker is to be extremely careful about how democracy is defined, a point Glickman addresses by discussing his definition of democracy. However, I would suggest that proposing a definition of democracy, however radical the definition, and then proceeding to build a view of educational reform (or societal reform) on that definition without taking serious and careful account of dominant social assumptions and practices, is dangerously naïve (and by "dangerously naïve" I mean that the naïveté itself is a social practice with dangerous effects).

I will illustrate what I mean. Affirmative action arose as a relatively limited policy to address the historical sedimentation of inequity that had become deeply embedded in a broad array of social practices, like hiring personnel or the letting of government contracts, and to redress the inequitable distribution of power, resources, awards, etc., like education, that resulted from that long-term sedimentation. Nonetheless, besides the fact that the policy chiefly benefited white majority women and besides the fact that the white public held exaggerated and distorted views of the policy and its limited effects, the majority has begun to move democratically against this policy. The most clear example of this is the passage by a democratic majority of Proposition 209, which makes affirmative action by the state government illegal in California.

Perhaps a more metaphorically compelling example is provided in a story called "The Space Traders," by Derrick Bell (1992), an African American legal scholar. In this story aliens come to the earth and offer to the United States gold, to bail out the almost bankrupt federal, state, and local governments; special chemicals capable of unpolluting the environment, which was becoming daily more toxic, and restoring it to the pristine state it had been in before Western explorers set foot on it; and a totally safe nuclear engine and fuel, to relieve the nation's all-but-depleted supply of fossil fuel.

And what do the space traders want in return for all of this? "To take back to their home star all the African Americans who lived in the United States." This "bargain" is put to a vote, and the democratic majority chooses to make the exchange. The aliens are democratically given all of the African Americans.

This story and the California move against affirmative action highlight the naïveté I mentioned earlier. To invoke democracy in the current societal context is not an innocent practice in its effects in contrast to the intentions of the speaker. It does not matter that the speaker wishes to provide a more radical definition of democracy; the discourse that the speaker speaks into, the receiving of the discourse, must be considered along with the speaker's intentions. It is socially naïve to believe that speech simply circulates as input from the individual speaker to reception by the individual listener. Speech (its meanings, categories, rhythms, etc.), as a social practice, circulates within social discourses that are structured by complex social assumptions (Bakhtin, 1986; Butler, 1993; Williams, 1991). What speakers say and what audiences hear is not only typically incongruent but also, and more importantly, socially structured or constructed.

In this specific case, the social structure in place is long-term inequities around the relationships between the majority and various minorities. In these historical relationships the majority has established what could be called a normativity, a standing ideology (or archaeology) of socially reinforced or iterated norms. For example, what this means in terms of race is that a white cultural normativity is and has historically been dominant, and this historical dominance is deeply embedded in virtually all aspects of social life, from the nature of an individual or of schooling to assumptions about what democracy is and means (for reference lists, see Banks, 1995; or Scheurich and Young, 1997). Consequently, when a speaker speaks to an audience, it is a mistake not to understand that the speech is spoken into this racialized normativity.

My contention is thus that within this racialized normativity, democracy discursively performs or circulates, whether it is consciously intended or not, as a code word for white majoritarian racial domination or supremacy. On the one hand, it is as if to whites the word *democracy* has this positive, appealing surface as it is circulated within the dominant normativity. It is seen by whites as the heart of a heroic story, an indication of the special character of U.S. society. It is central to what, to whites, makes the United States great in human history. It has thus become, in its invocation by whites, central to white nationalistic patriotism. However, while it is not on the surface, not explicitly discussed in public, whites know that democracy is, majority-wise, white power. And it is this understanding that politicians and others stoke with the promotion of fears about increases in immigrants, increases in the percentage of racial minorities in the national population, and "unfair" increases in minority gains in the job market through affirmative action. It is thus this understanding that drives the white majoritarian democratic attack on affirmative action.

On the other hand, members of historically dominated minority groups, like the Native American woman cited by Glickman, and like Derrick Bell, see democracy in a very different light. They see that democratic majorities historically supported the slavery of African Americans, the genocidal destruction of Native Americans and their ways of life, the murder and suppression of Mexican Americans, and the labor exploitation and oppression of Asians. People of color see and experience daily acts of racism, acts that are constantly being discounted by whites as "things are better," the exaggerations or paranoia of people of color; and other such dismissals. People of color see who has the largest proportions of population in poverty and relegated to a kind of geographical apartheid in substandard housing. They see whose kids are well treated and helped in school and whose are not. They see who bankers and real estate agents and supervisors treat well and who they do not. They see who the police favor and who they do not. That is, they constantly see the white normativity and its deleterious effects, while whites repeatedly state that they themselves are increasingly fair, open, and democratic—beyond racism or, at least, getting better. This, then, is the dark heart that travels, for people of color, within the circulations or invocations of democracy, whether the speaker intends it or not.

What I am addressing here is the politics of reality itself. Whatever is thought to be or taken to be reality is a social construction. Different groups historically come to construct reality differently. In a complex democratic society in which the majority—in this case, whites—has historically dominated and continues to dominate minority groups, such as Native Americans, African Americans, Hispanic Americans, and Asian Americans, over time reality itself (the normativity I spoke of before) comes to be defined by the dominant group, the racial majority in this case. Furthermore, the dominant group takes its view of reality to be real reality, to be natural, the nature of things. In contrast, minority groups see, live, experience, survive within substantially different perspectives, normativities, realities. Thus, what democracy means to the majority and what it means to a minority is often vastly different. This, then, is political because minority "realities" are dominated, suppressed, ignored by the majority "reality," hence a politics of reality.

Given this, it is crucial that we critically understand the reality politics of the dominant group in terms of democracy. In terms of analyzing and understanding these reality politics, it is naïve to invoke a key social concept, like democracy, without considering how it discursively functions and circulates within the reality politics (the dominant normativity) of contemporary U.S. society. Invocations of democracy, *in the terms of the contemporary and historical experiences of racial minorities*, easily sound like invocations of white supremacy. And, indeed, I would argue that these invocations, to a significant extent, act or perform in this way; invocations of democracy among whites ignite a complex discursive circuitry of supremacy, a circuitry that is woven into the individual subjectivities of whites and that links them as the dominant racial group.

In other words, when a white audience responds positively or warmly to invocations of democracy, the complexity of that response includes an invocation of the emancipatory gains of the past *and* white majoritarian power *and* the often deadly racial oppressions of the past and the present. Invocations of democracy do appeal to and stimulate whites, but what is being appealed to and what is being stimulated is not simple, is not just positive and emancipatory, but also is destructive and oppressive. Being unreflective about such invocations, then, is highly dangerous to racial minorities because the very utterance of the invocation turns on a racial dominance circuitry among whites, a circuitry that is not necessarily conscious, but a circuitry that is often highly dangerous to people of color in the United States.

I have said, then, my brief piece. I have tried to provoke some thinking together about a complex and central issue in U.S. society and in schools and school reform. I have tried, though my effort is in response to the piece by Glickman, to keep my comments away from individuals and directed at discursive enactments of democracy in the contemporary United States. For example, I know Carl and his work. I appreciate his voice, and I appreciate the work he does in schools. I believe that he is committed to schools that work well for both white children and children of color. That does not mean, however, that I do not think he is in some deep, dangerous waters with his invocations of democracy in his writing and in his work in schools. I hope then that I have been provocative and useful in that regard.

I know, though, from numerous past experiences, that it is at this point that I am expected to provide an answer, to provide suggestions about how we can address or, even better, change the situation as I have described it. What is my solution to the problem I have raised? I refuse to answer; I cannot answer. We whites and people of color are in a room together called the United States. We have a horrible history of the most destructive racial oppression. While in the present (which contains in complex ways our past together) the forms of that oppression have evolved in some cases and not in others, racial oppression continues throughout society and, especially, in schools, where children of color are overwhelmingly the least served and ill served by our schools, often to the point of the destruction of their very belief in themselves.

Indeed, we whites are in denial about our conscious and unconscious addiction to white majoritarian power and about the destructive effects of that addiction. If you "read" our democracy from the viewpoint of people of color—insane percentages involved in the "justice" system or prison, insane percentages failed by schools, insane percentages relegated to poverty, insane percentages exploited for cheap labor, insane percentages forced to live within apartheid-like geographical areas of substandard housing—which is how we whites must read it for it is by the least among us that we know ourselves, we are living a racial nightmare. That the media and much educational scholarship only provides and thus reiterates the dominant normativity as real reality and not the nightmare is but more of the same. In fact, to many whites my invocation of "the racial nightmare" may seem outlandish or extreme, but ask scholars of color, ask Cornel West, ask Gloria Anzualda, ask bell hooks, ask Richard Valencia, ask Francis Rains, ask Laurence Parker, ask Henry Trueba, ask Michelle Foster if I am being outlandish or extreme. That we whites do not see the nightmare is but racial reality politics at work inside our minds, business as usual.

Consequently, while I have no business offering an answer to people of color, I also have no answer for whites. For me to offer whites an answer would be to think that I could do the work we all need to do together. It would be to merely intellectualize. Intellectuality, such as that I have practiced here, is good for analysis; it is good for gaining an understanding or for critiquing the status quo. But it is not the doing of change, the journey of transformation. This journey cannot be prescribed, cannot be told or figured out ahead of time; it has to be lived. It has to be carried through by the people involved. It has to be done by you and me. Ending this racial nightmare is our journey; it is still the same one, the one that Sitting Bull and Sojourner and Martin Luther and Cesar and Rosa and thousands of others have repeatedly urged us to take.

COMMENTARY

A Response to the Discourse on Democracy:
A Dangerous Retreat

In the inaugural issue of the *International Journal of Leadership in Education*, I wrote an article (Glickman, 1998a) entitled "Educational Leadership for Democratic Purpose: What Do We Mean?" In the same issue, Jim Scheurich (1998) followed with a critique entitled "The Grave Dangers in the Discourse on Democracy." His response was that the word *democracy* used as a premise for educational change "circulates, whether it is consciously intended or not, as a code word for white majoritarian racial domination or supremacy" (p. 58).

He then writes that "it is naïve to invoke a key social concept, like democracy, without considering how it discursively functions and circulates within the reality politics (the dominant normativity) of contemporary U.S. society" (Scheurich, 1998, p. 59). And finally, he concludes with his concern that the promotion of the word *democracy* obscures the terrible issue of racial exploitation: "In fact, to many whites my invocation of 'the racial nightmare' may seem outlandish or extreme, but ask scholars of color, ask Cornel West, ask Gloria Anzualda, ask bell hooks . . ." (p. 60). He wanted me to know that my invocations of democracy for educational leadership and school renewal get me into "deep, dangerous waters" (p. 59).

Before I respond to his concerns, I want readers to know that I have great respect for Jim Scheurich—his thinking, his manner, and his work. He wished not to offend me personally, and I took no offence.

So without repeating my entire article, let me review a few of the major points. First, democracy has various definitions to different people, and as a guide to school change I believe that educators, students, and community members need to deal with the central question, "What should we be doing in our schools, our curriculum, our placement, our scheduling of students, our allocation of resources, and in our teaching that gives each child his or her inalienable right to life, liberty, and the pursuit of happiness?" (Glickman, 1998a, p. 49). Thus, I point out that democracy needs to be viewed as a governing means for achieving certain ends and that these ends are best achieved through classroom and school learning that is active, participatory, and contributory. I cited that such democratic-based pedagogy results in greater success for all students "across socioeconomic, 'race,' ethnic, and gender compositions of students" (Glickman, 1998a, p. 51). I conclude my essay by reinforcing my point that American democracy must be viewed as more than representative, majoritarian government—as a way of day-to-day life in schools that again achieve the democratic goals of life, liberty and the pursuit of happiness for all students (Glickman, 1998a).

Now let me respond to Jim's analysis. I understand Jim's argument. I agree that the word *democracy*, when not carefully explained, can be a comfort to those in a privileged position and keep the dominant status quo intact through majoritarian vote. There is a need for me, and others, to explain the progress, struggles, and failures of American democracy. There are two realities out there: one of great progress, the other, as Jim defines, of "insane" inequities. I concur with the statement of African American scholar Louis Gates, Jr., that "we need something we don't yet have, a way of speaking about race and poverty that doesn't falsify the reality of racial advancement, and a way of speaking about racial advancement that doesn't distort the enduring realities of poverty" (Gates and West, 1996, p. 33). The great tragedy of America today is that so many people have gained material wealth, and yet at the same time there are so many poor persons left in despicable conditions. I believe that any discussion about democracy needs to delineate the practice of American society—the good, the bad, and the ugly—with the espousal of democratic ideals.

Jim says that all education reformers—white or of color—are being naïvely dangerous in using the word *democracy* as central to educational improvement: "the promotion of democracy . . . in schools and school reform is not only particularly *harmful* to national minority groups, like African Americans or Mexican Americans, but also, in the long view, harmful to everyone" (Scheurich, 1998, p. 55). So in one stroke, Jim dismisses the work of democratic educators across the spectrum of human color as doing more harm than good to minority groups. Again, I understand Jim's perspective about institutional racism and unintended collusion with internalized power structures, but I could not disagree with him more. I simply have seen and studied the positive results of such democratic-inspired reform efforts on previously disenfranchised youth to believe that such work, in the present and long run, is not harmful. Rather, I would argue that a retreat from democratic education is what is most dangerous in the long run for minority groups and everyone.[1]

Lastly, Jim undercuts his own position by saying that examination of "insane" inequities can be found by listening to scholars of color, beginning with Cornel West. I suggest that Jim carefully read West; my work about democracy has been greatly influenced by him (see Glickman, 1998b). Cornel West puts American democratic ideals at the center of his hope for addressing the inequities of his own and other oppressed people. West wrote that "the greatest experiment in humankind began in 1776." He goes on: "It didn't apply to white men who had no property. It didn't apply to women. It didn't apply to slaves. . . . But that is not solely the point. It is in part the point. But it is not fully the point. The courageous attempt to build a democracy experiment in which the uniqueness . . . [and] sanctity of each and every one of us who has been made equal in the eyes of God becomes at least possible" (1993a, p. 8).

In another book, *Race Matters*, West wrote, "Since democracy is, as the great Reinhold Niebuhr noted, a proximate solution to insoluble problems, I envision neither a social utopia nor a political paradise" (1993b, p. 158). But, he continued, "we simply cannot enter the twenty-first century at each other's throats, even as we acknowledge the weighty forces of racism, patriarchy, economic inequality, homophobia and ecological abuse on our necks" (1993b, p. 159). So if we look to a scholar such as Cornel West, we don't retreat from the greatest experiment in humankind; we embrace it as our very best hope for a better society.

Finally, I disagree with Jim's postmodern, critical-theorist perspective on language usage. He attacks the concept of democracy as carrying imperialist, colonial baggage ("white cultural normativity" and "historical dominance") by citing an experience that I wrote about, the Native American woman who confronted me about a convocation address that I gave in which I discussed American democracy, Thomas Jefferson, and the Federalists' paper. She reminded me that what happened under that word, and time, was the systematic eradication of her people. She—as well as Jim and others—is correct to challenge all of us who use the word *democracy* to examine the hypocrisy of ideals of liberation versus practices of subjugation. But she didn't ask me to stop using the word; she asked me instead to explain it carefully and publicly. Jim wants me and others involved in educational leadership and school change not to use the word at all. Again, we are totally apart on this issue.

The ideals of a democracy—equality, liberty, fraternity; justice and freedom; life, liberty, and the pursuit of happiness—are, in my opinion, constantly worth struggling for. Perhaps Jim wants to replace the word *democracy* as a guide for educational leadership and school renewal with different terms, perhaps equity, emancipation, transformation, liberation? But where do those replacement words come from? Is he trying to find words that come from a tradition and culture free of exploitation and hypocrisy? If so, they won't be easy to find. Instead, I wish to keep the word (and concept of) *democracy*, recognized by virtually all Americans, and examine it in all its beauty and ugliness. It is only by doing so that we can revive the goals of democracy to accomplish more, for all its people, than ever before.

Democracy does not belong to white people alone, and to suggest that it does is an insult to all those people—of color and white—who have struggled to redefine it as being far more than voting rights or majoritarian government, but instead ideals that give a common hope to so many different people (Maier, 1997). For example, the Rev. Joseph Lowry of Atlanta, a lifetime civil rights leader and president of the Southern Christian Leadership Conference, recently received the Spirit of Democracy Award (Freda, 1997). He should be proud, not ashamed, to be recognized as an espouser and promoter of a better democracy. As feminist scholar Seyla Benhabib writes, "post modernism can teach us the theoretical and political traps of why utopias and foundational thinking can go wrong, but it should not lead to a retreat from utopia altogether" (1992, p. 230).

To conclude, I want to thank Jim for his critique. He has captured the paradox, dissension, and conscious and unconscious harm of democracy (Massaro, 1991). At the end, this argument is a dear one as it gets to the essence of what hopes and aspirations we have for education, individuals, and society. It is too important an issue to be bandied about by two white European male professors at American research universities who write papers to each other. Jim and I agree this discussion is not between us. It's really an issue about the future and the best ways of realizing it for all our children. It's an issue that needs to be confronted, defined, and practiced in every school and community in America.

Note

1. Educational reform and renewal that uses participatory, community-based ideals of democracy centrally can be found in the works of such contemporary thinkers as James Comer; Deborah Meier; Linda Darling-Hammond; Ernesto Cortes, Jr.; Hank Levin; Ted Sizer; Roger Soder; George Wood; and John Goodlad.

References

Aiken, W. *The Story of the Eight-Year Study.* New York: Harper, 1942.

Arendt, H. *On Revolution.* New York: Penguin, 1963.

Bakhtin, M. M. *Speech Genres and Other Late Essays*. (C. Emerson and M. Holquist, eds.; V. W. McGee, trans.) Austin: Texas University Press, 1986.

Banks, J. A. "The Historical Reconstruction of Knowledge About Race: Implications for Transformative Learning." *Educational Researcher*, 1995, *24*(2), 15–25.

Barber, B. R. *An Aristocracy of Everyone*. New York: Ballantine, 1993.

Bell, D. "The Space Traders." In *Faces at the Bottom of the Well*. New York: Basic Books, 1992.

Benhabib, S. *Situating the Self: Gender, Community, and Post-Modernism in Contemporary Ethics*. New York: Routledge, 1992.

Butler, J. *Bodies That Matter: On the Discursive Limits of "Sex."* New York: Routledge, 1993.

Dixon, D. A. "Conceptions of Democracy and School Reform: A Systematic Analysis of Prominent Democratic Education Reformers' Ideas." Unpublished Ph.D. dissertation, University of Georgia, 1997.

Freda, E. "Happening." *Atlanta Journal-Constitution*, Oct. 9, 1997, p. A19.

Gates, H. L., and West, C. *The Future of the Race*. New York: Vintage, 1996.

Glickman, C. D. *Renewing America's Schools: A Guide for School-Based Action*. San Francisco: Jossey-Bass, 1993.

Glickman, C. D. "Education as Democracy: The Pedagogy of School Renewal." Invited presentation to the annual meeting of the American Educational Research Association, New York City, Apr. 1996.

Glickman, C. D. "Educational Leadership for Democratic Purpose: What Do We Mean?" *International Journal of Leadership in Education*, 1998a, *1*(1), 47–53.

Glickman, C. D. *Revolutionizing America's Schools*. San Francisco: Jossey-Bass, 1998b.

Hill, N. "Reclaiming American Indian Education." In S. Elam (ed.), *The State of the Nation's Public Schools*. Bloomington, Ind.: Phi Delta Kappa Society, 1993.

Joyce, B., Wolf, S., and Calhoun, E. *The Self-Renewing School*. Alexandria, VA: Association for Supervision and Curriculum Development, 1993.

Joyce, B., and Weil, M. *Models of Teaching* (5th ed.). Needham Heights, Mass.: Allyn and Bacon, 1996.

Killens, J. O. "The Black Psyche." *New York Times Magazine*, Apr. 14, 1996, p. 108. (First published in *New York Times Magazine*, June 7, 1964.)

King, J. E. "The Purpose of Schooling for African-American Children." In E. R. Hollins, J. E. King, and W. C. Hayman (eds.), *Teaching Diverse Populations: Formulating a Knowledge Base*. Albany: State University of New York Press, 1994.

Ladson-Billings, G. *The Dreamkeepers: Successful Teachers of African American Children*. San Francisco: Jossey-Bass, 1994.

Maier, P. *American Scripture: The Making of the Declaration of Independence*. New York: Knopf, 1997.

Massaro, T. *Constitutional Literacy: A Core Curriculum for a Multi-Cultural Nation.* Durham, N.C.: Duke University Press, 1991.

Newmann, F. M., Marks, H. M., and Gamoran, A. "Authentic Pedagogy: Standards That Boost Student Performance—Issues in Restructuring Schools." (Report no. 8.) Madison: Wisconsin Center for Education Research, 1995.

Newmann, F. M., and Wehlage, G. G. "Successful School Restructuring: A Report to the Public and Educators by the Center on Organization and Restructuring of Schools." Madison: Wisconsin Center for Education Research, 1995.

Nieto, S., and Rólon, C. "The Preparation and Professional Development of Teachers: A Perspective from Two Latinos." Paper presented to the CULTURES conference Defining the Knowledge Base for Urban Teacher Education, Emory University, Decatur, Ga., 1995.

Raywid, M. A. "Rethinking School Governance." In R. F. Elmore and Associates (eds.), *Restructuring Schools: The Next Generation of Educational Reform.* San Francisco: Jossey-Bass, 1990.

Scheurich, J. "Highly Successful and Loving Public Pre-K–5 Schools Populated Mainly by Low SES Children of Color: Core Beliefs and Cultural Characteristics." (Unpublished paper.) Austin: Department of Educational Administration, University of Texas at Austin, 1995.

Scheurich, J. J. "The Grave Dangers in the Discourse on Democracy." *International Journal of Leadership in Education,* 1998, *1*(1), 55–60.

Scheurich, J. J., and Young, M. D. "Coloring Epistemology: Are Our Research Epistemologies Racially Biased?" *Educational Researcher,* 1997, *26*(4), 4–16.

West, C. *Beyond Eurocentrism and Multiculturalism.* Vol. 1: *Prophetic Thought in Postmodern Time.* Monroe, Maine: Common Courage, 1993a.

West, C. *Race Matters.* New York: Vintage, 1993b.

Wilder, M. A. "Professional Development Schools: Restructuring Teacher Education Programs and Hierarchies." In H. G. Petrie (ed.), *Professionalization, Partnership and Power: Building Professional Development Schools.* Albany: State University of New York Press, 1995.

Williams, R. "Base and Superstructure in Marxist Cultural Theory." In C. Mukerji and M. Schudson (eds.), *Rethinking Popular Culture: Contemporary Perspectives in Cultural Studies.* Berkeley: University of California Press, 1991.

Chapter Twenty-One

Going Public

The Imperative of Public Education in the Twenty-First Century

Carl D. Glickman, Derrick P. Alridge

The challenge of fully realizing democracy in twenty-first-century America depends heavily on the role that public education and schooling play in constructing democratic principles among students, the community, and larger society. American public education and schools have to respond to several important questions: What is the purpose of public education and schooling in the twenty-first century? How best can the public classroom facilitate democratic learning? What are some viable strategies for the public school and education to democratize society? What is the purpose and goal of the teacher in the public school, and what role can staff development play in furthering the goal? In this chapter, we explore these important questions by arguing that public education must play an important role in moving students and communities toward a more democratic society.

The Purpose of Public Education and Schooling

The chief writer of the Declaration of Independence was, not coincidentally, one of the first to propose that a common education for all children be tax-supported. Thomas Jefferson wrote, "If a civilized nation expects to be ignorant and free, it expects what never was and never will be." The idea of democracy in 1776, as proposed by Jefferson, James Madison, and others, was to break from the rule of royalty, aristocracy, and the priesthood and form a society in which citizens would rule; the free would rule the public domain rather than the king, thus the word "free-dom" rather than "king-dom." (See Arendt, 1963, for a fuller discussion of freedom.) The essential ingredient for governance by the people was to be a common education for all citizens. There was, of course, an obvious contradiction in the idea of democracy in 1776. Citizens of the United States were mostly white men with property. Women, African Americans, Native Americans, and the poor were not included as citizens. The African American activist and scholar W.E.B. Du Bois [1924], 1971 more than adequately addressed this contradiction when he wrote: "What do we mean by democracy? Do we mean democracy of the white races and the subjection of the colored races? Or do we mean the gradual working forward to a time when all men will have a voice in government and industry and will be intelligent enough to express the voice?" (pp. 257–258).

Contemporary thinkers such as Cornel West have echoed Du Bois's concerns about the current practice and the potential of democratic principles for all people. West (1993), a descendant of slaves who lived during the revolution, wrote, "The greatest experiment in humankind began in 1776 [because] . . . it made the sanctity of each and every one of us . . . at least possible" (p. 8). Thus the ideals of American democracy have, in time, created a moral consciousness that has been used to include others as citizens—that is, the common school movement, the women's suffrage movement, the elimination of Jim Crow laws and legally separated schools, and the civil rights movement. For example, the idea of free public education received an important boost during the post-bellum era when recently freed Negroes demanded universal, state-supported public education. Realizing that they were entitled to a democratic existence as stated in the Constitution, the Bill of Rights, and the Thirteenth Amendment, Negroes during the period believed that education was perhaps the most important means of obtaining their civil liberties. Education therefore had most important implications for democracy (see Anderson, 1988).

Education and Schooling

Mwalimu Shujaa (1994) points out the historically fundamental difference between education and schooling by stating that schooling has been intended to perpetuate and maintain existing power relations and institutional structures in society. Education, he notes, is the process of transmitting the knowledge of values, aesthetics, spiritual beliefs, and culture from one generation to the other. Although Shujaa's definition provides important insight into a *modus operandi* of an oppressive or liberative society, we borrow from his definition to construct our own. We believe that the practices of public schools must become congruent with beliefs of public education for a better and more inclusive democratic society. For us, *public schooling* consists of the institutional practices and administrative structures that guide how a school operates to educate its students. Schooling includes practices such as class scheduling, staffing, testing, grouping, learning methods, and discipline procedures. It nurtures the environment in which learning occurs (Glickman, 1993). *Public education* is the knowledge base; epistemological perspective; and teacher, parent, and community modeling that gives students the tools they need to participate in society.

Our ideal of public education is one in which students are engaged in reflection and action that constantly encourage them to move America toward a "truer" democratic society. A democratic society, we believe, is one in which people of all races, cultures, religions, genders, and sexual orientations have access to what the American founders called unalienable rights. One role of public education, as we shall explain later, is to challenge schools and society to live up to their claims of democracy and to address, head on, issues and problems that have historically impeded the realization of American democracy. We believe that the realization of democracy is a noble cause for public education; it can be readily found in the writings of a group of diverse people such as Thomas Jefferson, Benjamin Franklin, Martin Luther King, and W.E.B. Du Bois, as well as more recent theorists such as Amy Gutmann (1987), bell hooks (1994), and Cornel West (1993).

The Mission and Goal of Public Education

Ideally, all American public schools should have a mission, consistent with these words (Glickman, 1998c): "We hold these truths to be self-evident: that all students are created equal; that they are endowed by their creator with certain unalienable rights; that among these are an education that would ensure life, liberty, and the pursuit of happiness."

To our mind, the goal of public education is to enable students to become valued and valuable citizens of a democracy, learn to be free, have and make choices about their future, and govern themselves individually and collectively. All other outcomes (such as jobs; vocation; and intellectual, recreational, cultural, social, and aesthetic pursuits) are subgoals of this larger goal and are fully realized only in a classroom and school when connected to the larger goal. Obviously, to enact this "Declaration of Public Education" is a monumental challenge for teachers and other educators. It involves a core and diverse set of knowledge, skills, and understanding for all students. It ensures that they have the opportunity to pursue individual interests. And it requires that they demonstrate and apply their learning by contributing to a larger community, beyond classmates and teachers.

Democratic Learning

Democracy is as much a theory of learning as it is a political theory. It is a theory that when practiced in classrooms and schools shows astounding results in student achievement and advancement

(Newmann and Wehlage, 1995; Aiken, 1942; and Meier, 1995). A democracy strives for the progress of all its citizens by protecting general diffusion of knowledge, freedom of expression, a free press, the marketplace of ideas, and unfettered pursuit of truth. The idea is that the masses, when in an environment that supports open participation and human construction of knowledge, will learn more than if a king, an aristocrat, or the wealthy control and determine what they should learn. The idea of people being able to learn best through their own participation is a revolutionary concept about the educability of all humans as curious and self-seeking. Thus, the job of the public educator is to structure a learning environment developmentally to support the human capacity to seek for oneself. Paulo Freire (1970) stressed the importance of this type of guided autonomous learning as contrary to the "banking" practice of education, which merely "deposits" information into students' minds for the purpose of rote regurgitation. Instead, we suggest that democratic learning encourages students to take an active role in their own learning by giving them greater choice and more autonomy in their acquisition, production, and application of knowledge.

Democratic learning, however, is not without direction and guidance from the teacher. The teacher has the responsibility to use his or her unique attributes—position, experience, age, and wisdom—to guide students to the fundamental aim of a democratic society: learning to be free. Consequently, democracy and education are not separate concepts but two sides of the same coin. (In his classic work of 1916, *Democracy and Education*, Dewey rightfully claimed that the purpose of education is democracy, but he missed an important dimension of democracy as the most powerful form of learning. Thus we prefer the term democracy *as* education (see Glickman, 1998a, 1998b, 1998c).

Democratic learning consists of curriculum, methods, and assessments that demand student activity, purposeful choices, and tight connections between academics and community contributions (see Chapter Nineteen for further explanation).

Public Demonstrations of Student Learning

The impetus to knowing whether a teacher and school is teaching for democratic purpose is the set of classroom and school standards and visible assessments that determine how a student can integrate and apply his or her learning to make a contribution to a larger community. Here are some questions that lead to development of such public demonstration:

- What should virtually all students be able to know and do prior to leaving my classroom and our school?
- What should the product be: a portfolio, an exhibit, a project, a demonstration, a presentation?
- Who should review and assess learning beyond the immediate teacher: other faculty, staff, parents, peers, and other community members?
- What should the criteria be—for example, a study of a problem, issue, or topic that shows connections among three or more disciplines; the use of basic skills of reading, writing, arithmetic, and speaking; incorporation of technology; showing skills of study investigation and problem solving; and making application and contribution to a real setting at school or in the home, community, state, nation, or world?
- Finally, how do we judge the quality of the work, that is, accurate knowledge used; sufficient explanation of issue or problem; clear usage and grammatically correct reading, forms of writing, and speaking; appropriate use of technology as a tool to gain information and construct a display; application to a real setting being feasible and showing direct and immediate benefits? (See excellent examples of such public demonstrations in Meier, 1995; McDonald, 1996; Wood, 1998; Blythe, Allen, and Powell, 1999.)

The classroom and school should be a center of applied knowledge that extends learning to the community, and vice versa (Alridge, 1999). This type of communal education taps into the realities of the community and gives students a laboratory of sorts to conduct research; interact with community leaders; and examine real neighborhood, state, national, and world issues and problems. This *social action* and *communal education* approach, we believe, is an essential component in how public education should promote a more democratic society. (Jerome Morris [1999] has discussed the importance of communal schools in advocating what he terms communal bonds. In his recent field studies of several schools in St. Louis, Morris found that the community and community-school interactions facilitated better learning experience for students, particularly African Americans.)

Gloria Ladson-Billings (1994) wrote, in her study of successful teachers of African American children, that successful schools are responsive to the traditions of one's own community: "[The school] has one requirement—that its students be successful. The curriculum is rigorous and exciting. The student learning is organized around problems and issues. . . . The students have studied cities in ancient African Kingdoms, Europe, and Asia. They are studying their own city. They have taken trips to City Hall. . . . Groups of students are working on solutions to problems specific to the city" (pp. 140–141).

The same view of student learning combined with community is seen in the historic teaching methods of Native Americans. Norbert Hill (1993) wrote of the "Indian Way" that "the universe is the 'university.' The acquisition of [learning]] was largely a by-product of life experiences, including observation and participation in the activities of adults. . . . Assistance and guidance, rather than domination and control, were the way of our elders, our greatest teachers. . . . An enlightened teacher would encourage students to engage their curiosity through co-generating and participating in a variety of activities" (pp. 171–173).

What is being expressed by Ladson-Billings (1994) and Hill (1993), as well as by Morris (1999), Sonia Nieto and C. Rólon (1995), and others, is that student learning must be integral to adult issues of one's neighborhood and larger society. Thus, environmental, economical, social, historic, and civic issues of a larger community become the anchor for student application. For example, when students apply their learning of mathematics, science, and reading to solving issues of soil erosion, pollution, design of a local suspension bridge, creation of economic development activities, planning new housing, and discovering the lost history of elders, they come to know firsthand how their learning promotes a healthier neighborhood. It is well documented that when students apply their learning in a participatory and contributory way, their mastery of subject knowledge and skills is much greater than when no such application is expected or required.

In conceptualizing the role of public education and the connection to issues of community in the twenty-first century, we must also attend to the issues of race, class, gender, and culture that permeate American society and education. Given the recent number of hate crimes, the increase in stratification of the poor from the wealthy, and the growing number of ethnically and culturally diverse groups in the United States, public education must deal with the societal realities of our time and culture. Teachers and schools must assist students to provide real solutions to the problems of the lives of all people in an open, democratic society (see Banks, 1994). Racism, sexism, religious intolerance, and homophobia are a reality—an economic, social, and political one. These issues are controversial and difficult, but they cannot be ignored or merely marginalized if teachers are to promote the type of discourse that is necessary to realize a more democratic society (Delpit, 1995).

The Role of the Teacher and Staff Development

The role of a teacher or school is not to indoctrinate students into a certain perspective or way of thinking about social issues, but instead to give students the skills to analyze and think for themselves.

This proceeds through professional learning and staff development that opens a new window of understanding about students, teaching, learning, purpose, community, and oneself. To move toward more principled democratic learning, a teacher can begin in a number of ways: reading a journal; watching a video; seeking information and discussion on Websites; and attending a class, presentation, or conference. A teacher on his or her own might construct an individual, personal plan to include, annually, two components: information gathering and classroom practice—for example, (1) accessing information about democratic learning, multicultural perspectives, public demonstrations and assessments of students, and school and community bonds; and (2) setting and implementing classroom learning goals with one's own students.

In an experiential manner, a teacher might carefully select and participate with a group of people outside of his or her own friends and colleagues. He or she might visit classrooms, homes, and social and civic settings of people of different ethnicity, religion, economic class, gender, and ideology. The intent is to learn, use, and appreciate the differences among people and to have such experience guide working with one's own students and their parents or caretakers.

At another level, one might proceed with professional development plans with colleagues in one's own school, such as being part of a school study group, planning and implementing a school-based program of staff development, observing and coaching each other on jointly agreed classroom changes, having a critical-friends group of colleagues meeting monthly to share and assess the quality of student work, or being part of a schoolwide effort to better define democratic purpose and classroom practice. Participating with equally curious peers at the local, state, or national level in a teacher or school renewal network is a further, powerful way to support, learn, and act.

The quest to connect education, school, and democracy with the practices of learning is a never-ending challenge. All of these experiences can be exhilarating, at times exhausting, but always satisfying to know that professional and personal learning is an ongoing process. It is why most of us choose to be public educators in the first place.

Conclusion

Education with a public purpose has several important connotations: the purpose of education for democratic citizenship; the use of participatory learning and application for students; demonstration of student learning; and involvement of the larger public—colleagues, parents, citizens, students—in the life decisions of the school. For an individual or a school to do this work entails openness and vulnerability to criticism, revision, and constant change (Greene, 1973). It means taking scarce time to rethink, reconsider, reflect, and rework one's craft. To proceed means to find others—ideological friends and foes—to look at a classroom, judge student work, and change curriculum and learning together.

What appears to be a small change in increasing the involvement and participation of students in their learning might in actuality be a huge psychological step for a teacher who has been wedded to past routine. For educators to open their classroom and the nature of student work to others—colleagues and parents—can be fraught with anxiety. To work in a place where public purpose is encouraged and supported throughout the school and by its official leaders through provision of time and opportunities for professional development is the optimum learning community. Regardless, one who is an educator with a deep concern for public purpose cannot wait for others.

Education alone cannot bring about a totally just and democratic society. However, public education and schooling has historically played an important role in how we view and shape our future society, and its potential for furthering future democratic goals is unquestionable. Given the great diversity that America experienced in the twentieth century and the reality that the United States is one of the most ethnically diverse countries in the world, it is important that we stop and revisit the ideals of public education. As society becomes more racially, ethnically, religiously, and culturally diverse in this new century, we will be challenged in ensuring democracy for a plethora of groups with differing values and perspectives. We must search for more innovative and inclusive means of ensuring that public education is accessible to all Americans, that the process of schooling promotes democratic education for all, and that the end result of public education is further development of a more democratic society. No small task by any means—but after all, this is central to why we teach.

References

Aiken, W. F. *The Story of the Eight-Year Study, with Conclusions and Recommendations*. New York: HarperCollins, 1942.

Alridge, D. P. "Conceptualizing a Du Boisian Philosophy of Education." *Educational Theory*, 1999, 49(3), 359–379.

Anderson, J. *The Education of Blacks in the South*, 1860–1935. Chapel Hill: University of North Carolina Press, 1988.

Arendt, H. *On Revolution*. New York: Penguin, 1963.

Banks, J. A. *Multi-Ethnic Education: Theory and Practice* (3rd ed.). Needham Heights, Mass.: Allyn and Bacon, 1994.

Blythe, T., Allen, D., and Powell, B. S. *Looking Together at Student Work*. New York: Teachers College Press, 1999.

Delpit, L. *Other People's Children: Cultural Conflict in the Classroom*. New York: New Press, 1995.

Dewey, J. *Democracy and Education: An Introduction to the Philosophy of Education*. Old Tappan, N.J.: Macmillan, 1916.

Du Bois, W.E.B. *The Gift of Black Folk*. New York: AMS Press, 1971. (Originally published 1924)

Freire, P. *Pedagogy of the Oppressed*. New York: Herder and Herder, 1970.

Glickman, C. D. *Renewing America's Schools: A Guide for School-Based Action*. San Francisco: Jossey-Bass, 1993.

Glickman, C. D. "Educational Leadership for Democratic Purpose." *International Journal of Leadership in Education*, 1998a, 1(1), 47–53.

Glickman, C. D. "Revolution, Education, and the Practice of Democracy." *Education Forum*, Fall 1998b, 63, 16–22.

Glickman, C. D. *Revolutionizing America's Schools*. San Francisco: Jossey-Bass, 1998c.

Greene, M. *Teacher as Stranger*. Belmont, Calif.: Wadsworth, 1973.

Gutmann, A. *Democratic Education*. Princeton, N.J.: Princeton University Press, 1987.

Hill, N. "Reclaiming American Indian Education." In S. Elam (ed.), *The State of the Nation's Public Schools*. Bloomington, Ind.: Phi Delta Kappa Society, 1993.

hooks, b. *Teaching to Transgress: Education as the Practice of Freedom*. New York: Routledge, 1994.

Ladson-Billings, G. *The Dreamkeepers: Successful Teachers of African American Children*. San Francisco: Jossey-Bass, 1994.

McDonald, J. P. *Redesigning Schools*. San Francisco: Jossey-Bass, 1996.

Meier, D. *The Power of Their Ideas: Lessons for America from a Small School in Harlem*. Boston: Beacon Press, 1995.

Morris, J. E. "A Pillar of Strength: An African American School's Communal Bonds with Families and Community Since *Brown*." *Urban Education*, 1999, *33*(5), 584–605.

Newmann, F. M., and Wehlage, G. G. *Successful School Restructuring: A Report to the Public and Educators by the Center on Organization and Restructuring of Schools*. Madison, Wis.: Wisconsin Center for Education Research, 1995.

Nieto, S., and Rólon, C. "The Preparation and Professional Development of Teachers: A Perspective from Two Latinos." Paper presented to the CULTURES conference Defining the Knowledge Base for Urban Teacher Education, Emory University, Decatur, Ga., Nov. 11, 1995.

Shujaa, M. J. "Education and Schooling: You Can Have One Without the Other." In M. J. Shujaa (ed.), *Too Much Schooling Too Little Education: A Paradox of Black Life in White Societies*. Trenton, N.J.: Africa World Press, 1994.

West, C. *Beyond Eurocentrism and Multiculturalism*. Vol. 1: *Prophetic Thought in Postmodern Time*. Monroe, Me.: Common Courage, 1993.

Wood, G. H. *A Time to Learn*. New York: Dutton, 1998.

Chapter Twenty-Two

The Long Haul

Progressive Education and Keeping the Faith

> Your vision will grow, but you will never be able to
> achieve your goals as you envision them. My vision
> cannot be achieved by me. . . . It's a dream which I
> can't even dream. Other people will pick it up and
> go beyond.
> —*Myles Horton*, The Long Haul: An Autobiography

In these words from his autobiography (written with Judith and Herbert R. Kohl), Myles Horton was explaining the impact of the Highlander Center, which he founded in 1932. Long after his death, Highlander continues as one of the leading progressive education institutions for civil and human rights. In his words: "the problem [for a democracy] is not that people will make irresponsible or wrong decisions. It is, rather, to convince people . . . that the danger is not too much, but too little participation" (Horton, 1998, p. 134). The need to define the role of education and citizenship in furthering a participatory democracy is the crux of the matter for progressive educators; their schools have to be sustained so that "other people will pick it up and go beyond."

When a school is created around such ideas of education for democracy, it knowingly challenges the status, hierarchy, privilege, and control of mainstream society. Efforts to change the nature of learning in K–12 schools toward integrated, participatory, and performance-based education for all students typically meet opposition from many policy makers, school boards, parents, administrators, students, and the teaching profession itself. Education continues to be viewed mainly in economic and utilitarian terms, its purpose supposedly to produce skilled workers for large industries and corporations and concurrently to sort out a select group of academically talented students to take leadership roles in science, media, technology, government, and management. The pervasive norms of the classroom and school have been premised on student passivity, conformity, and competition, and many teachers have learned the role of covering predetermined curriculum, preparing students for narrow state or national tests, and keeping them conforming to prescribed rules and conventions. Hierarchical control imbues the entire system of public schooling, from state to district, from district to individual school, from principal to teachers, and from teacher to students.

Those who believe differently about the ultimate purpose of education—students learning to be free and responsible citizens—do so with great courage. The grand idea that public education is for life, liberty, and the pursuit of happiness and to judge the world for what it might be frightens those who know only how to control, protect, maintain, and reinforce the world as it is.

In Public Trust

In a convocation address I gave to the 2002 graduating class of a large state university, I reminded the class that their public education was not due to their efforts alone. Their university was established long ago "to serve the citizens of the state, nation, and world." The university was to be held in perpetual "public trust." Over two hundred years or more in existence, public schools and universities and states have repeatedly violated this public trust in terms of who is regarded as a citizen entitled to a quality education and who is not so regarded. Today, the statistics on educational access and quality of life for the poor across all ethnic populations is appalling; in many cases, the situation is more akin to the abject hopelessness of a devastated third-world society than the conditions one would expect for all citizens of the wealthiest country in the world. Of course, there are notable exceptions, but they should not obscure the continuing tragedy of young people attending schools in disrepair, with dispirited faculty and administrators, inadequate materials, and many teachers trying to instruct students in topics they hardly know themselves. These are the students who need the best; instead, what they most often get is the least.

I told the graduates of this rather elite public university that they are now the "we" who have benefited and succeeded from education. "We" need to be aware of the contributions and services that others have made for us. We are indebted to all the people of the state and the nation—from the poorest to the wealthiest—who paid their tax dollars so that we might be educated.

There are many people less well known to us that also deserve our appreciation: the neighbors who watched us grow up, the school bus drivers who transported us as small children to school, primary and secondary teachers who cared for us, the custodians who maintained our buildings, the police officers and firefighters who tried to keep us safe, the construction workers who built our roads to drive upon and buildings to learn in, farmers and agriculture workers who processed our food, postal service employees who kept us informed . . . the list goes on and on.

We, as the successful products of public education, should never walk by a citizen or resident without being aware of the contribution that person has made to us. Public trust of using our education well cannot be simply a rhetorical idea; it must be central to what we do. There are many other students just as bright and able as we are who have not had the same fortune or opportunity. This is not to make us feel guilty but to remind us that fulfilling the obligation of public trust remains our greatest challenge.

National Commission on Service Learning

The National Commission on Service Learning, on which I served as a member, was given the task to determine the form of education that every youngster in America should receive. The commission, chaired by former astronaut and U.S. Sen. John Glenn, consisted of eighteen members, including governors, members of congress, educators, parents, community and business leaders, entertainers, and students (one age eleven, the other seventeen). We represented the spectrum of political, regional, and ethnic diversity of America. Our group met every three months, for two years, and issued a report to local, state, and national leaders about what must be essential to any school, whether P–12 or a university or college that is publicly funded or guided by public purpose (National Commission on Service Learning, 2002).

In our report, we looked at such statistics as the nearly 50 percent decline over the past forty years in citizens participating in local, community, town, state, and world affairs. Regardless of educational attainment and economic success, the decline has been dramatic and steady across all groups. The average American does not engage in democratic citizenry; the majority of Americans do not attend a single public meeting. Rarely do Americans intentionally reach beyond their own economic, professional, religious, ethnic, racial, or social groups to be with others different from themselves to try to solve issues of a larger community.

Next, we looked at the achievement and economic gap that continues to widen in America between the wealthy and the poor as well as the resegregation and isolation between racial, religious, social, professional, and ethnic groups. We concluded that every student must learn that his or her education is not only for personal and career advancement, but for a larger purpose as well. Taxpayers at large, not just parents, pay the overwhelming percentage of education costs so that students can use their education as adults, not to feel superior or impose their beliefs upon others but to participate as equals with people different from themselves, to make decisions together to promote a better democratic society of life, liberty and the pursuit of happiness for all.

September 11, 2001, was an event that, in its horror and drama, symbolized to Americans the grappling for identity of a people who do not simply share a land but who share a common idea about the dignity and equality of all citizens to govern with and for themselves. After September 11, citizens and residents from almost all ways of American life became more tolerant and supportive of each other. (There was one notable extension to this new and higher level of trust: what we had with our Arab American and Muslim neighbors. The level of trust shown them was high with a majority of Americans, but at a lower percentage compared with other American ethnic and religious groups. At the time of the survey, a lower level of trust may be understandable, but it can never be acceptable.)

Educators in some schools saw the aftermath of September 11 as an opportunity for greater understanding about democracy, reciprocal obligation, and linking academics with public purpose. For example:

Following the terrorists attacks, students at the White Knoll Middle School in West Columbia, South Carolina, looked for a way they could help New York City. They learned that in 1867 a fire company in New York City had sent a fire wagon to their counterparts in Columbia as a peace offering to replace equipment lost in the Civil War. The gift was documented in a local museum, along with a pledge from a former confederate soldier that South Carolina's capital city would some day return the kindness "should misfortune ever befall the Empire City."

White Knoll students set out to honor this pledge; they launched a campaign to raise $354,000 to purchase a new fire engine for New York City. They studied the historical background of the gift in social studies class. They applied language arts skills as they wrote letters to firefighters in New York City's Red Hook Ladder Company 101 and to friends and family members to solicit donations. In art class, they created posters to advertise their fundraising efforts and made a huge fire truck mural to track incoming contributions in the school's front hall. Gifts and pledges arrived from throughout the state and beyond. Two months after the start of the campaign, they reached their goal [National Commission on Service Learning, 2002, p. 2].

These students indeed learned how to use their education to serve public purpose. All of us as progressive educators need to think of more powerful ways to link the academic and intellectual mission of the school with the responsibility of participatory citizenship.

Democratic Education:
To Learn, to Serve, to Question, and to Act

At some scale and in many ways, all those who attend a school with public purpose have to learn how to use their education in the service of others. If students don't learn to do so while in school, then most likely they will never know how education can advance a better society for all. The historic decline in citizen engagement continues and the ideals of a democracy remain as sound bites in political campaigns, but in reality, it will be a failed experiment among people.

To create and sustain schools where every student becomes a valued and valuable citizen of an improving democratic society means that students must be given the opportunity to apply their learning, from such noncontroversial issues as improving entertainment for the elderly or creating reading literature for a home with young children to the most provocative issues of our time in regard to environment, economics, health, cloning, life inception, welfare, and defining a good democratic society for all. The range of issues should be selected according to the student's age, experience, community; over time, students should be given wider choice as to how to use academics in the context of the pressing issues of our time.

The challenge of progressive education is to recenter schooling on intellectual inquiry and public engagement while respecting the student's capacity to come to his or her own conclusions. The noted and progressive educator Deborah Meier refers to this, in her own schools, as "habits of mind" (see Meier, 1995, p. 50). Student work must be assessed according to whether the student employed evidence, viewpoint, logic, supposition, and impact. The questions that guide the work are: How do we know what we know? Who's speaking? What causes what? How might things have been different? and Who cares?

The test of quality work is how well the student has studied, applied, and demonstrated understanding, not the conclusion itself. One of the most renowned progressive educators once said to me that "the test of a progressive education is whether students are free to come to their own conclusions and take stances in opposition to the predominant personal and political views of the teacher and other adults in the school." The responsibility of progressive educators is to demand intellectual study that results in a concrete contribution to others, not to convince students of the rightness of one's own political or personal stance.

Progressive Education for the Long Haul: Faith and Democracy

The record of sustaining progressive schools can appear discouraging.[1] There are many examples of such schools being created and thriving for a few years and then returning to a conventional pattern of passive and hierarchical education.[2] Yet I have found many other examples of hope in my visits across the country. I uncovered a number of K–12 schools in varied demographic settings and regions of the United States that are still surviving and thriving in the year 2002; all have been in existence for at least ten years and many for twenty to thirty years or more. I examined each school individually, and I have written about them in some of the previous chapters of this book. I detailed the common elements of planning, laying a foundation, refining pedagogy, making wise and careful use of politics in their work, and keeping the idea of education with public purpose central to what students learn and how students make a tangible contribution to their community.

Some of the schools I found stayed out of the glare of publicity and had the influence of internal school leaders and cheerleaders to protect them from the sway of district or state policy. Other schools prospered as the result of steady and supportive policy from the district and a mandate from local citizens and parents who wanted the school to always be part of the district and the reputation of their community. In all cases, the vision, principle, and practices of the school stood above dependency on a single charismatic individual; the educational program and culture of the school became a magnet. These schools attracted new leaders, faculty, students, and parents who wanted to be part of such a school and do as Myles Horton suggested: "pick it up and go beyond." I found no uniform steps or activities that could be used as a prescription for other schools to follow. Instead, what I did find was a set of common understandings about education, perseverance in pursuing such beliefs, and serendipitous happenings that formed a secular faith.

In a panel discussion about progressive education, I was politely upbraided by a prominent education reporter from one of the major newspapers in America. He said that the active, participatory, and contributory student learning that I spoke about and that is needed in schools to improve democratic society requires clear and compelling research showing that it works before other schools should make it part of their curriculum. I understood what he was saying, and I first replied by citing a list of references of studies on student achievement that he could review. However, I also told him that his statement about clear and compelling evidence was exactly what successful progressive schools do not wait upon. I told him that his critique totally missed the essential concept of a democracy.

For example, do we need convincing, "clear and compelling" proof that all people are born equal before we, as a society should act upon the notion as true? I would hope not, because the clear evidence is that we are not born equal. Some of us are born tall, some short. All of us differ in aptitude; intelligence; and physical, social, and aesthetic ability. My fourteen-year-old nephew knows numeric fluency in a way that will always be beyond me. It is obvious that we are not born equal, and it should be obvious that we must not rely on research to prove that this democratic belief is wrong. Regardless of what research says, we must strive as a society on the belief, not the empirical fact, that every human is born equal and to be accorded respect and dignity with the same rights and responsibilities as anyone else. Our job is not to prove the premise but to act on the belief in how we respond, educate, and live with one another.

Democracy is a sacred, secular belief about the breathtaking concept that people can live, care, and govern themselves more wisely than kings, tyrants, oligarchs, or benevolent dictators can do for them. Is there today clear proof that democracy is the best form of political life, so that we can then take action accordingly? Even today, America has not furnished clear and convincing proof that our current democracy provides the highest quality of life for all of its people. Perhaps it does so economically, for corporations, executives, and the professional class, and perhaps it does so for those individuals who have advanced and succeeded materialistically. But is it the best form of government for those who live homeless, in danger, in hunger, or in poor health without health benefits? Is American democracy the best form of society? Working hours here continue to climb compared to other industrial nations. The average person now takes less than two weeks a year in vacation for leisure time with children, family, and neighbors (Greenhouse, 2001). As Robert Reich writes, how do we measure success? (Reich, 2001). The United States is a wonderful country in many ways for so many people, but it is also a terrible country in many ways for so many people (see Rapp, 2002; and Reich, 2001). So maybe democracy does not have clear and compelling evidence that it is the best form of government. Do we stop trying it?

Cornell West wrote that "democracies are rare in human history, they are fragile, and historically they tend not to last that long. Oligarchic, plutocratic, pigmentocratic, patriarchal forces suffocate so easily democratic forces. And America has been so privileged because there has always been a prophetic slice across race, religion, and class, and gender, and sexual orientation, a progressive slice that says we are not going to give up on this fragile democratic project, it is incomplete and unfinished, but we are not going to give up on it, even against the grain of so much human history" (2000).

No, we do not wait or stop trying. The belief, not the empirical proof, leads us on. It is the job of progressive educators to demonstrate that democracy can thrive when students leave school knowing that an education can reinvigorate a democracy that promotes the dignity and well-being of all. It is the job of our generation to sustain the progressive dream of education. We can not possibly imagine what this wiser, healthier, and more caring world might look like, but the next generation will learn from our efforts and pick up our dream and remake it their own.

Notes

1. The story of Lord Byron Secondary School in Ontario is a sobering illustration about the track record of the sustainability of a progressive school. Dean Fink, the author of a case study of his once-famous school, joined the Byron staff in the early 1970s as a department chair. The school at that time was noted for its interdisciplinary curriculum, heterogeneous grouping, and activity-centered and participatory student learning. It was established as a "lighthouse" model for the future of progressive, secondary education. It attracted visitors from Canada, the United States, and other countries. It was staffed by a young, passionate faculty led by a brilliant and charismatic principal; it had the strong support of its school board and central office.

   Fink chronicled the demise of the original vision of the school through three overlapping periods. The first (1970–1978) was "creativity and experimentation," and the second period (mid-1970s to early 1980s) was an era of "overreaching" in which the school took on too many new innovations and "outstripped" the community's ability to comprehend and support the school. The final era, from the mid-1980s on, was one of "survival and continuity" by backtracking from the original vision and "joining the mainstream" of regimented and conventional high schools in the district and province (see Fink, 2000, especially p. 11).

The school fell victim to too much reliance on a single leader, perceptions of too much freedom given too quickly to students, a change in student enrollment numbers, the departure of key and talented faculty who were recruited by other schools, provincial swings in politics and economics, and growing animosity from faculty of other schools in the district who resented the attention given to and claims made by the Byron school faculty. Sadly, the picture of Lord Byron is the more common story about progressive schools, which typically have a beginning surge of creativity and afterward can no longer sustain their original vision. To read more of this discouraging research on progressive and innovative schools, see Elmore, 1996; Giacquinta, 1988; Hargreaves, Lieberman, Fullan, and Hopkins, 1998; McLaughlin, 1998; Miles, 1998, Levin, 1998; McDonald, 1996).

2. I also found a number of schools in the United States that had been pioneers for only a short time but literally spawned other progressive schools through partnership, professional development, mentoring, and hiring. These spawned schools continue to thrive today even though the original mother school is no longer operating as a progressive school. This phenomenon of spawning before death is an important and interesting issue for future study on progressive education.

References

Elmore, R. "Getting to Scale with Good Education Practice." *Harvard Leadership*, 1996, *37*(1), 15–24.

Fink, D. *Good Schools/Real Schools: Why School Reform Doesn't Last*. New York: Teachers College Press, 2000.

Giacquinta, J. "Seduced and Abandoned: Some Lasting Conclusions About Planned Change from the Cambire School Study." In A. Hargreaves, A. Lieberman, M. Fullan, and D. Hopkins (Eds.), *International Hand-*

book of Educational Change, Parts One and Two. Dordrecht, Netherlands: Kluwer, 1998.

Greenhouse, S. "Americans: We're No. 1 at Working." *New York Times*, Sept. 1, 2001. (In *Atlanta Journal Constitution*, same date)

Hargreaves, A., Lieberman, A., Fullan, M., and Hopkins, D. (eds.). *International Handbook of Educational Change, Parts One and Two*. Dordrecht, Netherlands: Kluwer, 1998.

Horton, M., with Kohl, J., and Kohl, H. *The Long Haul: An Autobiography*. New York: Teachers College Press, 1998.

Levin, H. "Accelerated Schools: Decade of Evolution." In A. Hargreaves, A. Lieberman, M. Fullan, and D. Hopkins (eds.), *International Handbook of Educational Change, Parts One and Two*. Dordrecht, Netherlands: Kluwer, 1998.

McDonald, J. P. *Redesigning School: Lessons for the 21st Century*. San Francisco: Jossey-Bass, 1996.

McLaughlin, M. W. "Listening and Learning from the Field: Tales of Policy Implementation and Situated Practice." In A. Hargreaves, A. Lieberman, M. Fullan, and D. Hopkins (eds.), *International Handbook of Educational Change, Parts One and Two*. Dordrecht, Netherlands: Kluwer, 1998.

Meier, D. *The Power of Their Ideas: Lessons for America from a Small School in Harlem*. Boston: Beacon Press, 1995.

Miles, M. "Finding Keys to School Change: A 40-Year Odyssey." In A. Hargreaves, A. Lieberman, M. Fullan, and D. Hopkins (eds.), *International Handbook of Educational Change, Parts One and Two*. Dordrecht, Netherlands: Kluwer, 1998.

National Commission on Service Learning. *Learning in Deed: The Power of Service Learning for Schools*. Kalamazoo, Mich.: W. K. Kellogg Foundation, 2002.

Rapp, D. "Social Justice and the Importance of Rebellious, Oppositional Imaginations." *Journal of School Leadership*, May 2002, *12*, 226–245.

Reich, R. B. *The Future of Success*. New York: Knopf, 2001.

West, C. "Democracies Are Rare." Keynote address, Coalition of Essential Schools' Fall Forum 2000, Providence, R.I., 2000.

Appendix A
Has Sam and Samantha's
Time Come at Last?

Reunion with an old friend, arriving late afternoon, hurried discussions about shared events, catching up on family and lost acquaintances, tales about graduate school . . . and the two of us laughing as old pictures are brought out. Each picture spins more stories, more laughter, and more reminiscing about the two years when we taught together and lived in the same community.

Then dinner is over, and the two of us remain seated in our chairs. I start thinking of how Sam and I began teaching together twenty years ago. We were both bright-faced twenty-two-year-olds eager to save the world. He came from the Southwest, from a large farming family; I was from the Northeast, from a suburban clan near a major city. That first year, we were joined by a third person, Samantha, from the West coast, a former Peace Corps volunteer.

The three of us—beyond being new, transplanted, and eager to be teachers—had little common history. We were of different races, religions, and backgrounds. But from 1968 to 1970, we became fast friends, teaching in the same school in a small rural community in the Southeast. We made naïve and tactless blunders with school administrators and community officials, but we also made some heartfelt connections with our junior high school students and their parents. Twenty years ago, I could see Sam and Samantha were talented educators; students clamored to be with them, and their students learned! They taught in unconventional and

---

The author is indebted to the writings of and conversations with Arthur Wise for clarifying the current state of educational reform.

boisterous ways, but everyone in the school—old-time teachers, administrators, students, and parents—concurred that these two could teach.

After dinner, Sam and I discussed the different paths taken by the three of us. Samantha had moved with her husband (and dogs) to upstate New York; she had become a career teacher in a village elementary school. On occasions when I've been to New York State, people who know Samantha narrate to me that she's become almost legendary in her classroom exploits. As for Sam, he's still in the same community and teaching in the same school district where we all began. He switched to the high school in 1973 and has been there since. He also is a career teacher. As for me, I moved back to New England to teach, then became a school principal, and eventually went into university work, first in Ohio and now in Georgia.

Later that evening, in the living room with our feet up, Sam and I discussed education and the impact of reform. The tone of our conversation became quite serious. I was somewhat taken aback by his views.

"I've been teaching for twenty years now," he said, "and I can't remember all the 'reforms' I've been through. I'm not sure that I can take another one! It seems that every three years, someone—whether it's a new hotshot superintendent, the state department, the governor, or a university professor—comes up with some great new idea of how American education is to be saved. What happens is that my colleagues and I become the punching bag recipients of someone else's plan.

"Why is it so hard for people outside the classroom, including you folks from the university, to understand that we teachers know at least as much about our students, teaching, and ways to improve as you do? To be blunt, I've seen these ideas come and go, and each reform dumps more work on us; and we're still left with our 125 students a day, working under the same work conditions that I had twenty years ago. Each new idea that comes down from on high doesn't improve my teaching; it often takes away from my teaching! Today I'm being forced to teach in ways that I know are not in the best interest of students."

I listened carefully because Sam was telling me almost verbatim the sentiments expressed by scores of other teachers that I highly respect. I read surveys showing that teachers as a group have had it up to their ears with paperwork, lesson alignment, teaching to test objectives, and being monitored and evaluated according to how closely they follow a lockstep sequence of instruction (Boyer, 1988). But hearing these remarks from Sam meant more to me than survey statistics. I knew him as a friend first, then as a teacher—he isn't a doomsayer, he isn't a radical. He's a sensible, sane, reserved person who cares about his students. He doesn't look for ways to make his job easier; instead, he looks for ways to do more for his students. When he spoke to me, friend to friend, I knew that his was not a union tactic or a special-interest plea. If Samantha had been with us, I suspect she would have concurred with Sam's sentiments in language even more forceful and colorful.

It took me several months after our reunion—talking with teachers and administrators throughout the United States and Canada, working with our demonstration school projects in Georgia, reading articles, and attending conferences with education policy analysts such as Arthur Wise (1988), Larry Cuban (1987), Susan Rosenholtz (1988), and Michael Kirst (1987)—to begin to understand the critical intersection of school reform now being played out. This intersection has to do with whether, at last, it is Sam and Samantha's time. If so, supervision in schools will become the vehicle to bring Sam and Samantha into the process of decision making about teaching. If not, supervision will remain what it has "usually been about: status, authority, and the peculiar evil of silence" (Glickman, 1988).

Two Reform Movements

In the early 1970s, the first reform movement, called *legislated learning* (Wise, 1987), began as part of school accountability, competency-based education, performance contracting, and the neoscientific view that research could uncover scientific principles and factors in effective schools and effective teaching. If students were not learning and if schools were not improving, it was because educators were not following the best available scientific evidence.

Therefore the spate of early 1980 reports, which painted a bleak picture of public education and student achievement, added fuel to the scientific reductionist view of reform: the need for installing "best practice" in the schools. *A Nation at Risk* (National Commission on Excellence in Education, 1983) deplored the mediocrity of education and stated unequivocally that schools as they exist have done a ruinous job on the economy and society: an "unfriendly nation" who wished to undermine the United States could not do a better job than what we have done in our schools. Such inflammatory language transformed legislative initiatives into an array of requirements enacted through the prodding of governors throughout the land. The banner words for legislative learning were *academic excellence* (Kirst, 1987). We were to become schools of excellence, centers of excellence, and have excellent education. The way this was to be accomplished was that the states (by way of their department of education) were to take control of local schools with "standards" and "requirements." Legislative mandates of statewide curriculum, statewide tests, statewide teacher evaluation, statewide promotion and retention policies, and statewide mentor career ladder plans were enacted (Cornett, 1987).

To be sure, such renewed interest in education created benefits: more equitable funding formulas for schools, improved salaries, scholarships and career incentives, facility upgrades, and the like. But the legislated learning and academic excellence reform was primarily a top-down, philosophically essentialist movement that viewed teachers and administrators as *the problem* of poor schools. The feeling was that schools left to local educators and local boards could not be trusted.

Since the early 1970s, there have been nearly two decades of increased regulation and tightened external control over school operations. The typical action for determining a solution to school improvement has been to appoint a state blue-ribbon commission of political and corporate leaders (with token representation from educators). The commission then listened to research experts develop a list of requirements for schools; it then had the list revised and approved by the state legislature, signed by the governor, and enforced by the state department. Every three to five years, when education results are publicized as still unsatisfactory, the next blue-ribbon commission is impaneled and another round of legislated learning occurs.

The second and more recent reform movement is entitled *empowerment* and the banner that flies over it reads *restructuring schools* (Pipho, 1988). For various reasons—increased dissatisfaction with the results of legislated learning, less state money than expected to fund legislated mandates, and a political climate shifting to domestic issues of poverty and disenfranchisement—there is now a different experimental and pragmatic view of school reform. The new view is that local teachers and administrators are *the solution to,* rather than the source of, school problems. Therefore, to give local educators maximum flexibility to address the particular educational and instructional concerns of their students and community, schools must be deregulated.

This bottom-up view of school reform—where the district and the state provide resources, money, and knowledge to the local schools in facilitating their own instructional decisions—is an attempt to promote variety rather than uniformity of practice across schools and districts. The premise is that there do not (and never will) exist scientifically validated best practices of supervision and teaching. Rather, best practice means what is best for students by those teachers closest to them. Reports by the Carnegie Forum on Education and the Economy (1986) and the Holmes Group (1986) have stimulated much discussion about this grassroots approach to school improvement whereby teachers are the primary instructional decision makers in the school. The principal is not seen as the sole instructional leader but rather as the leader of instructional leaders. Teachers are jointly responsible for supervision of instructional tasks in a school and direct assistance with staff development, curriculum development, group development, and action research.[1]

The tension in education, at the moment of this writing, is that two totally contradictory reform movements are going on at the same time. Educators are hearing two antithetical messages. One says, "You have district and state requirements you must comply with." The other says, "You are the professionals, do what you think is best, we'll work with you." It's no wonder that educators feel a bit schizophrenic at this time.

Whether or not education reform remains primarily legislative (although in some states there simply isn't much more that *can* be legislated, short of hiring full-time inspectors for each school) or tilt more toward empowerment has much to do with the initiative and preparation of those in instructional leadership roles. Empowerment sounds the overwhelming bell of approval with most educators, but if it is to succeed, many issues, nuisances, and perils must be personally and professionally faced up to and resolved. If the function of supervision is to empower rather than to enforce compliance of teachers, we must be fully aware of the revolutionary change necessary in how we think about ourselves, teachers, and schools. We also need to consider the transition steps in moving from external control and uniformity of practice to internal control and divergence of practice.

Reform One: The Answers; Reform Two: The Questions

Most reform efforts do not fundamentally alter the prevailing organization scheduling, curriculum, or structure of teaching (Cuban, 1987). For twenty years, legislative learning reforms have applied certain answers by adding more to what is already taking place. Certain answers and uniform answers to reform are readily proposed by laypersons and embraced by the public because they fit into the public notion of teaching and schools. Therefore the practices that are proposed, passed, and regulated to improve schools are characterized as scientifically "derived," "research-based," and "proven answers" that will work if only the local school implements them correctly. However, the answers themselves largely call for doing more of what is already being done. Most legislated reform enacts:

- More direct teacher-centered instruction
- More homework
- More standardization and restrictions of the curriculum
- More testing of students
- More alignment of lesson plans with test objectives
- More uniform lockstep retention policies
- More and tighter evaluation of teachers

As such practices are implemented, if noticeable improvements in student achievement, success, and attitude are not forthcoming, the next blue-ribbon commission, state superintendent, or district superintendent comes forth with a further plan to tighten, standardize, and demand more of what has previously not worked. As Plank (1987) observed, legislative reform answers tend to "reinforce rather than challenge the present structure . . . [and] have ensured that the main consequence has been further homogenization . . . among schools both across and within states" (pp. 16, 17).

The troublesome point is that as such practices fail to improve learning for students, the answer has been to enforce more of what is not working. For example, there have been only slight gains in basic skills achievement in the past decade as reported in a national survey (Boyer, 1988). Further, Educational Testing Services (1987), in reviewing three National Assessment of Educational Progress Surveys, reports that "evidence is mounting that Americans are not learning to read and write with more than 'surface understanding' whether . . . fourth-grade . . . or young adults, their ability to dissect ideas and defend positions is limited."

Furthermore, seven hundred thousand functionally illiterate adults continue to graduate each year, and an equal number of students drop out of school. The dropout rate in the United States remains alarmingly high. According to Hodginson (1985), "since 1980, the national figure for all students has declined from 76 percent high school graduation to 73 percent. The unintended fall-out from . . . state reforms undoubtedly will cut the number even further" (p. 13). Nearly every month, a new national study reports the poor performance of U.S. students in another academic area (see Rothman, 1989).

Why has legislated reform based on applying more of the same persisted at a time when evidence indicates little progress, and when recent research suggests that successful schools are not a template of homogeneous, standardized, and conventional practice? Legislative top-down reform revolves around authorities' having scientific certainty about improvement, getting Sam and Samantha to do it right.

Empowerment reform raises questions of uncertainty with school practitioners and allows them to work through difficulties toward their own answers. Empowerment reform asks questions that defy the conventional norms, structures, and pat answers of schools:

- Why have grade levels?
- Why have grades?
- What is the best curriculum?
- What are the best locations for education in and out of school?
- Why teach in fifty-minute time periods, six and a half hours a day, five days a week?
- Why have subjects—why not integrated projects?

- Why not evaluate portfolios of student work?
- Why rely on textbooks?
- Why have one teacher, one classroom?
- Why use Carnegie units?

Such questions of uncertainty challenge the fundamental structure of schools.

Albert Shanker, commenting on the reason for students' poor higher-order thinking skills, says that "it is the way schools are pretty universally structured now, that not all kids can sit still and listen to somebody for five or six hours each day" (O'Neil, 1988, p. 6). What Shanker was echoing is a conception of education that has been largely lost in the legislated reform of our schools according to Piaget: "The goal of intellectual education is not to know how to repeat or retain ready-made truths. It is in learning to master the truth by oneself at the risk of losing a lot of time and going through all the roundabout ways that are inherent in real activity" (1973, p. 106).

Some readers may take such question posing as heresy, while others may already work in schools where the questions are raised and answered routinely. They are not meant to shock, simply to indicate that empowerment reform opens the boundaries of acceptable practice and with excitement comes discomfort, dissent, controversy, challenge, and at times fear.

Let's take the mundane convention of the school lunchroom as an example. Students wait in line with their trays, receive their food, and sit at institutional tables. Why? There are a few schools where lunch is an aesthetic, pleasant learning experience, with piped-in music, tablecloths, and family-style serving. Most summer camps operate this way—why not more schools? In the same manner, there are a few high schools in the country that don't use Carnegie units or fifty-minute class periods—why aren't there more? There are elementary programs that don't use basal readers, don't have grade levels, don't use standardized texts; and they are successful. Why aren't there more? There are successful school districts that don't evaluate teachers according to six or seven elements of effective instruction; some evaluate according to three elements: "due regard," "due process," and "due diligence" (Swift Current Public Schools, 1985). Why aren't there more?

The reason there aren't more is that we are rarely challenged to raise questions about conventional practices for new possibilities to emerge. The point of empowerment reform is not that conventional answers should be rejected and that all schools should innovate; the point is that when schools are not regulated by the outside, all instructional practices are fair game for discussion and action. When we open schools to question, we also open schools to responsibility for answers.

Are we willing to identify, ask, and act upon such questions? Do we want the power to do so? Not an idle question—because in doing so, the locus of accountability, responsibility, and comfort changes.

Rhetoric or Reality of Restructuring

Educators think of empowerment as the heady nectar of fragrance, beauty, and strength—but when the state begins to give the district the opportunity to restructure the schools, will we do it? That some schools fight for restructuring in their district and state while others passively complain about external mandates is an indication that when schools are given more freedom, many will probably "talk a good game" but stay within the same conventions. Regrettably, if history is our guide, most people in controlling positions in a school or district would rather complain about education than do something about it (Cuban, 1984; Reid, 1987).

To put ourselves at risk by taking responsibility for change is another matter altogether. What does it mean to prepare ourselves to truly improve schools? I say *truly* because schools will not improve until those people closest to students—teachers—are given the choice and responsibility to make collective informed decisions about teaching practice. The arena of choice, responsibility, and decision making may be small and restrictive for some staff, to begin with, but the direction should be to enlarge choice, responsibility, and decision-making overtime.

Supervision must shift decision making about instruction from external authority to internal control. This is the *only* way, on a large and long-term scale, that supervision will improve instruction. As long as decisions come down from authorities far away from those who teach, we will have a dormant, unattractive work environment that stymies the intellectual growth of teachers and the intellectual life of students.

Teachers are the heart of teaching. Without choice and responsibility, they comply, subvert, or flee; motivation, growth, and collective purpose remain absent. What motivates people to work harder and smarter is not money but a work environment "that lets [professionals] make decisions and nurtures a free exchange of ideas and information" (Harris Survey, 1988).

Transcendent Wisdom, Unleashed Potential

Sam and Samantha taught with me twenty years ago. They have stayed in the classroom, and I have left. I don't come close to possessing the wisdom they have gained about their teaching, their schools, their students, and their communities. Their wisdom is not less than that of their supervisors, principals, central office directors, and state officials. All things considered, it is amazing that they have persevered for so long in schools where they are viewed as workers—not as competent professionals capable of participating in decisions about teaching and learning.

Sam and Samantha represent most teachers: caring and wise, with unleashed potential for making a school what it truly can be: an educative community. Can we acknowledge that teachers possess expertise, knowledge, and concern and will demonstrate a far greater sense of purpose or a cause beyond oneself if decisions are made with, rather than for, them?

Now that the rhetoric of restructuring schools is upon us, the next decade will tell if we are only flirting with change or ready to make a profound commitment to improving schools. At last, is it time for teachers to be equals, rather than perfunctory advisers, in the remaking of education? Is it Sam and Samantha's time?

Note

1. Examples of second-wave reform can be found in the Washington State Schools for the Twenty-First Century Program, the Massachusetts Carnegie School Program, the National Coalition of Essential Schools, the National Network for Educational Renewal, the Georgia Program for School Improvement, the National Education Association's Mastery in Learning Project, the American Federation of Teachers' Research-into-Practice Practitioners Network, and the ASCD's Consortium of Restructured Schools.

References

Boyer, E. *Report on School Reform: The Teachers Speak.* New York: Carnegie Foundation for the Advancement of Teaching, 1988.

Carnegie Forum on Education and the Economy, Task Force on Teaching as a Profession. *A Nation Prepared: Teachers for the 21st Century.* New York: Carnegie Forum on Education and the Economy, 1986.

Cornett, L. "More Pay for Teachers and Administrators Who Do More: Incentive Pay Programs, 1987." *Career Ladder Clearinghouse,* Dec. 1987, pp. 1–27.

Cuban, L. *How Teachers Taught: Constancy and Change in American Classrooms, 1890–1980.* White Plains, N.Y.: Longman, 1984.

Cuban, L. "The District Superintendent and the Restructuring of Schools." Paper presented to the Conference on Restructuring Schooling for Quality Education, Trinity University, San Antonio, Texas, Aug. 1987.

Educational Testing Services. "Learning to Be Literate." *ETS Developments,* 1987, 33(1), 2.

Glickman, C. D. "Supervision and the Rhetoric of Empowerment: Silence or Collision?" *Action in Teacher Education,* 1988, 10(1), 11–15.

Harris Survey. "Rating the Work Place." In *Burlington [Vermont] Free Press,* July 23, 1988, p. 18a.

Hodginson, H. L. *All One System: Demographics of Education—Kindergarten Through Graduate School.* Washington, D.C.: Institute for Educational Leadership, 1985.

Holmes Group. *Tomorrow's Teachers.* East Lansing, Mich.: Holmes Group, 1986.

Kirst, M. W. "Rethinking Who Should Control Our Schools." Paper presented to the Conference on Restructuring Schooling for Quality Education, Trinity University, San Antonio, Texas, Aug. 1987.

National Commission on Excellence in Education. *A Nation at Risk: The Imperative for Educational Reform.* Washington, D.C.: U. S. Government Printing Office, 1983.

O'Neill, J. "Restructured Schools: Frequently Invoked, Rarely Defined." *ASCD Update*, 1988, 30(1), 6.

Piaget, J. *To Understand Is to Invent: The Future of Education.* New York: Viking Press, 1973.

Pipho, C. "Restructured Schools: Rhetoric on the Rebound?" *Phi Delta Kappan*, 1988, 69(10), 710–711.

Plank, D. W. "Why School Reform Doesn't Change Schools: Political and Organizational Explanations." Paper presented at the Annual Meeting of the American Educational Research Association, Washington, D.C., Apr. 1987.

Reid, W. A. "Institutions and Practice: Professional Education Reports and the Language of Reform." *Educational Researcher*, 1987, 16(8), 10–15.

Rosenholtz, S. "Improving the Quality of Work Life in Teaching." Paper presented to the Conference on Restructuring from Within: The Next Reform Agenda for School Improvement, University of Georgia, Athens, June 1988.

Rothman, R. "U.S. Pupils Earn Familiar Low Scores on International Math, Science Tests." *Education Week*, 1989, 8(20), 5.

Swift Current [Saskatchewan] Public Schools. *Instructional Improvement: A Policy Framework.* Swift Current, Saskatchewan: Swift Current Public Schools, 1985.

Wise, A. "The Two Conflicting Trends in School Reform: Legislated Learning Revisited." *Phi Delta Kappan*, 1988, 69(5), 328–333.

Wise, A. E. "The Teacher as Professional: Policy Implications for Quality Schooling." Paper presented at the Conference on Restructuring Schooling for Quality Education, Trinity University, San Antonio, Texas, Aug. 1987.

Appendix B
Reflections on Facilitating School Improvement: Issues of Value

As a facilitator in school-improvement efforts, I'm often wrestling with a sixties cliché: if you're not part of the solution, you're part of the problem. On many occasions, I participate in critical debate about educational change taking place in the shared-governance meetings of our public schools. At times, I feel strongly that the direction of the decision being taken is wrong. How hard should I try to convince others of the rightness and educational soundness of my views? When should I retreat to a more modest stance that might soften and minimize the harm of the direction? When do I let others convince me that I might be wrong? Finally, at what point should I take a walk?

If I push too hard, alienate, and harden other people's position, am I then part of the solution? If I clarify, help others understand my feelings—but then back off—am I then still part of the solution? If I take a walk because I'm opposed to the decision being made, am I now part of the problem? These issues of value stay with me long after meetings and workdays are over.

I make no claim of moral rightness in my resolution about these dilemmas. Instead, in this Appendix, I'd like to examine how I deal with these issues and offer a forum for you the reader to think about how you likewise facilitate school change. I'd like to draw out several scenarios and then reflect on the value tug, possible responses, and personal resolution.

Scenario One: Out There

Eliot Wigginton, high school teacher of twenty-five years and founder of the nationally acclaimed Foxfire program in Rabun Gap (Georgia), wrote in his semiautobiographical book, "I know that the public schools are not ideal learning environments but that they are here to stay; that the public schools will continue to be the front lines—the institutions to which most of our nation's young people will continue to be sent despite any rhetoric advocating the opposite; and that despite the fact that we've been given an almost impossible job, there are strategies we can use to make the situation work if we can both find them and summon enough energy from within ourselves to implement them" (1985, p. 190).

Wigginton makes clear that his value stance to improve education is by working within the system. John Puckett (1989) explains how Wigginton realized that the critics of public education he had admired as a beginning teacher no longer worked in public schools. They all had either quit or been fired after a brief classroom stint. These critics' scathing books and articles had done little to change the public school. Wigginton instead chose to reform from within public schools and to establish how to sustain innovative pedagogy and curriculum. Over the years, therefore, he had to compromise to implement his point of view: "Men and women of great strength and compassion are chewed up and spit out of the public school system every day, their confidence in themselves and the future of our schools shaken to the core. I've seen things happen to adults and children in that system that would curl a hardened cynic's hair, and so have you. Plainly, the job will not tolerate much wide-eyed idealism" (p. 190).

Scenario Two: Close in

A colleague of mine, an educational consultant known as an expert in designing instructional resources, served on a public school committee charged with reexamining and recommending teaching materials for the next five years. Certain influential committee members wanted to keep the current text materials. After lengthy debate and fiery discussion, my colleague gave an eloquent, forceful appeal about research supporting a multimaterial approach. To do less, she emphasized, was to consign a high percentage of students to failure. The influential members of the task force did not respond and showed through their stony silence an unwillingness to change their opposition. Other group members who believed in the multimaterial approach asked the consultant to be quiet. They believed that they could get some movement away from a single-text approach if the traditionalists did not become defensive. The more the consultant pressed, the more the sympathetic members felt their cause was being lost. She was at a loss for what to do: desist, or press on? The two of us discussed the issue at length.

To interpret this scenario as a good-versus-bad or educated-versus-ignorant debate is much too simple. All the committee members advocated the position they did because they each believed it to be in the best interest of students. The issue was not which members cared more. They all cared. Furthermore, which position the research supports was not uniformly clear. Most often, we can find research to support either position in a debate. Rather, as in most educational debates, the decision came down to philosophical or value differences among well-intentioned people. Should the consultant have backed away from staunch advocacy to allow more moderate change to take place? Should she have persisted even if all change might be lost? Or might she have stuck to her stance as a calculated ploy to give maneuvering room for other members to negotiate between the polarized positions? She finally resolved to stand her ground, not back down, and persist in arguing for what she thought was right. Her conscience remained intact even as all was lost. The instructional materials remained the same.

Scenario Three: Within

One school that I've worked with for several years has a twenty-year history of grouping students in a particular way. The teachers and principal have established a shared-governance (empowerment) process, set school goals, and made immediate changes that have improved the school climate and the achievement of students from a poverty background. When we first agreed to work together, I openly admitted discomfort with the grouping practice and, to my surprise, found that the faculty felt likewise. They had already identified the need to change it. After a year of study, the school faculty proposed eliminating the grouping practice to the school board. It said no. The board had a general written policy that the members interpreted to establish grouping and saw no need to change the interpretation. Since then, the school has discreetly made modifications to keep within the words of board policy but to be more flexible in practice. Still, even with discreet change, after several years of working with this school, a practice that I don't like remains. The staff still wants to formally change it, the board doesn't, and I'm still uncomfortable. Some colleagues of mine, who are great supporters of our work with public schools, have reservations about being involved with any school that uses an educational approach that they personally and professionally believe is unsound.

The Common Issues

All three scenarios—out there, close in, and within—raise common issues of value to any facilitator of school improvement:

- Should we fight from within, or from outside the school system?
- Should we press our position, or back off?
- Should we view ourselves as more enlightened than others?
- What, ultimately, is the highest good?

The inside-outside issue has long raged and will rage for eternity. Allan Bloom, in his controversial book *The Closing of the American Mind* (1987), argues that university thinkers should stay outside of the real world. They should clarify and debate issues to better inform future directions of society. On the other hand, Larry Cuban argues (1987) that most outside reformers set off ideological bombs that make great noise and activity on the surface of education but have little impact on the deep structural currents of the schools. Most educators advocate a middle course that links those outside of school and those inside of school. But if we believe in linking (theory and practice, research and application, or coalitions and partnerships), then by definition we must get inside. We can't have linkage unless we link inside another link. The question becomes one of extent.

I believe that insiders bring about school change. If I personally don't want to get inside, then I can criticize and wax eloquently, but I shouldn't expect much to happen (unless, of course, I can find others who are willing to go inside for me). I am highly impatient with people who criticize from afar, do not become engaged in schools, and then criticize some more. To my mind, they've built a comfortable career of intellectual whining—"no avail and no responsibility." So I want to get inside, but I don't want to be an insider. I don't want "to go native" in this sense. I don't want to be so much a part of school practitioners' lives that I perceive the world exactly as they do. Nothing is wrong with their perception; I just want mine to come from a further distance.

Yes, I want to eat my cake and have it too! After all, I chose not to be a native when I left the full-time employment of public schools for academia, not because I was superior but because public school life as a full-time enterprise was too hard and university life was more desirable. In fact, I have often worked to make public school lives more discretionary, flexible, and autonomous—more like lives in the university. I try not to deceive myself. Good practitioners do their job in public education at a level of competence and endurance beyond mine. Good public school teachers and good public school administrators are better at what they do than I was or would be. I'm not troubled by this admission; I'm grateful for it.

I'm aware of my choice to work inside but not be an insider, but now how hard do I fight inside a public school for what I believe? I'm somewhat knowledgeable about educational research. Again, to be honest, my beliefs tend to screen the research I use. I'd like to say that the research shapes my beliefs, but in reality my beliefs shape the research I use. My philosophy of education is reflected in how I teach, the studies I conduct, the schools I've led, and the curriculum and instruction I value for my children. In other words, I don't come into schools with an unbiased mind.

As a public school teacher and administrator, I was strongly influenced by the open education movement of the sixties. In my early university years, I worked with many older colleagues who were involved in the progressive laboratory schools of the thirties. My particular view of education has been influenced by experiences in my formative years. I believe in project-centered, experiential, and guided (rather than centered) student learning. Classifying me as a progressive, a constructivist, a developmentalist, and a liberal educator with a bent toward great democratization of classroom and school would fit most of the bill (not that I don't have a few conservative views that drive others of similar classification crazy).

How hard should I fight for what I believe? Should the empowered schools I work with believe in the same things I do? To assist school-empowerment efforts but want assurance that teachers and administrators in a school will toe a certain philosophic line imposed by an outsider is a bit of a contradiction. So now I'm caught in my own contradiction: I believe strongly in certain educational premises, but I want the school to be a collection of professionals who make their own educational goals on behalf of students.

Let's return to the previous scenarios. Should Wigginton have continued in public education when the school carried out student policies "that would curl a hardened cynic's hair"? Should the consultant have been quiet and let her carefully articulated and researched position about teaching materials be ignored? Should I take a hike from a school that continues to use a grouping practice when I believe these practices have mostly negative effects on students? Should I allow the practices to occur with my active participation? Should I make a scene? Should I call in the investigative reporters? Should I sue, or should I leave?

My first response is to ask myself a question: What do I gain by leaving? Will the objectionable practice be discontinued? Unless my departure is of such an earth-shaking, traumatic loss to a school (which it is not), the objectionable practice will continue. What do I gain by staying? I'll continue to be uncomfortable with my presence being seen as a possible endorsement, and yet it's possible I'll have a greater influence on change in the next round of decisions. Of course, those who continue to belong to intolerant groups could also use this rationale. Surely, at some point I should leave— but how do I know when I reach that point? My basic posture is to be patient, stay inside, press, understand, reclarify, and then (if I detect no influence) back off. To back off means I can stay in the schools; I can continue to work with them. But there are times when I should get out. When do I tell myself that enough is enough?

I get out when I no longer have hope of honestly escalating the troublesome issue. I don't mean hope that the decision will eventually go my way; I mean hope that the group remains open to asking questions, gathering additional information, and reformulating their thinking. When I lose hope, I've lost confidence in my ability and the group members' ability to entertain other possibilities. Therefore, when I no longer have hope in our capacity to learn from each other, that is my signal. Hope, as the sole signal, may be too simple an answer.

After writing this last paragraph, and reading it to others, I realize that prior understandings also are important. Did I accept the conditions that bothered me when I agreed to work with a school, and the school with me? If so, has the school and have I honestly worked to try to change those conditions, and are we still working? I'm getting back to hope.

Finally, I realize that urgency is another signal for when to walk away and try to orchestrate a change from the outside. If I'm knowingly aware and certain that students are being abused, mistreated, and ill-educated and people are unaware or indifferent, then I should try to press for immediate change; if change is not forthcoming or the problem taken to a higher authority, then I should walk. If a school acknowledges problems and is trying to right inequities, I won't walk.

The View of Enlightenment and Higher Control

Life is a series of choices, more so for people with the luxury of options. School educators, consultants, and university faculty have more opportunities than many less-skilled and less-educated persons. Predeterminism never seemed an adequate explanation of most people's lives in America. If anyone would like to explain in a predictive manner how it could be determined that a Jewish boy, the son of a furniture proprietor from Boston, would marry a Protestant woman, become a university professor, have an older daughter dating a fellow from Germany, and live in Athens, Georgia, I'll be intrigued. Most educators I know have similar stories of unexpected occurrence leading to further choices and creating a novel story.

With choice, I must consciously take responsibility for accepting the consequences of my actions. I have chosen, at least for now, to remain on the inside as I try to influence the direction of school improvement. Rarely do I choose to push issues of educational practice to the breaking point. That choice probably explains why I'm viewed as a facilitator and mediator (and only at times as a leader) of school change. I knowingly try the patience of colleagues who wish me to be a stronger advocate of a particular curriculum, pedagogical, or staff development approach that they know I personally favor. I won't because I have a view of enlightened education that, to me, is a higher good than any particular pedagogical position. That view, in fact, is my pedagogical position.

The line where I walk and will not stray is the advocacy of school teachers and administrators as caring and decent people who need to be part of the collective, oral decision making about the education of their students. I am certain that our only hope for improving education, for retaining our best and brightest practitioners, and for attracting curious and intellectual teachers is to have schools that can fulfill the intellectual as well as affective needs of adults. Therefore, in any isolated meeting about a particular educational issue not going my way, I will back down, even if I believe the decision to be not particularly wise, because I believe wisdom comes with time.

As teachers and administrators acquire the capability and confidence to raise questions, seek further information, listen to others, and debate ideas, their decisions for students become as enlightened as anyone else's. They in turn learn to cultivate their own students' capability and confidence to raise questions and deliberate over ideas as a source of enlightenment. Enlightenment is not the province of one group (that is, university people). People who are deliberate, informed, and wise will disagree with each other. But the disagreement is resourceful, intelligent. I have a hard time abandoning hope. Only when I'm in meetings with others who see that they alone have the answer to school change, who believe they can ministrate from on high, and who view school practitioners' capabilities with contempt will I certainly take a walk.

References

Bloom, A. D. *The Closing of the American Mind.* New York: Simon & Schuster, 1987.

Cuban, L. "The District Superintendent and the Restructuring of Schools." Paper presented to the Conference on Restructuring Schooling for Quality Education, San Antonio, Texas, Aug. 1987.

Puckett, J. L. *Foxfire Reconsidered: A Twenty-Year Experiment in Progressive Education.* Urbana: University of Illinois Press, 1989.

Wigginton, E. *Sometimes a Shining Moment: The Foxfire Experience.* Garden City, N.Y.: Anchor Press/Doubleday, 1985.

Original Sources of Selected Essays by Carl Glickman

(Chapter One) Glickman, C. D. "What Do We Mean by an American Education: A Dollar or the World?" Adapted version as Forum essays appearing in University of Georgia *Columns*, 29(20), p. 7; and *Athens Banner Herald*, Jan. 27, 2002, p. 7. Glickman, C. D. "More Than a Dollar: Education with Public Purpose." *International Journal of Leadership in Education*, in press.

(Chapter Two) Glickman, C. D. "Leadership for Navigating Great American Schools." Originally published as "The Courage to Lead." *Educational Leadership*, 2002, 59(8), 41–44.

(Chapter Three) Glickman, C. D. "Sustaining a 'Sacred' Education: Symbols, Stories, and Ceremonies." Previously unpublished.

(Chapter Four) Glickman, C. D. "Good and/or Effective Schools: What Do We Want?" *Kappan*, 1987, 68(8), 622–624. Used by permission.

(Chapter Five) Glickman, C. D. "Pretending Not to Know What We Know." *Educational Leadership*, 1991, 48(8), 4–10. Copyright 1991, Association for Supervision and Curriculum Development. All rights reserved. Reprinted with permission.

(Chapter Six) Glickman, C. D. "Pushing School Reform to a New Edge: The Ironies of School Empowerment." *Kappan*, 1990, 72(1), 68–75. Used by permission.

(Chapter Seven) Glickman, C. D. "Unlocking School Reform: Uncertainty as a Condition of Professionalism." *Kappan*, 1987, 68(10). Used by permission.

(Chapter Eight) Glickman, C. D. "The Essence of School Renewal: The Prose Has Begun." *Educational Leadership*, 1992, 50(1), 24–27.

(Chapter Nine) Glickman, C. D. "Developing Teacher Thought." *Journal of Staff Development*, 1986, 7(1), 6–21. Reprinted with permission of the National Staff Development Council, 2002. All rights reserved.

(Chapter Ten) Glickman, C. D. *Leadership for Learning*. Alexandria, Va.: Association for Supervision and Curriculum Development, 2002, pp. 1–8, 9–23.

(Chapter Eleven) Glickman, C. D. "The Supervisor's Challenge: Changing the Teacher Work Environment." *Educational Leadership*, 1984, 42(2), 38–40. Copyright 1985, Association for Supervision and Curriculum Development. All rights reserved. Reprinted with permission.

(Chapter Twelve) Glickman, C. D. "Democratic Education: Judy and the Dance." In S. Schapiro (ed.), *Higher Education for Democracy*. New

About the Author

Carl D. Glickman holds the Roy F. and Joann Cole Mitte Endowed Chair in School Improvement in the College of Education at Southwest Texas State University (San Marcos), where he is involved in a unique interdisciplinary Ph.D. program for public-spirited community and school leaders. In addition, he is president of the Institute for Schools, Education, and Democracy and University Professor Emeritus of Education at the University of Georgia.

He began his education career in 1968 as a Teacher Corps intern in the rural South. Since then, he has been a principal of award-winning schools, taught at four universities, and held faculty appointments in departments of curriculum and supervision, educational leadership, and foundations of education. In 1997, he was awarded the highest faculty career award of the University of Georgia for bringing, "stature and distinction" to the mission of the university, and in 1999 students honored him as the faculty member who had "contributed most to their lives, inside and outside the classroom."

Glickman serves in many leadership roles on university, state, and national commissions to improve schools, teacher education, and academic programs. He was the founder and chair, and remains senior adviser of the Georgia League of Professional Schools. Most recently, he served on the board of the National Commission for Service Learning (chaired by former astronaut Sen. John Glenn), a countrywide initiative to revitalize democratic citizenry by connecting student academic learning with service to local communities.

He is the author of twelve books on school leadership, educational renewal, and the moral imperative of education. His previous books with Jossey-Bass include *Renewing America's Schools* (1993) and *Revolutionizing America's Schools* (1998).

Glickman has worked with schools and communities throughout the United States, Canada, the Mediterranean, Asia, and Africa. He and his spouse, Sara, a former middle school teacher and currently adult educator, have lived in the South for nearly thirty years but find time in the summer every year to spend with their widely dispersed family and grandchildren in a small fishing camp in St. Albans Bay, Vermont. He may be contacted via email at isedinc@aol.com.

Index

Educational authority domains, 256t

"Educational Leadership for Democratic Purpose: What Do We Mean?" (Glickman), 294

Educational Testing Services, 331

Educational theory of democracy, 266–268

Effective vs. good schools, 41–46

Elite schools, 60–61

Elmore, R. F., 249

Empowered schools: described, 329; effects of reform through, 81–84; gains/losses in, 77–78; hesitation linked to, 75–77; individual differences and collective, 73–74; model impracticality of, 74–75; questions asked by, 332–333; response of nonempowered schools to, 72–73; school improvement and, 71–72; using democracy in, 79–81, 83–84

Equal access to knowledge, 213–215fig

Erickson, V. L., 106

External teacher incentives, 52–55

F

Facilitator/leader of peer coaching, 136–137

Faculty. See Teachers

Federal Hocking High (Ohio), 16–17

Feedback ("warm" and "cool"), 138, 140

Festinger, L. A., 47

Fink, D., 322n.1–323n.1

Floyd, K., 91

Foster, M., 293

Foucault, M., 243, 243n.6

Four Seasons Project, 220

Fowler Drive Elementary School (Georgia), 69, 76

Foxfire Network (Georgia), 53, 179–185

Franklin, B., 304

Freda, E., 298

Freire, P., 305

Fried, R. S., 178

Fullan, M., 32, 116, 118, 249, 259

G

Gage, N. L., 44

Gaines, G. F., 253

Gallagher, C., 227, 237

Gallup/Phi Delta Kappa poll (1989), 66

Gamoran, A., 48, 268, 284

Garmston, R. J., 130

Gastright, J. F., 49

Gates, H. L., Jr., 235, 295

Generative curriculum development, 113

George, P. S., 48

Georgia League of Professional Schools, 23n.3, 47

Georgia Program for School Improvement, 214

Glenn, J., 9, 315

Glickman, C. D., 4, 17, 18, 23, 42, 66, 67, 82, 89, 110, 112, 123, 127, 130, 135, 146, 154, 170, 195, 197, 220, 229, 233, 240, 243n.8, 246, 267, 268, 271, 281, 282, 286, 287, 288, 290, 294, 295, 296, 303, 304, 327

Glickman, S. O., 102n.1, 154

Goals 2000 legislation, 221

Goddard College (Vermont): compared to University of Georgia, 154–156, 157, 163–167; democratic education at, 169–172; described, 153–154; diversity of field experience at, 165–166; experience as visiting faculty at, 156–159; intellectual diversity of, 166–167; introduction to students of, 159–161; Judy couldn't dance story and, 159–160; last memory of Judy dancing at, 172; learning/teaching applications at, 167–169; personalization of learning at, 165; relationship with students of, 161–165

Goldhammer, R., 130

Good education: debate over, 195; goals of, 195–196; teaching practices and, 196–197

Good schools: beginning with elite schools, 60–61; effective vs., 41–46. See also Great American schools

Goodlad, J. I., 50, 102, 107, 146, 192, 243n.8

Gordon, S. P., 110, 123, 130, 135

Governance structure: curriculum planning scheduling conflict and, 20–21; Dade County schools use of shared, 60; democracy and empowered school, 79–81, 83–84; individual differences and shared, 73–74; as part of school renewal framework, 19fig; schoolwide decisions and, 17

Grade levels, 51–52

Graham, P., 167

"The Grave Dangers in the Discourse on Democracy" (Scheurich), 277, 286–293, 293

Great American schools: building the foundation of, 17–19; criteria for defining, 23n.3; examples of staying on path, 19–21; imbued with public purpose, 12; preparation/appraisal of, 15–17; school renewal framework and, 19fig; standing firm on commitments by, 13–15. See also Good schools; Schools

Greene, M., 270, 310

Greenhouse, S., 321

Guthrie, J. W., 267

Gutmann, A., 3, 196, 240